Weaving the Net

Weaving the Net

Conditional Engagement with China

edited by James Shinn

COUNCIL ON FOREIGN RELATIONS PRESS

NEW YORK

COUNCIL ON FOREIGN RELATIONS BOOKS

The Council on Foreign Relations, Inc., is a nonprofit and nonpartisan organization devoted to promoting improved understanding of international affairs through the free exchange of ideas. The Council does not take any position on questions of foreign policy and has no affiliation with, and receives no funding from, the United States government.

From time to time, books and monographs written by members of the Council's research staff or visiting fellows, or commissioned by the Council, or written by an independent author with critical review contributed by a Council study or working group are published under the designation "Council on Foreign Relations Book." Any book or monograph bearing that designation is, in the judgment of the Committee on Studies of the Council's Board of Directors, a responsible treatment of a significant international topic worthy of presentation to the public. All statements of fact and expression of opinion contained in Council books are, however, the sole responsibility of the author.

If you would like more information on Council publications, please write the Council on Foreign Relations, 58 East 68th Street, New York, NY 10021, or call the Publications Office at (212) 734-0400.

Library of Congress Cataloging-in-Publication Data

Shinn, James.
Weaving the net : conditional engagement with China / James Shinn, editor.
    p. 284 cm.
    Includes bibliographical references
    ISBN 0-87609-190-7   (pbk.): $19.95
    1. China--Foreign economic relations.   2. China--Economic conditions--1976-   3. International economic integration   4. United States--Foreign economic relations--China   5. China--Foreign economic relations--United States   I. Shinn, James.   II. Council on Foreign Relations
HF1604.F57 1996
337.51--dc20   96-2302
                                                                    CIP

TABLE OF CONTENTS

Foreword • *Harold Brown*

Foreword

CHINA HAS NOT ONLY awakened, it has arisen, albeit decades after Mao announced the birth of the People's Republic in Tiananmen Square on October 1, 1949. The form China will take in the 21st century is far from certain. Two decades from now, China will probably be more modern, more technologically advanced, richer, more prominent in trade and international investment, and more assertive beyond its borders. China's rates of economic growth, inflation, and, especially, progress toward a more pluralistic society are less easily forecast. No one knows how the tension between central authority and localism will be resolved, how strong its military will be, and whether it will cooperate in the international security system.

By historical standards, China's economic transformation is remarkably fast. Within 15 or 20 years, in most scenarios, China's relations with other nations on economic, security, and transnational issues will be of great importance, and therefore the stakes in China's internal development will be high. Accordingly, during the last few years scholars in the West and in Asia have focused their attention on the region's—especially China's—economic revolution and its implications for policies of the United States.

Few in 1975 would have predicted China's configuration and direction in 1996. Thus U.S. planners and policymakers ought to be thinking about the wide range of possibilities for the China of 2015. China's highly authoritarian succession process, no matter how foreordained it may appear, is always subject to uncertainty. Internal political difficulties could change China's attitude toward the external world and slow its economic growth. Even if the succession is smooth, economic mismanagement also could taper the phenomenal growth rate of the last decade. In any event, China's average growth rate is likely to moderate to the level of its East Asian neighbors over the last decade, say, seven or eight percent a year. And on international security issues, China could be a cooperative player or an angry nationalistic disruption depending on the nature of its future political leaders, the issues that drove their accession, and their perceptions of how China's interests—and their own authority—will best be preserved.

Even if it has a seven or eight percent growth rate over the next two decades, China will have a massive effect on the world economy, energy consumption, and trade and investment flows—measured, as these effects should be, in terms of exchange rates. China's growth in capability to design, build, field, and support a world-class military will correspond to the growth of its gross domestic product.

What are the implications of all this for U.S. policy toward China? China does not now have the weight in any of these dimensions that is ascribed to it by journalists. It is not in a class with the United States economically, militarily or technologically, or in international affairs. But two decades hence it could begin to approach that status, and its relationship with the United States could be either cooperative or adversarial. China's relative weight will be determined primarily by internal forces and events, but U.S. policy, especially over the next few years, will have a significant effect also. Policymakers should be prepared for either outcome in each dimension.

The effect of China's economic progress on its internal political development and international behavior will be a crucial factor in such policy considerations. The policy of conditional engagement with China that James Shinn proposes in the first five chapters of this volume, and to which the six authors respond in subsequent chapters, acknowledges this fact. This detailed and careful study of the risks and rewards of conditional engagement is precisely the sort of input that decisionmakers need as they formulate U.S. policy toward this rising power.

Harold Brown
Washington, D.C.
January, 1996

Weaving the Net

*Better
to Weave a Net,
than to Pray
for Fish*

- Chinese Proverb

1

Introduction

Better to Weave a Net than to Pray for Fish
- Chinese Proverb

CHINA'S ASCENT on the world stage presents great risks and huge potential rewards for the United States. A wealthy and peaceful China would immeasurably enrich the world community, in cultural as well as commercial terms. But a wealthy and belligerent China, or a China in chaos, would destroy Asian stability and threaten vital American interests.

Will the growing web of trade and investment successfully enmesh China in the world community, and ensure the peaceful integration of this emerging power? Or will China's path be shaped by the cruel calculus of great power rivalry, leaving the rest of the world no choice but to stand by hopefully, and to prepare for the worst? In other words, should the United States weave a net to engage China, or should it be resigned to merely pray for fish?

There is wide disagreement on these crucial questions among China-watchers and policymakers alike. One major school of thought, unconditional engagement, argues that

China's integration into global trading and financial systems will gradually but inexorably moderate the behavior of the People's Republic of China (PRC).[1] Jonathan Pollack notes in chapter 6 that, "The results of this approach are presumed to be cumulative: success will beget success, ultimately leading to a systemic transformation that will sharply diminish or altogether eliminate the pursuit of national security by unilateral means."[2] The other major school of thought, preemptive containment, contends that relying on economic integration to moderate Chinese behavior is naive and dangerous. It views the PRC as an assertive emerging power with regional reach and global aspirations. Since China's leaders have a sharp realpolitik view of the world, a "rational policy toward a rising, threatening China would have . . . two components: 1) containing China as it tries relentlessly to expand its reach, and 2) undermining its pseudo-Marxist but still ruthless dictatorship."[3]

There is an alternative to the two major schools of thought in China policy. It is a moderate, rules-based, essentially empirical strategy for dealing with China that the authors of this volume have termed conditional engagement.

Conditional engagement welcomes China's integration into the global trading and financial systems and proposes ways in which the United States and other Asian states can not only accelerate the process but amplify its moderating effect on PRC behavior. It includes some modest proposals for sustaining economic engagement by having China, the United States, and U.S. allies agree to a set of principles to guide their behavior. The policy would provide an objective measurable means of tracking China's political trajectory. A high-level, sustained, comprehensive dialogue between Washington and Beijing would be necessary to communicate and reinforce these principles. Conditional engagement also advocates security engagement in Asia in which the United States, U.S. allies in Asia, and Association of Southeast Asian Nations (ASEAN) maintain a countervailing diplomatic and military structure to encourage the PRC to comply with these principles. It would also be a hedge against the risk that economic integration fails to moderate Chinese behavior.[4]

The strategic choice for the United States and its Asian allies is not between engaging China economically and confronting it militarily; that is a false dichotomy and impractical as the perpetual debate between liberal-institutionalists and neo-realists. While seeking a close economic relationship with China, the United States has maintained a military presence in the region built on political partnerships with some of China's neighbors. In sum, conditional engagement works toward economic integration while pursuing stabilizing security relationships.

An emerging economic power, China is likely to account for more than 10 percent of gross world product within a decade. An emerging political power on a regional level, China clearly intends to play a global role as well. Admittedly, China is still poor in terms of per capita income and has enormous social problems, which has kept sustained economic development Beijing's overwhelming priority. In doing so, the leadership has abandoned communist economics in favor of a mixed-market economy, but it has not abandoned authoritarian politics. The political system appears to have slowly loosened up from the totalitarian state of Mao Zedong, to the hard authoritarian state of Deng Xiaoping, to the soft authoritarian state of Jiang Zemin.

Integrating an emerging power into the world system is a wrenching and risky process, however, and there are few historical examples where it has been managed without violence. Political transformation is riskier still: no communist state has been able to manage the process without the abrupt collapse of its regime. Therefore, the trajectory of China's multiple transformations is extremely difficult to forecast.

China may pose a serious problem for the rest of the world regardless of which trajectory it follows. If the PRC disintegrates, the mass social chaos and human suffering could well result in waves of refugees, rampant crime, weapons and nuclear arms proliferation, and staggering economic losses.[5] If China remains united and strongly authoritarian, a coalition of party ideologues, state capitalists, and xenophobic People's Liberation Army (PLA) officers could gather the reins of power in Beijing while constructing a new legitimacy based on Han nationalism and an aggressive foreign policy. If China remains united and mildly authoritarian, it could well become a destabilizing force in the international system, and in any case would still be difficult to deal with—as Washington has lately discovered. However, even a pluralist, quasi-democratic China, given its sheer size, the volatility of its domestic politics, and the depth of its aggrieved nationalism, would pose an enormous problem. As Jianwei Wang points out in chapter 7, "The challenges China will pose to American policymakers and U.S. national interests in the coming decades are largely those that would be posed by any emerging power. Attributing them exclusively to China's authoritarian political system is misleading. It is also naive to assume that the "China problem" will disappear as soon as China becomes a democratic country."[6]

Compounding the uncertainty about the PRC's political trajectory, the strategic anchor of the bilateral relationship—the alliance of the United States and China against the Soviet Union—is gone. The problems presented by an emerging China are not the same as those presented by the Soviet Union. China does not pose an ideological threat to the rest of Asia or to the United States. Communist ideology is dead, Marxist-Leninist theory is bankrupt. In fact, the ideological risk is posed by ideas flowing *into* China—hence, the sensitivity of Chinese officials to the consequences of "peaceful evolution," a term that seems benign to Americans. As they struggle to manage the political and economic transformation of China, with no legitimate authority, with a bankrupt ideology, and with the legacy of collectivist brutality and cyclic repression weighing on their shoulders, the leaders in Beijing are acutely aware that neither time nor history is on their side.

Nor does the PRC pose an immediate military threat to its

neighbors. There is no Chinese equivalent to the massed War-saw Pact divisions that once were poised to charge through Germany's Fulda Gap into Western Europe. It will be a decade or more before the PLA can project enough power to seriously threaten the rest of Asia, much less the United States. China's small nuclear arsenal is growing, but it is currently a minimal deterrent. America's annual defense expenditure is *10 times* greater than even the most liberal estimate of the PLA's budget. Conditional engagement is therefore premised on keeping the "China problem" in proper perspective.

China does not exist inside an economic shell. There is no Chinese equivalent of COMECON, the Soviet economic bloc. To the contrary, by most measures of trade and investment China is remarkably integrated in the global economic system and steadi-ly becoming more interdependent. However, this difference between China and the Soviet Union is much less reassuring than the previous two. The United States will not be able to force the PRC to spend itself into bankruptcy in a competitive arms race. Unlike Gorbachev's economically imploding Soviet Union, Jiang Zemin's China is growing at a 10 percent annual rate. And given the fact that the United States and Europe are no longer the world's center of economic gravity—the bulk of the PRC's trade and investment is within Asia—the cold reality is that the Unit-ed States cannot isolate China economically.

The problem of dealing with China is the problem of deal-ing with a renascent nationalist state with a rapidly expanding economy, one more like Wilhelmine Germany than Bolshevik Russia. As with Bismarck's Germany, the outside world will have only limited political influence in shaping the course of events in China or affecting the pace of its domestic evolution. As Arthur Waldron observes, "China is not Germany, but it is undeniable that such Bismarcks as China has produced—Zhou Enlai and Deng Xiaoping among them—have left or are about to leave the scene. How long the gendarmerie can control the streets is an open question."[7] Although the web of economic interdependence between China and the rest of the world widens, economic growth, as in the Germany of a century ago, is the basis of China's increasing power.

The thrust of conditional engagement is to bring China into the community of nations through an accord on basic rules for international conduct. The proposed ten principles for acceptable behavior are realistic guidelines reasonably congruent with current behavior and international undertakings. They will accommodate the emergence of the PRC as a world power and protect the vital interests of the United States and China's neighbors. Conditional engagement is also aimed at accelerating China's economic integration into the global trading and financial systems through negotiations to improve access to China's markets, further enmeshing the PRC in multilateral trade and financial regimes, and shunning commercial sanctions to achieve political or security goals. But the United States and its Asian allies will have to be clear-eyed about the limits of economic integration, patient with the political transformation in China, and aware that economic engagement alone will not solve all the bilateral problems. The United States and its allies will also have to follow a parallel strategy of security engagement to encourage Chinese compliance with the ten principles, give economic integration an opportunity to work its long-term moderating effects on Beijing, and, above all, prepare military and diplomatic countervailing structures in Asia as a fallback in the event China

---

THE TEN PRINCIPLES OF CONDITIONAL ENGAGEMENT

1. No unilateral use of offensive military force
2. Peaceful resolution of territorial disputes
3. Respect for national sovereignty
4. Freedom of navigation
5. Moderation in military force buildup
6. Transparency of military forces
7. Nonproliferation of weapons of mass destruction
8. Market access for trade and investment
9. Cooperative solutions for transnational problems
10. Respect for basic human rights

repeatedly violates the rules of acceptable behavior.

In sum, conditional engagement consists of a set of objectives, a strategy for attaining those objectives, and tactics (specific policies) for implementing that strategy.

- The objectives of conditional engagement are the ten principles, which were selected to preserve American vital interests in Asia while accommodating China's emergence as a major power.

- The overall strategy of conditional engagement follows two parallel lines: economic engagement, to promote the integration of China into the global trading and financial systems; and security engagement, to encourage compliance with the ten principles by diplomatic and military means when economic incentives do not suffice, in order to hedge against the risk of the emergence of a belligerent China.

- The tactics of economic engagement should promote China's economic integration through negotiations on trade liberalization, institution building, and educational exchanges. While a carrots-and-sticks approach may be appropriate within the economic arena, the use of trade sanctions to achieve short-term political goals is discouraged.

- The tactics of security engagement should reduce the risks posed by China's rapid military expansion, its lack of transparency, the proliferation of weapons of mass destruction, and transnational problems such as crime and illegal migration, by engaging in arms control negotiations, multilateral efforts, and a loosely-structured defensive military arrangement in Asia.[8]

This volume is organized in two parts. In the first part (chapters 1-5) the elements of conditional engagement are laid out. In the second part (chapters 6-11) this strategy is tested from a number of perspectives. The objectives of conditional engagement, and the ten principles for measuring the behavior of the PRC and trajectory of its political evolution are outlined in chapter 2. The tactics of economic engagement with China are the subject of chapter 3, which examines the moderating influence of economic integration on China, how this is likely to ensure Chinese compliance with the ten principles, and the degree to which economic engagement can be a tool of public policy. The tactics of security engagement, or how to encourage Chinese compliance with those principles not buttressed by economic integration and hedge against the failure of economic engagement, are discussed in chapter 4. The risks inherent in a strategy of conditional engagement from the perspectives of the PRC, the Asian states, and the United States, and the contrasts between conditional engagement and so-called "constructive" or "comprehensive" engagement, are explored in chapter 5.

In chapter 6, Jonathan Pollack defines the criteria for a successful American security strategy in Asia, and compares conditional engagement to several alternative strategies, including strategic autonomy, liberal internationalism, and preemptive containment. The authors of the next four chapters test the logic and the geopolitical context of conditional engagement from various national perspectives: Jianwei Wang, from the perspective of the PRC in chapter 7; Masashi Nishihara, from the perspective of Japan in chapter 8; Byung-joon Ahn, from the perspective of the Republic of Korea in chapter 9; and Amitav Acharya, from the perspective of ASEAN in chapter 10. Paul Evans concludes in chapter 11 by examining principles of behavior and how such principles can be formulated in the context of multilateral organizations.

The authors in this volume concentrate on a single complex problem—how to deal with an emergent China. Although the literature on China and the United States is rich in descriptions of the complexity of the problem, with much hand-wringing about the current state of affairs, the strategy of conditional engagement discussed in these pages represents an effort to get beyond hand-wringing and propose a constructive alternative solution for dealing with an emergent China peacefully and prudently.

NOTES

1. See Takashi Inoguchi's "Five Scenarios for Asian Security: Affluence, Amity and Assertiveness in its Changing Configuration," (paper written for the Council on Foreign Relation's Asia Project, 1994).
2. Jonathan Pollack, chapter 6, p. 108
3. Charles Krauthammer, "Why We Must Contain China," *Time*, July 31, 1995, p. 72.
4. As Paul Evans notes in chapter 11, p., "The adjective 'conditional' refers not to American engagement in the region (with the possibility that America will disengage if China does not meet particular conditions) but to the kind of policy that will be pursued as part of a continued American presence."
5. See Jack A. Goldstone, "The Coming China Collapse," and Yasheng Huang, "Why China Will Not Collapse," *Foreign Policy*, no. 99 (summer 1995), pp. 35-52, 54-68.
6. Jianwei Wang, chapter 7, p. 134.
7. Arthur Waldron, "Deterring China," *Commentary* 100, no. 4 (October 1995), p. 18.
8. Conditional engagement's recommended tactics of tit-for-tat responses are equivalent to using carrots and sticks in response to foreign policy actions by China. Economic engagement calls for what is described as symmetric tit-for-tat and security engagement for asymmetric tit-for-tat. A symmetric response is one that counters a move by China in the same place, time, and manner; an asymmetric response might occur in another place at another time, and perhaps in another manner. A symmetric tit-for-tat would be for Washington to counter a Chinese tariff of 10 percent on imports for the United States with a tariff of 10 percent on imports from China. An asymmetric tit-for-tat would be for the United States to counter a Chinese shipment of missiles to Iran with an American shipment of F-16s to Vietnam (John Lewis Gaddis, *Strategies of Containment: A Critical Appraisal of Postwar American National Security Policy*, New York: Oxford University Press, (1982). This is also cited in Fareed Zakaria, "The Reagan Strategy of Containment," *Political Science Quarterly* 105, no. 3 (1990), pp. 383-88).

2

The Principles of Engagement

THE PROPOSAL TO engage China on the basis of a set of agreed-upon principles is driven by the need to forge a new strategic anchor for the bilateral relationship that can withstand the battering of periodic setbacks. These principles are guidelines for the behavior of nation-states.

THE TEN PRINCIPLES OF CONDITIONAL ENGAGEMENT

1. No unilateral use of offensive military force
2. Peaceful resolution of territorial disputes
3. Respect for national sovereignty
4. Freedom of navigation
5. Moderation in military force buildup
6. Transparency of military forces
7. Nonproliferation of weapons of mass destruction
8. Market access for trade and investment
9. Cooperative solutions for transnational problems
10. Respect for basic human rights

These principles are ranked in order of importance—violations of the first are more likely than violations of the last to lead to war. The application of these principles is limited to Asia; no claim of global applicability is made. Currently, no single treaty or agreement incorporates all of these principles, but elements of them are embodied in bilateral agreements between the United States and China, the charters of organizations such as the ASEAN Regional Forum (ARF), and multilateral accords under the auspices of the United Nations. These are the concentric rings of U.S. policy in Asia that Amitav Acharya discusses in chapter 10.

The ten principles set modest expectations and focus largely on the external behavior of states, with three notable exceptions. The first exception is the principle of market access for both trade and foreign investment, which constrains domestic commercial policies. The second exception is the principle of cooperation on transnational problems such as crime, drug trafficking, illegal migration, and the environment, which are usually tackled as domestic issues. The third exception is the principle of respect for human rights, which denies states a free hand in the treatment of their citizens, particularly with regard to arbitrary imprisonment, torture, and abuse. The human rights principle is emphatically not equivalent to democratization, however, which is an issue of political, as opposed to personal, rights.

THE FORMULATION OF POLICY

RETHINKING FIRST principles is useful for clarifying the objectives of U.S. policy. Selecting these principles can force Washington to examine its priorities and to reevaluate goals that may be inconsistent or conflicting. A set of clear principles such as those proposed here can serve as a scaffold for public debate on American policy toward China. An extensive and vigorous public debate is the precondition for building a public consensus on the need for common sense and reasonable goals in dealing with China and for creating public awareness of the sizable rewards of a stable relationship that may be imperiled by a wrongheaded strategy.

By focusing on the ten principles, Washington will be able to communicate better its policy objectives to China and to other states in Asia, including allies and neutral third parties. A persistent problem of current U.S. strategy is its fundamental ambiguity; Beijing seems to understand neither the overall strategy nor the relative importance of American goals. Many Asian allies are equally confused.

The ten principles can serve as the basis for the text of joint communiqués and other formal agreements with China. Communiqués and agreements usually begin with a statement of common principles and proceed to a statement of principles by each party, including those points on which the parties agree to disagree. Such principles are also embodied in a range of charters of great import to China such as the loan criteria of the World Bank and Japan's Overseas Development Assistance program.

Building the U.S.-China relationship on a foundation of the ten principles will allow both countries to emphasize common interests, not the vast gulf of differences between them. Their common interests may not be strong enough to support the edifice of a strategic alliance, as they did during the Cold War, but they should bear the weight of a normal long-term relationship. In this sense, conditional engagement is a direct descendant of the Nixon-Kissinger rapprochement with China in 1971. Most important, the ten principles can serve as a gauge of how well China integrates into the world community. A status quo China will adhere to them; a revolutionary, belligerent China will not.

Conditional engagement is premised on the conviction that the anchoring principles of America's strategy toward China must be realistic, modest, and reasonably congruent with current behavior. These principles must be as unambiguous as possible, reciprocal, and consistent with current treaties and other international undertakings. They must also be elastic enough to accommodate China's drive for recognition as a regional and, ultimately, global power, and strong enough to protect the vital interests of the United States and China's Asian neighbors.

MEETING THE TEST

How WELL DO the ten principles correspond to these criteria? The first four principles taken as a group—the national integrity principles—have a long history of elaboration in diplomatic practice and international treaties. Both China and the United States have repeatedly subscribed to these principles, including the proscription of the unilateral use of force, the peaceful resolution of territorial disputes, respect for sovereignty, and freedom of navigation. These principles are modest, reciprocal, and clear. The saber-rattling of the PLA troops, in conducting missile tests off Taiwan, does not violate these rules. But launching PLA troops across the Taiwan Strait would be a blatant violation. The disputes over Taiwan and the South China Sea are likely to be the severest test of these national integrity principles.[1]

China has used force as "diplomacy by other means" in border disputes with Vietnam, the Soviet Union, and nations with claims in the South China Sea, and it has threatened to use force against Taiwan. "The PLA will not undertake to eschew the use of force, and will not sit idle and let it go unchecked if foreign forces meddle in China's international affairs to effect an 'independent Taiwan,'" remarked Chi Haotian at the reception to mark Army Day on August 1 last year.[2] In an interview with the *Asahi Shimbun* several months earlier, Jiang Zemin stated unequivocally that China would not renounce the use of force against Taiwan, claiming that such a pledge would prevent the island's peaceful reunification with the mainland.[3] China's official position is that Taiwan is not a sovereign state, that Taiwan's status is "an internal matter of national unification," and therefore no international principles apply.

Taiwan presents such a knotty problem because the principle of national sovereignty, in this case the PRC's vital interest in national unification, collides with the principle of national self-determination, which would arise were Taiwan to demand de jure independence. The United States has no formal relations nor any security alliance with Taiwan, but it does have strong economic ties and a residual political relationship. Thus it has nothing to gain (and much to lose) from Taiwanese independence. China, however, has much more to lose. It is unlikely that any ruling group in Beijing could survive a successful Taiwanese declaration of independence: it would destroy their legitimacy as patriots, nationalists, and the nominal rulers of a united China.

To deal with this conflict of principles, conditional engagement would refine these national integrity principles according to a proposal by Jianwei Wang in chapter 7. Wang suggests that the United States recognize the legitimacy of China's goal of national unification but remain neutral on the "internationalization" of Hong Kong and Macao, Tibetan separatism, and independence of Taiwan. In turn, China would promise to reunify through peaceful means and respect the political and economic systems and cultural heritage of these places. The harsh imposition of the mainland social system on Hong Kong and Macao or an unprovoked attack on Taiwan (in the absence of de jure independence or foreign intervention) would be seen as threats to the stability of the region, hence to U.S. interests.

The South China Sea disputes, however, require no such refinements of principle. This is a crystal-clear measure of China's willingness to resolve problems as a status quo great power and peaceful member of the international community rather than as a belligerent state employing deception, intimidation, and force. The ASEAN states have vital interests in the South China Sea, and they have all staked claims and placed troops on various islands. But they are apprehensive about China's intentions.[4] (Ironically, in a rare gesture of solidarity with the mainland, Taiwan has sent troops to the largest island in the disputed area, Taiping Dao, to support the Chinese claim). The United States, Japan, and Korea have no vital interests in these reefs and islands, but they worry that the dispute may infringe on freedom of navigation in the region.[5]

With regard to the three "military principles"—moderation in military buildup, transparency of military forces, and nonproliferation of weapons of mass destruction—the third is the least ambiguous in terms of compliance, although there are still some uncertainties about verification.

But what is an immoderate military buildup? And how much transparency is enough? It is hard to argue that China's current defense expenditures as a percentage of gross national product are immoderate. In absolute terms, even expansive estimates of China's military expenditure suggest that the PRC spends less than Japan and eight times less than the United States.[6]

Conditional engagement focuses on the future threat. The debate over China's conventional force modernization centers on the PLA's acquisition of power-projection capabilities, which will enable China to pose a credible threat beyond its land borders, especially toward Taiwan and the South China Sea. The projection of sea power requires aircraft carriers, ships with advanced missile and electronics capabilities, amphibious warfare capability, and advanced attack submarines. The projection of power requires air transport for troops and equipment, air-to-air refueling technology, and aircraft equipped with such sophisticated technology as "stealth," electronic countermeasures, and an airborne warning and control system.[7] The PLA has none of these capabilities on a large scale but hopes to acquire them.

The hard fact is that the PRC's ongoing economic growth in the 8-10 percent range will allow Beijing to modernize and expand much of its military at a steady pace. As a rising great power, China has been explicit about its intent to acquire a powerful military machine. American military experts have stated that, "the question for American strategy and diplomacy is not whether China will possess a modern military force or not. The only questions are when it will have one."[8] In any event, the PLA's acquisition of conventional power projection will pose a major threat to China's neighbors and indirectly threaten U.S. forces in the region.

A dramatic expansion of China's nuclear arsenal, currently estimated at about 300 warheads, and of the missile delivery systems for these warheads, which includes intercontinental ballistic missiles (ICBM) targeted at North America, could be a direct security threat to the United States. The PLA continues to develop and refine its nuclear capabilities and is reportedly adding missile-equipped submarine and mobile launchers. China continues to improve the technical capability of its ICBMs, developing solid-fuel rockets and more sophisticated warheads, such as multiple intercontinental reentry vehicles—ostensibly the reason why China must continue to conduct nuclear tests.[9] The goals and limits, if any, of China's nuclear program are not clear.

There is some limited but disturbing evidence that China may be moving from a strategic doctrine of minimal deterrence toward the more dangerous and complex doctrine of limited deterrence: "Minimum deterrence refers to a small, purely countervalue second strike capability. Limited deterrence, on the other hand, refers essentially to flexible response, whereby China should have a range of strategic and substrategic capabilities to deter any level of nuclear conflict, and in a nuclear war to contain escalatory pressures."[10]

On the issue of transparency, China could provide outsiders with some insight into the PLA's capabilities and intent in many ways: the publication of detailed defense "white papers," accurate and complete defense budgets and documents on military doctrine, participation in the U.N. arms registry, and a variety of related confidence- and security-building measures.

China's military planning is opaque and secretive, and the transparency of the PLA's buildup is low, which magnifies Asian worries. According to PLA expert Paul Godwin, "Beijing's leaders have become aware in recent years that transparency is a central tenet of arms controls measures and regimes—a notion antithetical to lifelong habits and natural impulses. As with every modern totalitarian and communist country, the paramount importance of secrecy and compartmentalization in national security affairs reaches a level of paranoia in China scarcely equaled and unlikely to be surpassed in other states, with the possible exception of North Korea."[11]

The PLA's long-awaited defense white paper was issued in November 1995 but was incomplete, rhetorical, and largely pro forma.[12] Recent visits by Pentagon officials to China and PLA officials to the United States and exchanges of information on capabilities and doctrine have yielded little of value. China's participation in confidence and security-building measures is very limited. Progress on further Chinese transparency within the ARF and related "track-two" discussions has been slow.[13] This slow pace is complicated by the fact that several ARF participants, particularly within ASEAN, are also uncomfortable with a high degree of transparency. This limits the transparency that conditional engagement can demand from China; it would be unreasonable to demand more transparency from the PRC than from Indonesia, for example.

The principles of nonproliferation are an easier case because there are detailed conventions for measuring China's performance. There is an alphabet soup of agreements encompassing nuclear weapons, chemical and biological weapons, missiles and space weapons, and conventional weapons. The United States has a vital interest in the extension and enforcement of these nonproliferation regimes. As a regional and emerging global power, China likewise has a vital interest in these regimes and the responsibility to uphold them.

China is in compliance with the nuclear weapons Nonproliferation Treaty (NPT), although there are some questions surrounding Beijing's involvement in Pakistan's weapons development program, and with the International Atomic

Energy Agency safeguards, even though China is not a formal member of the Nuclear Suppliers Group.[14] Two other pivotal nuclear nonproliferation agreements are still under negotiation, the Fissile Material Production Cutoff and Control Treaty and the Comprehensive Test Ban Treaty (CTBT) under the aegis of the U.N. Conference on Disarmament. Beijing has indicated that it will accede to the CTBT after 1996, or when the treaty is ready to sign.

China is complying with the Chemical Weapons Convention. However, signatories to the Biological Weapons Convention suspect China may be violating the pact by continuing some of its research programs. There is no evidence that China is involved in the proliferation of biological weapons.[15] China is not a formal member of the Missile Technology Control Regime (MTCR), although it "affirmed its commitment" to MTCR guidelines in an October 1994 joint statement with the United States. However, there is some question as to whether China is violating these guidelines by shipping advanced missile systems to Pakistan.

China sells far fewer conventional arms on the international market than the United States, although the PLA's customer base may be less savory. However, as Jianwei Wang points out in chapter 7, "Some would insist that the United States sells arms to good guys while China sells weapons to bad guys, but China would argue that such a distinction is without merit. How can you determine what kind of weapons, sold to whom, will have stabilizing or destabilizing consequences?"

It is unrealistic for the United States to expect to dictate the definition of rogue regime and have China refrain from weapons sales accordingly. From Beijing's perspective, Taiwan is a rogue regime. Beijing would argue that by selling F-16s to Taiwan, Washington has violated the principle of nonproliferation, as well as the 1982 Arms Sales Communiqué. U.S. weapons sales to Taiwan are likely to be a factor in negotiating nonproliferation principles with China. The equation is delicate: the United States threatens the PRC's vital interest by supplying weapons to Taiwan, China threatens a vital American interest by supplying weapons to the Persian Gulf states. Complicating matters further, Beijing argues that Taiwan's military aircraft pose a nuclear delivery threat, albeit different than that of missiles. Therefore, the Chinese insist that the sale of long-range fighters should be subject to a control regime similar to MTCR.

Turning now to the first of the three "interdependence principles," market access for trade and investment is a principle of vital importance to both the United States and China, as well as to the PRC's other trading partners. China's economic transformation, the source of its reemergence as a great power, has been accelerated by international trade and investment, which in turn depends on a liberal trading order. China's compliance with market access principles can be measured crudely on a macroeconomic basis and more closely on a sectoral microeconomic basis.

Trade data since 1978 shows that China's current account varies between a modest surplus and a modest deficit, and there is little evidence that Beijing is following macroeconomic policies that will result in perpetual trade surpluses, as Japan did. The renminbi, or national currency, is not yet fully convertible into other major currencies, but the Bank of China has neither the inclination nor the ability to sustain an artificially undervalued exchange rate to promote exports over the long term. The U.S. balance of payments deficit with China approached $40 billion in 1995, but it was created by fundamental macroeconomic factors, principally differences in savings and investment ratios, and the imbalance between the relatively open American market and the Chinese market, which is garrisoned behind trade barriers. The deficit figures are also distorted by an accounting anomaly. Almost 75 percent of Chinese exports to the United States flow through Hong Kong, where their nominal value is markedly increased. Without that value added step, the U.S. trade deficit with China would decrease by as much as $10 billion.[16]

The argument that China's market is closed is not supported by other macroeconomic indices, such as the ratio of foreign
investment to total domestic investment, and the level of foreign
trade as a percentage of GDP. By these measures China is
arguably more open and more integrated into the global economy than South Korea or Japan.[17] Many of China's Asian neighbors run a permanent balance of payments surplus (Japan's is
two to three percent of GDP), and almost all practice a variety of
trade and investment restraints. It is unreasonable to demand of
China more conformity to the principle of market access than is
demanded of South Korea or Japan, for example.

In specific sectors of the Chinese economy, however, compliance is much more negative. The pervasive state intervention,
left over from the days of the command economy, as well as the
garden-variety protectionist measures, some driven by local corporatist interests, some by state industrial policies, are the source
of arbitrary and inconsistent tariffs, restrictive licenses, discriminatory standards, exclusionary procurement, and a lack of transparency and due process. In pursuing structural goals, such as the
building of an indigenous automotive industry, Chinese officials
routinely force foreign investors to transfer technological know-
how to local industrialists and to enter into "shotgun marriages"
with Chinese industries in exchange for investment licenses.

The multilateral forum for dealing with such protectionist
measures is the World Trade Organization (WTO). The WTO's
trading rules are clear-cut, with detailed mechanisms for measuring and redressing violations. China has been negotiating
for permission to join the WTO, so it can qualify for the waivers
and delays of trade regulations accorded to a less developed
country (LDC). A policy of conditional engagement would
mean a strong recommendation that China become a full
member of the WTO, but on a footing with other great powers
rather than as an LDC. There should be some flexibility on
phase-in periods but no compromise on China's adherence to
the principle of market access—the foundation of the liberal

trading system—or on the honoring of WTO commitments at every level of the Chinese government.

But WTO rules are still relatively ineffective in dealing with many of the structural and nontariff market barriers in China and elsewhere in East Asia. The challenge of breaking down China's protectionist local corporatism, which is described in more detail in chapter 3, will still fall upon bilateral negotiations for some time to come. It is a double-barreled problem: negotiating a reasonable bilateral agreement and enforcing it at the local level. The recently signed intellectual property rights agreements between the United States and China are a case in point: negotiated agreements are in place, but the jury is still out on whether they will be enforced at the provincial and local levels.

Increased access to China's markets is vital for American exporters and the only way to forestall protectionist backlash in the United States against China. Such protectionist moves would not only reduce American profits, they would threaten the economic integration of China, the cornerstone of conditional engagement. A widespread public perception that the United States is hobbled by an uneven playing field in trading with China, combined with a popular suspicion that Washington is tolerating the arrangement for reasons of security (as it has with Japan for almost three decades) would destroy domestic political support for conditional engagement.

The principle of cooperative solutions for transnational problems, the second of the "interdependence principles," is hard to nail down because such problems—drug trafficking, illegal migrants, environmental hazards—are fairly new to the diplomatic agenda, having traditionally been dealt with as domestic policy problems in Asian states and the United States. China's inability to police its borders and the inefficient and frequently corrupt Chinese law enforcement permits the outward flow of illegal migrants and drugs. The U.S. government's inability to control its own borders and the inefficient and frequently corrupt American system of law enforcement permits the inward flow of illegal migrants and drugs. As such problems occur with increasing frequency, they provoke intense public reactions. However, there are few comprehensive international agreements that deal with crime and migration, and there is a spotty history of enforcing the ones in existence.

It is difficult to measure Chinese compliance with the principle of cooperative resolution. The number of illegal migrants in Asia has exploded from about 200,000 in 1980, to a total of 2-3 million today. There is a lack of reliable statistics on how many of these illegal migrants are from China, but rough estimates suggest there are some 100,000 illegal Chinese migrants in Thailand, 30,000 in Taiwan, 50,000 in Japan, and tens of thousands scattered around the rest of northeast and southeast Asia.[19] As many as 300,000 reside in eastern Russia; up to 400,000 in the United States. These migrations have caused cultural clashes, public health problems, increased activity in organized crime, and rising concerns over political stability.[18]

While the number of Chinese illegal immigrants is significant, it represents a modest percentage (between 15 and 20 percent) of the total number of illegal migrants in Asia. It pales in comparison to the number of migrants within China, the "floaters," currently estimated at 100 million.[20] The current number of Chinese illegal migrants in Asia is a mere trickle compared to the potential number who could come flooding out of the 1.2 billion-person nation. If China were to loosen its border controls, either to let off steam from domestic dissent or to intimidate a neighboring state, or were it to collapse into political chaos—as has happened in Russia—the borders would be deluged.

Organized crime is an enormous problem in China and its groups (known as "triads") have spread their tentacles throughout Asia and the United States.[21] It has benefitted immensely from Beijing's loosening of controls on the life of the average citizen, the widespread official corruption, and the booming Chinese economy. The so-called "snakehead" triads, who dominate the smuggling of people, transport an estimated 100,000 illegal migrants into the United States annually. At a fee of $20,000 per migrant, it is a $2 billion business. Southeast Asia is also the origin of most of the heroin smuggled into the United States—some 400 tons per year. The effects of the drug trade are showing in China too. Chinese police are increasingly seizing narcotics and illicit chemicals in transit. There are an estimated 250,000 known addicts, and perhaps one to two million other users, in China.

Narcotics smuggling is covered by numerous international agreements that could prove useful in evaluating China's participation in cooperative solutions for transnational problems, including the United Nations Convention against Illicit Traffic in Narcotic Drugs and Psychotropic Substances of 1988. The convention and the related activities of the U.N. Drug Control Program and the International Narcotics Control Board are of too recent a vintage to permit an assessment of their usefulness. China and the United States are parties to the convention, but enforcement is obviously difficult for both.

China has signed several international agreements on environmental pollution, such as the Montreal Convention on Chlorofluorocarbons, and the Rio convention on "greenhouse gases." The problem with measuring China's compliance is that these agreements have no bite, that is, they will not impose economic costs on China for several years. Currently, China has serious environmental problems on all fronts—polluted water supplies, shrinking water tables, poor air quality—that are beginning to have a serious impact on its neighbors. Although China has very progressive environmental legislation on the books, corruption and economic dependence on polluting industries has meant poor enforcement.

On respect for human rights, the last of the ten principles, China's violations are widespread, brutal, and well documented, particularly with respect to its political dissidents. Personal freedom and security for the average Chinese citizen, however, has expanded enormously over the past 15 years, especially compared to the totalitarian horrors of the preceding decades. There is no doubt, however, that China does not honor the elementary definition of human rights implicit in the U.N. charter it signed in 1979.

The United States has historically taken a strong stand on human rights issues in China and elsewhere in Asia, a sharp contrast to the passivity of other Asian states, including democracies like South Korea and Japan. Most of the members of ASEAN also have been mute, on occasion even approving, of Beijing's repressive policies. As Amitav Acharya points out in chapter 10, the ASEAN countries argue that respect for human rights should conform to "Asian values," in particular the priority of societal rights over individual ones. While much of this talk about Asian values is merely a transparent attempt to justify ruling regimes' monopolies on power, conditional engagement argues that China should not be held to a human rights standard much higher than that expected of Indonesia or Vietnam, for example.

Conditional engagement will not work unless Washington has realistic expectations with respect to Beijing's acceptance of and compliance with the ten principles. The principles themselves are so broad that they should not be contained within a single agreement. It is unrealistic to expect, at least for the next few years, that there will be some sort of comprehensive Shanghai II Communiqué that would cast these principles in bronze. Leaders in both Beijing and Washington are still wary of each other, and the political risks involved in such a comprehensive negotiation of principles are too high at the moment.

Aside from bureaucratic obstacles, getting China to place much faith in international principles at all is a tall order. Many of China's leaders are suspicious of the world's political economy ("in which the rich bully the poor"), international law ("which recognized the unequal treaties that dismembered Qing China"), and multilateral organizations ("a tool of the West"), and they point to the lessons of the eighteenth and nineteenth centuries, when China was ruthlessly exploited by imperialist powers. Nevertheless, the PRC does have a fairly principled foreign policy in the sense that its rhetoric has a strongly moralistic tone. This approach is a product of the regime's concern for domestic legitimacy and international prestige as well as residual Confucian attitudes regarding the proper exercise of power. Moreover, the clarity of these principles permits the small group of leaders in Beijing to communicate them more effectively to the 60 million members of the Chinese Communist Party and the 1.2 billion Chinese citizens.

As China scholar Samuel Kim observes, "The challenge of 'remaking' the hard facts of its international behavior to validate its professed self-image leads to a constant reformulation, renumbering, and redramatization of China's basic foreign policy principles (e.g. the Five Principles of Peaceful Coexistence, Mao's three-worlds theory, Deng's Four Cardinal Principles, etc.)."[22] Another gradual reformulation, toward the ten principles outlined here, is all that conditional engagement would require, but if the reformulation somewhat constrained China's foreign policy, so much the better. There is no expectation that China's rhetorical agreement to these principles alone would lead Beijing to alter its foreign policy practices. The main purpose in eliciting agreement to the ten principles is to create a reasonable benchmark against which China's integration into the world community and its subsequent behavior can be measured.

It is only fair to acknowledge that hostility to internationalist principles as a guide for foreign policy is not limited to China. Many political groups in the United States, including elements of the new Republican majority in Congress and traditional conservative groups, are deeply suspicious of any approach to American foreign policy that implies a diminution of sovereignty, even in principle. And as a practical matter, American policymakers are not comfortable in accepting constraints on America's ability to act unilaterally, particularly in the security realm, or in observing reciprocity in principled behavior. American behavior in Latin America, for example, generally falls short of the standards that conditional engagement would demand of the Chinese in Southeast Asia.

America's leaders, like China's leaders, are attracted to a principled foreign policy for some of the same reasons, such as domestic political legitimacy. This is compounded by the streak of Wilsonian idealism that runs through American foreign policy. The United States is unwilling to cede the moral high ground to anyone, much less China, and needs to justify its actions, however expedient, with reference to some principles. Conditional engagement's ten principles should fit the bill.

Unfortunately, the fractious American political system makes it difficult for other countries to deal with the United States on the basis of shared principles. Diplomats and foreign leaders find it exceptionally hard to pin down which principles the United States is prepared to act on since there are many powerful voices recommending a wide range of actions based on widely different principles on any given problem, particularly the China problem. This cacophony is particularly hard for Chinese leaders and other Asian leaders to interpret. Almost all the states on China's periphery are receptive to a principles-based approach to foreign affairs, because an appeal to principle can marginally tame the great powers or at least make them more predictable.

Principles alone will not tame China, nor will they make China's political trajectory any more predictable. But these ten principles do provide an objective means of measuring the direction and the speed of that trajectory, and its likely impact on the world outside of the Middle Kingdom. The ten principles proposed by conditional engagement are moderate enough to accommodate Chinese assertiveness while defending the vital interests of the United States and China's Asian neighbors, and they pass the reality check of compatibility with current behavior. The ten principles can provide the basis for a consistent and practical American domestic consensus on how to deal with the great imponderable of Asian politics, the People's Republic of China.

NOTES

1. The national integrity principles are treated in detail in chapter 4.
2. Reuters, "China's army cannot rule out force against Taiwan," July 31, 1995.
3. Reuters, August 15, 1995.
4. See Amitav Acharya's discussion of this issue in chapter 10. "Beijing's current commitment to the peaceful settlement of disputes is dismissed as a tactic to buy time . . . Proof of this can be found in the contradictions between China's declared policy and its actions on the Spratly Islands issue. While recognizing the disputed status of the islands and supporting a negotiated settlement, China has steadily increased the number of islands under its occupation and claimed sovereignty through national legislation."
5. U.S. Department of Defense, "National Security and the Convention on the Law of the Sea." pp. 3-6.
6. According to the U.S. General Accounting Office, "Since 1989, the official Chinese defense budget increased annually at a double digit pace, but . . . when adjusted for inflation there has been almost no real growth in the official defense budget. Major categories of defense spending, such as weapons acquisition and research and development, are not part of the official budget. To date, few new weapons systems have been acquired, and other improvements, such as better training, have benefited only a few units." See GAO, *The Impact of China's Military Modernization in the Pacific Region* (Washington, D.C. 1995), p.2. PLA budget estimates vary widely, however; the GAO is not the final word in this debate.
7. See Ashley J. Tellis, "Military Technology Acquisition and Regional Stability in East Asia," in *East Asia's Potential for Instability and Crisis*, ed. Jonathan D. Pollack and Kim Hyun-Dong (Santa Monica, Ca.: RAND, 1995).
8. McNamara *et al*, "Sino-American Military Relations: Mutual Responsibilities in the Post–Cold War Era," *National Committee China Policy Series* 9 (November 1994), p. 11.
9. Dunbar Lockwood, "The Status of U.S., Russian, and Chinese Nuclear Forces in Northeast Asia," *Arms Control Today* 24, no. 9 (November 1994), p. 24.
10. See Alastair Iain Johnston, "China's New Old Thinking: The Concept of Limited Deterrence," *International Security* 20 (Winter 1995), and "Learning versus Adaptation: Explaining Change in Chinese Arms Control Policy in the 1980's and 1990's," *The China*

Journal 35 (January 1996).

11. Paul Godwin and John Schulz, "China and Arms Control: Transition in East Asia," *Arms Control Today* 24, no. 9 (November 1994), p. 10.

12. "China White Paper on Arms Control and Disarmament," *Xinhua News Agency*, November 18, 1995.

13. Track-two discussions are expert discussion groups on security matters which government and military officials attend in an unofficial capacity, such as the Northeast Asia Cooperation Dialogue, which is organized by Dr. Susan Shirk.

14. U.S. Arms Control and Disarmament Agency, *Report to Congress 1994*, p. 74.

15. Ibid., p. 71.

16. See Richard R. Garbaccio, "U.S.-China Trade Relations," (unpublished manuscript prepared for the Program on International Economics and Politics, East-West Center, September, 1995).

17. Nicholas Lardy, *China in the World Economy*, (Washington, D.C.: Institute for International Economic), p. 111.

18. See Paul J. Smith, "Asia's Economic Transformation and Its Impact on Intraregional Labor Migration," *Asia Project Working Paper*, (New York: Council on Foreign Relations, March 1995).

19. These are recent migrants, as opposed to the *hua qiao* in Southeast Asia, most of whose families have resided outside China for several generations.

20. By way of contrast, there are at least one million illegal Indonesian migrants in Malaysia alone, more than half of one percent of Indonesia's current population.

21. Stephen Flynn, "Ailing Sovereignty: Drugs and Organized Crime in the Far East," *Asia Project Working Paper*, (New York: Council on Foreign Relations, June 1995).

22. Samuel S. Kim, "China's International Organizational Behavior," *Chinese Foreign Policy: Theory and Practice*, ed. Robinson and Shambaugh (Oxford: Oxford University Press, 1994), p. 402.

3

Economic Engagement

ON THE SURFACE, the economic engagement of China is tempting: the emerging Chinese power is persuaded to moderate its behavior and comply with the ten principles, and every trading partner involved is enriched in the process. However, the assumption behind conditional engagement is that trade with and investment in China may encourage compliance with some of these principles, but may actually undermine others.

For example, as China moves toward full integration in the global economy, it has a strong incentive to respect the four national integrity principles; those on the use of force, the resolution of territorial disputes, respect for sovereignty, and freedom of navigation. Their violation would impose a direct and immediate risk to China's sustained economic growth. Moreover, this incentive will increase as China grows more dependent on international markets and the costs of reversing such integration rise.

But economic integration will not have an equally salutary effect on Chinese compliance with the principle of military moderation; the People's Liberation Army (PLA) may become more of a threat as it accumulates more money and better technology. This negative effect may well increase over time if China's economy continues to barrel along at a 10 percent annual growth rate. Similarly, economic integration will not solve the problem of transparency, and it may increase the risk of proliferation.

Economic integration will encourage China's conformance with the market access principle, although local corporatism and losses by state-owned enterprises will continue to obstruct market reforms and deregulation. At the same time, however, freer markets and the corrosion of Beijing's command economy will make it harder for China to solve the transnational problems discussed in Chapter 2, at least in the short run. A weak central administration, local corporatism, rampant corruption, and yawning income disparities among provinces will compound illegal migration, crime, and pollution.

The impact of economic integration on the recognition of basic human rights in China has been positive and is likely to grow. But because its effects are diffuse and indirect, marked improvement will take a long time. Democratization may spread to higher levels of authority throughout China, but only as a result of fundamental change in the domestic political environment, not as a result of economic integration alone, and emphatically not as a result of external political pressures.

FOUR MODERATING FACTORS

THESE CONCLUSIONS about the effects of China's economic integration that underlie conditional engagement were reached by tackling three knotty questions. First, are the changes caused by economic integration apt to be irreversible? Second, will they encourage Chinese compliance with each of the ten principles? Lastly, can they be used as a tool of public policy?

The tyranny of markets will have the bluntest impact on decisionmakers in Beijing. China's economy is becoming increasingly dependent on world markets for essential inputs: energy, food, technology, and capital. The tyranny of markets means that immoderate international behavior and breaking the rules impose an economic cost on China, either by cutting off the supply of these critical inputs from abroad or by raising their price.

Capitalism, over the long term, can be corrosive to traditions and institutions in subtle ways: the spread of the rule of law, standardized public financial disclosure, and managerial accountability. Foreign traders and investors expect these rules of the road to be observed in their commercial dealings with China. Corrosive capitalism means that these international commercial practices will have a spillover effect on Chinese domestic economic activities, and ultimately on domestic political activities as well, in ways that will enhance compliance with the ten principles.

The ongoing devolution of power from Beijing to provincial authorities and even more so to municipal and other local authorities is the result of marketization, wherein resources are allocated by markets, not bureaucrats in Beijing; privatization, wherein the state-controlled sector is transferred to private owners; fiscal decentralization, wherein revenues and expenses of the state are increasingly controlled at provincial and local levels; and the erosion of the state's control over information. All four of these processes are accelerated by international trade and investment. The loss of power by the central government should make the leadership more accountable, less able to uni-

---

THE TEN PRINCIPLES OF CONDITIONAL ENGAGEMENT

1. No unilateral use of offensive military force
2. Peaceful resolution of territorial disputes
3. Respect for national sovereignty
4. Freedom of navigation
5. Moderation in military force buildup
6. Transparency of military forces
7. Nonproliferation of weapons of mass destruction
8. Market access for trade and investment
9. Cooperative solutions for transnational problems
10. Respect for basic human rights

laterally engage in risky or provocative behavior, and thus more likely to comply with the ten principles.

The effects of economic integration are showing up in the changing composition of China's elites, the growing personal stakes of the elite in the international integration process, and the expanding involvement of the PLA in business activities. These trends should enhance the odds of China's compliance with the ten principles.

Any discussion of the four moderating factors with respect to Chinese behavior must confront one inconvenient but inescapable caveat, however. The Chinese leadership's secretive decisionmaking obscures the calculus of tradeoffs between economic and security objectives. Senior-level decisionmaking is particularly opaque on security questions, making it difficult to trace the connection between an action in the economic arena and a decision in the political arena, much less to argue that there was a clear causal connection.[1] Given China's enormous government apparatus, it is likely that the broad authority to make tradeoffs between economic and security goals is exercised only at the highest levels. Moreover, the tone of public political discourse in China, which is heavily rhetorical and freighted with ideology, thoroughly clouds the picture of economic and political causation.

The leadership in Beijing is not particularly troubled by issues of economic efficiency; it is primarily motivated by the desire to keep itself in power and secondarily by the need to create a framework for comprehensive security, as expressed in the phrase *fu guo qiang bing*, "rich country, strong army." The strength of China and its military depends on a strong economy; wealth creation is not viewed as an end in itself.[2]

International economic integration is not endorsed by some of the Communist Party's old guard, who fear that entangled mutual interests will override national political differences and constrain China's ability to act unilaterally. Ironically, and unfortunately, the common translation of "peaceful evolution" in Chinese, *he ping yan bian*, is a code phrase for "capitalist plot" in Chinese political discourse.[3] The Chinese decisionmakers who view the world through the lens of interdependence and ascribe to the liberal-institutionalist school comprise a very small minority. As China scholar Michael Swaine of RAND points out, "China's emerging leadership is increasingly supportive of a state-centered form of patriotic nationalism. This notion, intended to compensate for the all-too-evident weaknesses of socialist ideology and to rally support behind the communist regime, seeks to defend the vested interests of the current authoritarian political system, not to challenge it in the name of an enlightened 'modern' or 'liberal' nationalism."[4]

THE TYRANNY OF MARKETS

THE CHINESE economy depends on international markets for two of the essential factors for economic growth, capital and technology, as well as two critical commodities, petroleum and food grains. This external market dependence is increasing at a remarkable rate.

China changed from being a net exporter to being a net importer in 1995, at a rate of about 200,000 barrels per day, or 7 percent of domestic consumption. By the year 2000, China will be importing about 1.2 million barrels per day, an amount estimated to comprise 22 percent of domestic oil consumption.[5] Moreover, half of China's petroleum imports are refined products, which increases China's dependence on oil refineries located offshore, mostly in Southeast Asia.

China is one of the world's largest grain producers, and it imported only 10 million tons in 1994, or less than 3 percent of the domestic demand. But by the year 2000, annual consumption will have risen to more that 520 million tons, of which 5 to 10 percent will have to be imported.

Although China has traditionally shunned the world capital markets, in recent years it has borrowed large sums in the commercial capital markets and become, relative to other developing nations, the largest recipient of loans from the World Bank. China's total foreign debt reached $93 billion by 1995, 75 percent of which was incurred by government agencies and state-owned financial institutions. This represented an 11 percent increase from 1993, an amount roughly equivalent to China's GNP growth rate.[6]

China restricted foreign investment and technology transfer until the Deng reforms in the late 1970s, but it is now the biggest recipient of foreign direct investment in the developing world, bringing in between $30 billion and $40 billion each year. Again, the rate of increase is roughly proportional to GNP growth rates.

China's dependency on these external markets certainly cannot be reversed without incurring huge political and economic costs.

In terms of capital, the Chinese authorities are constrained by the simple mathematics of funding high economic growth rates and huge infrastructure investments. The alternatives to external borrowing are limited, and there is little room to squeeze domestic consumption because the Chinese domestic household savings rates of 30 to 40 percent are already sky-high. The government could cut back on public and private investment, but that is a crude tool that would reduce job creation and drive up unemployment, possibly to politically explosive levels. Or it could try to reduce its fiscal deficit by cutting off subsidies to money-losing firms in the state sector (amounting to 5 percent of GDP), which would dump millions of workers into the streets.

China's energy planners cannot substitute coal for oil, since 70 percent of China's power is generated by coal, a level of output requiring over 1.2 billion tons of coal per year. No significant new domestic oil reserves have been found, and, in any case, tapping and transporting any such reserves takes a decade or more. China therefore has no alternative but to import more oil, unless it is willing to shut down most of its transportation, kill its embryonic auto and truck industry, and cripple the PLA.

As China has industrialized, the inexorable loss of arable land and shrinking of water tables has been the downside of its modernization miracle. However, its reduced agricultural capability is only part of the problem. Population growth is swelling the demand for food grains (China's population increases by 14 million each year, despite draconian population control policies). China will have to continue importing food grains to avoid drastically squeezing the already modest diet of its citizenry.

There is no practical alternative to technology transfer from abroad, given China's state of development. Without foreign designs and manufacturing expertise, which China has been getting through both direct investment and arms-length licensing agreements, productivity would stagnate.

If the tyranny of markets is indeed irreversible, then how will China's growing dependence on these markets—capital, technology, petroleum, and food grains—lead to more moderate political behavior and thereby buttress compliance with the ten principles? And how long will this take?

Any violation of the national integrity principles would require the use of military force on China's part. All four of these external markets react anonymously and unambiguously to aggression either by imposing a risk premium on all transactions or by drying up their resources entirely. These markets cannot be reasoned with or bullied into suspending the costs they impose on states for belligerent behavior. Even under the tightest international sanctions regime, there are always potential suppliers of oil and food, of course; it is merely a question of price. But the price can be very high indeed and the supply uncertain. Like Japan, China is becoming inescapably vulnerable to a long thin line of oil tankers streaming eastward from the Persian Gulf. Organized violence can easily rupture this line, but force alone cannot sustain it.

Capital markets can be fragile too. International lending institutions are not eager to deal with belligerent states, and firms that would otherwise be eager to invest in China and transfer their technology can get cold feet. Decisions involving direct investment take longer to make and implement, and therefore direct investors generally react more slowly than commodity or capital markets, but they are also more sensitive to the political and social climate in China. It takes much longer to restart a flow of foreign direct investment than to restart either commodity selling or capital borrowing. The tyranny of markets may also undermine Chinese compliance with the principles of moderation, transparency, and nonproliferation, since the free flow of capital and technology may accelerate the PLA's modernization efforts.[7]

The tyranny of markets is unleashing a host of forces within China that bolster the market access principle. Once foreign investors are inside the door with product or service operations, their presence begins to corrode protectionist regulations and other trade barriers from the inside out. Foreign investors are delighted to profit from state monopolies erected on their behalf, but they object to paying high prices charged by someone else's monopoly and work to surmount such barriers. Many foreign firms in China start out with an export focus but soon look to the domestic market as well, where their competitors, especially among the state-owned enterprises, are hampered by high prices and low-quality products.[8] The mobility of foreign investors can serve as a countervailing force to local corporatist protectionism in China: if the downstream costs of a local monopoly become high enough, downstream producers will lose their competitiveness, and new investors will shy away.[9]

Unfortunately, the tyranny of markets is of little use in solving such knotty transnational problems as illegal migration, crime, and environmental pollution, and it may well make these problems worse. For example, the globalization of markets has been a boon to organized crime in Asia. This globalization process has made it much easier to smuggle drugs and people and a lot easier to hide, launder, and transport the profits from illicit activities. Market interdependence loosened China's control of its borders and thus contributed to illegal emigration. In the long run, continued high economic growth and domestic job creation is the only solution to the river of Chinese economic refugees.

The tyranny of markets will also reduce environmental pollution in the long run. Poor regulation and the anything-goes boomtown atmosphere in China has attracted polluting factories. But eventually, foreign investors in manufacturing plants are more likely than indigenous firms to use more efficient, less polluting production technologies. These technologies are often cheaper once standardized throughout a firm or an industry and result in better quality control. Also, the managers of international firms are deeply averse to potential pollution liability.

One exception may be power-generation plants owned or operated by foreign investors. In that industry, pollution abatement can take a big a bite out of profits. However, over the long run the tyranny of markets, by pressing for the rational pricing of energy inputs, helps alleviate pollution. Suppliers will demand the prices set by world markets for energy inputs, so any subsidies to China's consumers, such as those for kerosene fuel, will quickly snowball into huge losses for the state enterprises involved.

International commodities markets have little if any effect on human rights issues. Few commodity suppliers give much thought to how Chinese citizens are treated by the state. But international investors generally do care about the basic rights of their local employees in China. They are also aware of the risks involved in investing in a repressive nation. Such regimes are inherently unstable, a fact that shortens the investment horizon and raises the discount rate in any investment calculation.

Firms that produce brand-name consumer goods in China, particularly apparel and sporting goods, also care about human rights. They run the risk of costly consumer boycotts in the United States and Europe during well-publicized spates of repression in China. Their brand name is their most precious asset, and human rights abuses can threaten that asset. In response, these firms can vote with their feet, or at least with their production contracts, and move to a less controversial location even if it has slightly higher costs.

CORROSIVE CAPITALISM

THE RULE OF LAW, public disclosure of financial data, and managerial accountability corrode command economies. These liberal practices are necessary for sustained growth in a market economy and, it is argued, will inevitably spill over into civil society and the world of politics, thus leading to a more moderate China.

In the 15 or so years since China's economic reforms began, foreign traders and investors have exposed their counterparts in China—partners, investors, workers, and officials—to these liberal practices. Capitalism has direct effects on how a society is fundamentally ordered. For example, contracts are critical to the conduct of international business; they must be enforced by the courts and recompensed if they are breached. Financial disclosure is essential for all commercial transactions, public or private, and is a cornerstone for the operation of stock and debt markets. Basic financial disclosure is built on double-entry accounting and standardized procedures for estimating assets, liabilities, and profitability. Accountability, by which managers are responsible for results and the proper stewardship of resources, is also fundamental to international commerce. (It is not so fundamental for managers in command economies, where making jobs can be more important than making anything else.)

In practice, how far have such liberal practices permeated China, and how irreversible are they? If the number of lawyers and cases in court is one measure, the rule of law in China has expanded by leaps and bounds since 1980. New laws are being written at various levels in China at a dizzying pace, including several national codes that will have a major impact on international trade, such as the Foreign Economic Contract Law and the Administrative Litigation Law.[10] But as Chinese legal scholar Jerome Cohen points out, "It is relatively easy to adopt legislative frameworks and regulatory regimes . . . It is much more difficult and time-consuming to put those laws into practice . . . 15 years is a very short period of time to develop the web of rules, customs, practices, institutions, habits and attitude that make up a legal system."[11]

There has been a similar burst of progress in the standardization of accounting since the beginning of this decade. Three major steps forward were taken from 1992 to 1993; a groundbreaking revision of the Accounting System for Foreign Investment Enterprises, enactment of the new Accounting System for Joint Stock Companies and the sweeping General Accounting Standard for People's Republic of China Enterprises. These three acts, plus subsequent refinements, brought the rather rudimentary accounting of Chinese enterprises closer to international practice.

A major force driving the improved accounting has been the public disclosure required by stock markets: the domestic exchanges, mainly in Shanghai and Shenzhen, the Hong Kong exchange for some firms, and the New York exchange for an even smaller set of Chinese firms. The market capitalization of listed Chinese firms is relatively small by international standards, but the rate of growth will probably continue to be explosive. The market capitalization of listed firms in China was roughly equivalent to 10 percent of GNP in 1995, compared to an average of 150 percent of GNP for listed firms in the ASEAN emerging equity markets. This suggests that the value of listed Chinese firms could well increase tenfold over the next decade, thus driving even more standardized reporting and public disclosure.[12]

How reversible are these liberal practices? The rule of law would be hard to turn back. According to Jerome Cohen, "When Deng Xiaoping assumed the leadership he and his colleagues in the Politburo and Central Committee made it clear that the construction of a legal system would be an indispensable element of the newly-proclaimed modernization policy."[13] The bureaucrats in Beijing have had enormous problems reconciling the patchwork of deals and exceptions that characterized the modernization reforms with the imperatives of rational administration. Given the benefits of increasingly efficient enterprises, which provide tax revenue and jobs, China's leadership is beginning to realize that it cannot roll back the practices of disclosure and accountability without paying a big price, and it cannot manage the economy without good information on economic performance. It has learned from the Soviet experience that poor statistics lead to poor decisions. The authorities in Beijing simply cannot regulate the provinces on many issues, ranging from monetary policy to environmental policy, without good information and more bureaucratic regularity.

Provincial and municipal party leaders in the local corporatist machines have found in the rule of law a means of protecting themselves from the arbitrary rulings of the central government, and their experience in touting their provinces abroad has taught them that these liberal practices are important in attracting foreign investment. And these liberal practices, particularly the freedom from arbitrary administrative levies and other abuses, can protect local interests as interprovincial trade and investment grow, eliminating the need for a bureaucracy to mediate.

If corrosive capitalism, as with the tyranny of markets, is also irreversible, then how will it lead to compliance with the ten principles? The most obvious and direct positive impact of increased capitalism will be on market access; the spread of the rule of law, standardized accounting, and disclosure will make it easier to spot pockets of protectionism. Under standard accounting practices, even a minimal amount of public disclosure can make it difficult to hide the windfall profits of monopolies.[14]

These liberal practices provide the grounds for injured commercial parties, both foreign and domestic, to seek redress for arbitrary nontariff barriers and other such impositions and for a reliable means of measuring damages and levying fines. And more important, the rule of law provides a mechanism for the enforcement of trade agreements, such as the 1995 intellectual property rights agreements between China and the United States.

These practices can also help resolve transnational problems. Environmental abuses will be more easily tracked and pollution fees will be assessed in a more systematic way. The rule of law will help China deal with its burgeoning crime problem, not least because the adoption of more consistent and less draconian practices by China's law enforcement agencies would make it easier for the FBI and other foreign agencies to cooperate in attacking such problems as drug and migrant smuggling.

Liberal practices may be of some marginal use in improving Chinese compliance with basic human rights principles, but only if there is a spillover from commercial law to civil law and criminal law. The reversion of Hong Kong in July 1997 and its subsequent governance as a special administrative region may be an object lesson in this regard.

The Chinese government has acted so far with restraint in its dealings with the United Kingdom over the reversion because Hong Kong is enormously valuable in economic terms; the colony's moneymaking machinery could be quickly damaged by harsh treatment. The Basic Law governing the reversion of Hong Kong is not limited to commercial law, but also guarantees an extensive amount of civil and criminal due process.[15] If China's leaders honor the Basic Law for the promised period of 50 years and Hong Kong is preserved as an island of political moderation and bureaucratic regularity within China, they will have created a model of quasi-federal governance that could be applied to Taiwan as well. Such an accomplishment would be a powerful example to Beijing of the practical rewards of principled behavior and reinforce compliance with the ten principles.

Two serious reservations must be kept in mind about the likelihood of a spillover from commercial affairs into the political realm. The first is that economic growth may not depend on the rule of law, public disclosure, and accountability quite as much as the West assumes. Singapore and South Korea have proven that authoritarian politics is not necessarily incompatible with fast economic growth. China's economy has grown more than 10 percent annually for over a decade without these liberal practices, and economic reforms have been desultory and scattershot, without much reference to the rule of law or uniform administration of rules. Disclosure has generally been limited to party conferences. Economic reforms addressing accountability were executed under a system that China scholar Susan Shirk refers to as "particularistic contracting."[16] In other words, the pace, sequence, and economic effect of reforms were tailored to enhance the personal wealth and political power of party officials. This striking aspect of the Chinese economy, referred to as local corporatism, is a dense network of local political machines made of party officials, bureaucrats, managers, and bankers who repay their special commercial privileges with political loyalty and financial kickbacks.

Local corporatism is not based on the rule of law, at least as defined in Western terms. Although it may depend on fairly accurate accounting, it certainly does not encourage public disclosure. There may be a semblance of accountability, but there is no equivalent to the standards of Western corporate governance.[17] According to legal expert Stanley Lubman, "Legality remains an ideal only inconsistently supported by the leadership, and current Chinese groping for the rule of law may become confused with the search for bureaucratic regularity."[18]

The second reservation about the spillover of these liberal practices into the political realm in China is that the Chinese Communist Party for all practical purposes remains above the law. The judiciary is viewed as an administrative arm of the government, more or less coequal with other state bureaucracies, and the bureaucracy remains accountable only to the Party.[19]

LOSS OF CONTROL BY THE CENTER

THE CONVENTIONAL wisdom is that economic integration with other nations has accelerated the loss of control by the core of political power in Beijing and that this control has devolved to the provinces and the private sector. The central government is thought to have less power to act unilaterally on both economic and political issues. This loss of control is attributed to several aspects of China's economic transformation: marketization, privatization, fiscal decentralization, and a freer flow of information.

Marketization, as measured by the percentage of transactions based on market prices rather than officially established prices, is very far along in China. By 1994, the Chinese government was setting prices for less than 15 percent of capital goods, 10 percent of agricultural products, and 5 percent of retail prices, and these percentages continue to fall. In contrast, when the economic reforms began in 1978, the government set over 90 percent of prices by administrative fiat.

Industry in China has been extensively privatized, as evidenced by the declining share of industrial output by state-owned enterprises; in 1978, the share was 78 percent, now it is 40 percent. Enterprises with private or foreign proprietors expanded their share of output to almost 20 percent over the same period, after starting near zero.

The balance of the industrial output share has been taken over by collective enterprises, which includes so-called "township and village enterprises," which are not owned by the central government, but are clearly not privately owned either. The collectives' share of output has grown to almost 40 percent from 22 percent in 1978.

Fiscal decentralization is also well along, with the central government's share of total tax revenues having declined to around 40 percent from 60 percent in 1978. In doing so, the center has pushed not only revenues but expenditures down to the provinces, which are now responsible for food subsidies, healthcare, education, government-run corporations, and a host of other major responsibilities. As a result, many provincial and local governments throughout China are in parlous financial condition. These local governments have retaliated with a variety of countermeasures to protect and increase their own revenues, including tax evasion, creation of extra-budgetary accounts, and revenue-sharing with the Ministry of Finance, which controls taxation formulas. The most prevalent countermeasure is to increase the local tax base by aggressively developing local industries under collective or government control as quickly as possible.

The central government has also lost much of its control over the flow of public information; marketization and privatization have affected the media industry as well. The loss of control was not what Beijing intended, of course. As émigré scholar Minxin Pei notes, "The Chinese opening in the mass media in the early 1980's was aimed at reducing financial losses and not at freeing public discourse. The government slashed subsidies to media organs and allowed the introduction of market forces, including financial autonomy, management decentralization, deregulation, and diversification."[20]

Market forces have had dramatic results on the media. For example, the government-owned media giant Xinhua's share of book sales has fallen to less than 30 percent from 95 percent in 1978. Ninety percent of Chinese citizens have access to a television, and nonstate channels now broadcast in several urban markets. More than 10 percent of urban households own a videocassette recorder, and millions more are sold annually; tens of millions of videotapes are in circulation. The government still tries to censor the news, particularly in the broadcast media, but leakage from the outside world is increasing. The number of phones and faxes per capita is still low by world standards but growing at an extraordinary rate. The number of telephones installed grew by over 30 percent from 1992 to 1993, to 26 million, and the number of wireless and mobile phone subscriptions almost doubled, to 6 million, in the same period.[21]

Are any of these four factors reversible by the central government, perhaps as part of a neonationalist crackdown? If so, at what cost to the leadership in Beijing? Beijing could not reverse marketization without throwing the economy into chaos. It has taken the government almost 20 years to gradually introduce pricing reforms. Privatization could be reversed only by clamping down on the high-growth firms in favor of the money-losing state enterprises. Beijing could reverse fiscal decentralization, and may in fact be doing so, given the nominal effect of the 1994 tax reforms. But it would be very difficult to reverse the trend toward the freer flow of information, for both economic and logistical reasons. The government would have to clamp down on several key growth sectors, including telecommunications, computers, information services, and the entertainment business. Keeping the censor's hand on all sources of print and broadcast copy would require a monitoring apparatus of colossal scale. Recent moves to grant Xinhua a domestic monopoly on economic news reporting have run into fierce opposition.

How will the loss of central control shape China's compliance with the ten principles? The loss of control by the central government should improve compliance with the four national integrity principles. There is some anecdotal evidence that the emergence of "natural economic territories" for Asian countries has constrained the ability of the central government to engage in confrontational diplomacy with the states on China's periphery. These territories arise from extensive cross-border commercial interests, and several of them include China. Those encompassing regions of China, ranked by level of economic activity, are: Guangdong with Hong Kong, Fujian with Taiwan, Shandong with South Korea, Dalian with Kyushu in Japan, and Guangxi and Yunnan with the Greater Mekong region. Provincial authorities, protective of their economic interests, have been known to counter belligerent statements from Beijing with more moderate and occasionally flatly contradictory statements of their own. Such back-channel diplomacy is likely to increase as these economic territories expand.

The freer flow of information is likely to moderate Beijing somewhat as the Chinese public has access to more objective news reporting, especially regarding national integrity issues or border disputes. A freer Chinese media, however, may not be a less nationalistic media. Chinese nationalism could be inflamed by irredentist tensions over Taiwan, Tibet, and other traditional trouble spots.

The devolution of power from the central government may have similarly mixed results on Chinese compliance with the principles of military moderation and transparency. Marketization may reduce the buying power of the PLA, and the military will have to compete for resources at market prices with other buyers. The PLA may have less control over its contractors as they increasingly focus on civilian markets; 60 percent or more of the output of China's defense industry is now devoted to civilian production. Nonetheless, marketization may improve the efficiency and the technical expertise of the PLA's suppliers, providing the military with access to more sophisticated equipment. More important, fiscal reform is leading to a more robust central government budget. As the central government sheds local responsibilities (and local losses), it will not necessarily become weaker. It may be able to focus on a smaller list of missions, such as national defense, and have more flexibility in spending to achieve its ends.

The freer flow of information is unlikely to improve compliance with the transparency principle. Military affairs are still considered taboo by the Chinese media; draconian punishments have been meted out to journalists for reporting "secret" economic data, much less truly secret military data. The forces lending to the central government's loss of control over prices, company ownership, and taxes can hardly be expected to lead to a loss of control over state security matters.

The devolution of power may not increase market access, since most stubborn trade barriers in China are due to local corporatism. The local authorities' appetite for tax revenue fuels local protectionism, not just against foreign imports, but against imports from other provinces.[22] They evade central government regulations, including international trade agreements, which makes it tough for China's trading partners to negotiate effective trade agreements with Beijing. Local enforcement provisions must be incorporated into the agreements. State enterprises are also roadblocks to free trade, which is often devastating to their market positions. They still have a disproportionate weight in the government's economic decisions. Most of the technocrats in the government rose through the ranks of the state enterprises sector, and have strong claims on the personal and institutional favors of the leadership.

Still, in the long term the loss of control by the central government will probably have a positive effect on market access. Collective and private sector firms are increasingly unwilling to purchase inputs from state enterprises above market price; and to see the fruits of their research and licensing agreements ripped off by domestic competitors. These firms may coalesce into a domestic lobby for compliance with market access and other free-trade principles. There is anecdotal evidence that such a coalition helped push the Chinese government into inking the intellectual property rights agreement with the United States.

The loss of control by the central government will have many more negative implications with respect to the handling of transnational problems. The emergence of local corporatism, stimulated by marketization and fiscal decentralization, has made local authorities prone to use expedient measures to maximize local revenues. Thus they are more inclined to take bribes for ignoring crimes, labor abuse, and pollution. Fiscal decentralization may also exacerbate the problem of migration because it has destroyed one of the mechanisms for interprovince transfer payments, whereby the central government was able to partially alleviate widening interprovince income differentials. Similarly, marketization is squeezing employment in state enterprises, leaving millions of workers who cannot be reabsorbed into the rural economies with few prospects. As censorship eases, China's mass media will increasingly broadcast the glitter of big city lights into remote villages, enticing a tide of surplus workers to surge into the big cities. Local governments are already putting up barriers to illegal internal migrants, such as strict local residence requirements. If China's economy crashes, this problem could swamp neighboring countries and send tens of thousands of illegal immigrants toward North America's shores.

The devolution of power from the central government has given citizens more freedom in their personal, day-to-day affairs; they no longer are dependent on the government for jobs, housing, and education, all of which were channeled through the *dan wei*, or work-unit, system. This economic "personal space" is a vital step toward the recognition of basic human rights by the state. And that progress will be reinforced by the freer flow of information, so that repression of dissent will increase the political risks at home and the financial penalties abroad.

THE CHANGING ELITE

THE COMPOSITION of China's elite is changing to include more technocrats and provincial leaders, both of whom seek to keep the PRC on a more pragmatic course and even keel. The membership of the powerful Central Committee is a case in point. Elections to the Central Committee take place every five years, the Fourteenth Central Committee having been assembled in 1992. Although the Central Committee does not choose the general secretary of the Communist Party, it does play a key role.[23] Thirty-five percent of the Fourteenth Central Committee membership has a technocratic background, slightly more than the Thirteenth Central Committee. Provincial representation is up as well, particularly from the eastern provinces, which account for 74 of the 189 members.[24] More of the elite also have a personal, as opposed to professional, stake in seeing that China's international relations and trade continue to run smoothly. These stakes may be direct, affecting how much money an official receives in bribes or other emoluments, or indirect, affecting profit-making opportunities for family members or scholarships for family members to study or travel abroad.

There is no reliable data on corruption in China, needless to say, but there is general agreement that it is endemic, involves huge sums, and is probably growing. There is some data on patterns of nepotism and rent-seeking by officials' family members, which is clearly extensive. Data on the number of Chinese students abroad, which in 1994-95 was nearly 40,000 in the United States alone or 8.7 percent of all foreign students in the United States, is more reliable.[25] Anecdotal evidence suggests that the children of China's elite leadership comprise a disproportionate share of those working or studying abroad, and that they are concentrated in the United States, Western Europe, and Japan.

The elite is also being affected by the burgeoning commercial role of the military in China. The PLA's joint ventures with foreign firms and their intermediaries may lead the PLA to become more cosmopolitan, less xenophobic, and more sensitive to the benefits that the armed forces can reap from a stable trading order. As an indirect benefit, the outside world may gain insight into the relatively closed world of Chinese security activities.

Data on the PLA's business activities is hard to obtain and even the leadership in Beijing may not have reliable data. Estimates suggest there are more than 20,000 PLA-owned firms, employing more than one million workers and generating revenues ranging from $3 billion to $6 billion per year.[26] The PLA participates in more than 200 joint ventures with foreign firms. And PLA businesses are concentrated in the transportation, real estate, civil engineering, and construction sectors.[27]

Given the emphasis on investment in infrastructure in China and the attractiveness of such projects to foreign investors, the PLA will continue to grow as an economic player despite the occasional warnings from the central government to cut back or restrict the scale of military businesses.

Are these changes in the composition of China's elite reversible? Whatever factional infighting may be taking place at the top and in the Politburo, the Central Committee has a degree of staying power because of its five-year selection cycle. Of course, a new secretary-general can try to reshuffle or pack the Central Committee with his supporters but even that is constrained by consensus politics. It is unrealistic to expect any serious reduction in China's endemic corruption. There are very few true believers in Marxist-Leninist-Maoist ideology in China any more, and there is a limit to which official exhortation and selective prosecution can inhibit corruption, given the ideological bankruptcy of the ruling party itself. The PLA's involvement in business could be reversed in theory, but to do so would probably require much bigger PLA budgets, extensive privatization of its existing firms, and a combination of financial incentives and crackdowns to wean PLA officials from their lucrative deals.

How will these shifts in elite composition affect China's compliance with the ten principles? The impact of these shifts on the national integrity principles will be marginally negative. Economic technocrats are not necessarily political moderates, nor will technocratic leaders be any less firm in dealing with challenges to Beijing's foreign policy. They may be slightly more cosmopolitan than the ideologues because of their personal exposure to foreigners in the course of managing the economy, but that does not necessarily make them liberal internationalists. In fact, assuming that technocrats continue to gain power both within the Central Committee and the Communist Party generally, political control over the PLA may erode. None of the third-generation party leaders have military credentials, and Jiang Zemin's control of the military still requires the cooperation of the old soldiers on the Central Military Commission. An expanding technocratic bias could make the leadership more sensitive to challenges to its nationalist credentials, less able to reign in party hawks and the military, and thus less moderate in foreign policy.

This tendency may be partially offset by the elite's growing personal stakes in economic integration. Many members of China's elite, both civilian and military, own assets in Hong Kong, including the prized asset, real estate. They have much to lose if Hong Kong's economy crumbles after the 1997 reversion. The leadership's families also would suffer if international tensions were to jeopardize the welcome of Chinese students abroad.

Technocrats may be more pragmatic than ideologues in

making the economic tradeoffs between civil and defense expenditures, and more easily persuaded by the argument that transparency will allow them to reduce military expenditures without imperiling security. Nevertheless, their experience in state enterprises has made them sympathetic to the needs of China's military industrial complex. In any case, they will have to contend with provincial representatives whose budgets have already been squeezed by fiscal decentralization and who begrudge the resources allocated to the military at their expense.

China's emerging technocracy may promote nonproliferation as well as transparency. The personal relationships among scientists of many nations during the Cold War and the personal relations between Soviet scientists and their leadership was important to progress in arms control with the Soviet Union. There is now some evidence of an embryonic arms control community forming within China, with links to the technocrats.[28]

The commercial activities of the PLA will have a mixed impact on defense moderation and nonproliferation. The sizable off-budget revenues from the PLA's businesses allow the military to buy advanced weaponry with few constraints from civilian decisionmakers. There is no evidence that these revenues are being used for large-scale weapons procurement, but PLA-related businesses may push Beijing to expand China's weapons exports trade. Chinese exports of politically sensitive items such as missiles and nuclear technology are still tightly controlled by the central government. Yet the leadership's personal stakes in the success of the defense industry may become a negative factor; money can buy anything, including export permits. Children of China's leaders (known as the "princelings") have been closely involved in China's weapons trade.

The changing composition of the elite has produced mixed results in terms of China's compliance with the market access principle. Technocrats are more inclined to seek market efficiencies and comparative advantages. However, the growth of local corporatism creates barriers to free trade and market access. If the PLA's commercial empire continues to expand and the "law of avoidance" (by which PLA commanders are rotated regularly in posts other than their home provinces) for military commanders is loosened, the PLA could become further entwined with local corporatist entities throughout China, adding layers of complexity and corruption to the already dense networks.

In addition to protecting local collective enterprises, artificial monopolies created by local corporatist interests are an easy source of "administrative rents," as are licensing requirements, discriminatory standards, arbitrary taxation, and thickets of bureaucratic red tape. Local corruption does present foreign investors with an opportunity to share in these rents, either as a partner or junior partner in a joint venture, but this type of arrangement, however profitable, is a far cry from free trade. Such protectionism worsens all the way up the ladder of power; many princelings thrive financially by cutting through Beijing's ministerial red tape.[29]

China's inclination to engage in cooperative solutions to transnational problems has been diminished by the changes in the elite. Pervasive corruption and nepotism undercut the very reforms they have prompted. Although technocrats may prefer pragmatic solutions to such problems and provincial representatives know the impact of such problems as environmental pollution, neither group favors accountability to third parties, such as environmental organizations. Crime, migration, and pollution are not just weak-state problems, but are deeply rooted in local corporatism.

The new elite may bode well for human rights protection. China's new technocrats are not closet Jeffersonian Democrats, but they could be more squeamish than other elites about the use of state power to torture and murder dissidents, particularly intellectual dissidents of like educational and family backgrounds. And the children of the leadership studying or working abroad may well turn out to be the most powerful moderating influence.

Several caveats should be kept in mind. First, technocrats are still a minority in the Central Committee, which is better described as a technocratic-bureaucratic alliance, and the Central Committee is only one of many decision-making institutions in China. There is, for example, the informal influence of party elders and various small groups that interlace the matrix of party and bureaucracy. And the technocrats' managerial experience is usually derived from their work for state enterprises, which are not exactly hotbeds of innovation, free thinking, or open-market competition.

Second, corruption has pervaded officialdom in China for a long time. Marketization may bring money, even colossal amounts of money, into the perpetual power struggle in Beijing, but money does not necessarily spawn moderation. Money does not make the power struggle at the top any more pluralistic or accountable, nor does it help institutionalize negotiation, power sharing, or power succession in Beijing.

Third, the transformation of the PLA from warriors into hoteliers is unlikely to be smooth. As Michael Swaine notes, "The military's business involvement has generally served to exacerbate particularistic interests and corrupt tendencies within the ranks . . . producing a division between those officers who place a priority on professionalism and view business activities as corrosive . . . and those officers who gain greatly from such activities."[30] Envy is compounded by a loss of PLA prestige—hardly a recipe for moderation.

In sum, economic integration has had—and likely will have—an uneven influence on China's compliance with the ten principles, so it cannot be seen as a panacea. Compliance with the four national integrity principles has been enhanced by China's increasing dependence on external markets such as petroleum, grain, capital, and technology, which are sensitive to belligerent foreign policies, and these constraints will increase over time.

WHAT GOVERNMENTS CAN DO

TO WHAT DEGREE can the economic integration of China be a tool of state policy? That is, how can the United States and other nations adjust their policies so that economic integration encourages or reinforces China's compliance with the ten principles? Government policy can make a modest difference through market-access agreements, both bilateral and multilateral; trade promotion; financial assistance; and cultural, technical, and educational exchanges.

However, there is relatively little that can be done to enhance the effect of the tyranny of markets. It is important for governments not to interfere with China's growing market dependence. One of the most emphatic recommendations of conditional engagement is that the slowly developing benefits of China's economic integration should not be put at risk or interfered with in favor of short-term political objectives. Linking most favored-nation status (MFN) with human rights performance is a classic example of such a shortsighted policy. Free markets often enforce better discipline than governments or quasi-government agencies and are less susceptible to political pressure. For example, capital markets can raise the cost of doing business in China in response to provocative PRC behavior; it is much harder for the World Bank, the Asian Development Bank, or, for that matter, the Japanese government to call China's leadership to task. Official grants are substitutes for commercial borrowing, and they reduce China's reliance on financial markets. This suggests that concessionary loans to China by quasi-official or public agencies should be discouraged.

As power devolves from China's central government and the elite class is transformed, economic integration will help create opportunities for retooling policies. It makes sense to expand government-to-government links with provincial authorities throughout China based on trade policy, commercial cooperation, and investment promotion. It also makes sense to build bridges to the PLA's businesses, since the military will have a strong impact on issues of strategic moderation, transparency, and nonproliferation.

The tyranny of markets, corrosive capitalism, and decentralization all buttress the principle of market access, but given the legacy of China's command economy and the thickets of local corporatism, they do not guarantee it. Therefore the United States must have a strong, activist trade policy toward China to promote U.S. exports and negotiate its way through the web of protectionist barriers.

On this score, the World Trade Organization (WTO) is a potent force for trade liberalization, and Chinese participation in the WTO is highly desirable, but only under conditions that are consistent with the organization's basic mission. The Chinese economy is too big and the WTO's infant industry exceptions are already too protectionist to warrant a relaxation of the rules of admittance, other than some flexibility on phase-in periods. The WTO has established incentives and sanctions, which Beijing should not be able to twist with political pressure. Over the long run, encouraging China's involvement in the WTO—a rather cut-and-dried rules-based negotiating forum where ideology counts for little and pragmatism for much—is an excellent way to promote China's peaceful integration into the global community and encourage principled behavior. Therefore, it is important for the United States and other nations to accommodate China's membership in the WTO.

Unfortunately, the current scope of the WTO is too narrow to deal with the types of nontariff barriers characteristic of China's local corporatism and residual state intervention. As a result, the office of the U.S. Trade Representative must remain engaged with Beijing to ensure implementation of existing accords, such as the intellectual property rights agreement and work toward additional liberalization. This will require ample resources, patience, and negotiating leverage, such as the ability to block Chinese exports to the United States if American exports to China are blocked, as permitted under Section 301 of the Omnibus Trade Act. Chinese trade negotiators will not make meaningful concessions—ones that will "break somebody's rice bowl"—unless they have strong incentives or no alternatives. This is why conditional engagement recommends measured but strict reciprocity on trade issues, including selective trade sanctions, when Beijing is uncooperative in negotiations or backpedals on agreements.

Trade promotion and other merchandizing efforts by the U.S. Department of Commerce appear to be effective, particularly for new-to-market American firms in China, and they should not be swept away in the efforts to streamline the Washington bureaucracy. Economic engagement requires official trade promotion in China, at both the national and provincial levels. Official interaction with Chinese buyers on behalf of American suppliers, and with Chinese authorities to obtain licenses for American investment, must be key elements of bilateral trade promotion. Chinese government agencies will continue to exercise a great deal of influence on many purchasing decisions, especially on big-ticket items, such as aircraft, power-generation equipment, transport equipment, and telecommunications systems—the products with which U.S. manufacturers are most competitive worldwide. These government agencies also issue licenses for foreign direct investment in sensitive sectors such as finance, insurance, media, telecommunications and automobiles. Direct investment is a necessary condition for sustained U.S. exports to China because sophisticated products need distribution, marketing, and local service and engineering support.[31] To encourage cooperative Chinese behavior, economic engagement recommends more flexible U.S. licensing and export approval policies, including a pragmatic approach to technology transfer. Only the transfer of the most sensitive military-use technologies should be blocked.

The positive effects of corrosive capitalism in China can be amplified by helping to build new institutions. Two excellent examples of such initiatives are New York University's training program for Chinese judicial authorities and the Syracuse University program for Chinese administrators. These activities are usually controlled by NGOs and funded by private foundations. The U.S. government could help the programs in minor ways, but in private hands they are probably more effective and less vulnerable to political pressures.

Conditional engagement's benefits for human rights are even more indirect and will be slow in bearing fruit. Unilateral efforts to hold China's exports hostage to American standards of human rights are rarely productive. Pressing the case for human rights and political pluralism in multilateral fora and a context of economic engagement will be more effective, since it is much harder for China's leadership to deflect such pressures when they come from other Asian states, especially big aid donors like Japan, or a group of fellow U.N. member states.

Private actors, businesses and NGOs, may be even more effective than governments in pressing China to improve its human rights record and labor standards. Consumer boycotts are a potent but underused weapon with which NGOs could convince corporations to enforce codes of conduct in their manufacturing and product-sourcing activities in China.

However, education will be more effective than coercion in the long run, and conditional engagement places the most hope for transplanting the principles of human rights and political pluralism to China on its next generation of leaders, who are currently being educated in the West and Japan. That the leaders of China, who are nominally hostile to Western values, have entrusted the education of so many of their children to Western universities is remarkable. By the same token, cadres of Chinese business managers, technicians, and administrators are being trained in the United States, Japan, and Europe. The U.S. government and American NGOs should provide visas, financial support, and any other reasonable inducements to the growing body of Chinese students in the United States, especially the children and grandchildren of the leadership, to encourage the transmission of this vital principle of human rights—the most elusive of the ten principles, but also the most uncompromising test of civilized behavior by states.

NOTES

1. There is only a small amount of anecdotal evidence showing how commercial transactions have led to the creation of "communities of interest" within China and how such communities express their agenda to the authorities. Contrast this with American ties of interest, such as midwestern wheat farmers, who want to sell food grains to China, or aircraft manufacturers, such as Boeing or McDonnell-Douglas, who want to sell airplanes to China. They have many venues for expressing their concerns clearly and loudly to Washington.

2. This concept is identical to the Japanese notion of *fukoku kyohei*, or "rich country, strong military," a popular phrase during the Meiji Restoration. The Meiji modernizers harnessed economic growth for the task of arming a Japan that was perceived to be backward and surrounded by avaricious imperialist powers who were carving up a proud but defenseless Qing Dynasty China.

3. As Thomas Christensen observes, the *he ping yan bian* problem is not one of transiton, but of etymology. It was first used by John Foster Dulles in the 1950s as a strategy of destabilizing the CCP.

4. Michael Swaine, *China: Domestic Change and Foreign Policy* (Santa Monica, Ca.: RAND, 1995), pp. 8-9.

5. Frank Tang, "China's Petroleum Market in 1995: Mid-Year Review, and Import Surge and Smuggling Outlook," *IAEE Newletter* (summer 1995).

6. China State Administration for Exchange Control, "1994 Debt Statistics."

7. This does not mean that China will necessarily become a big arms purchaser. The PLA's past behavior suggests that China will again license foreign military technology but depend on local production and reverse-engineering.

8. David Zweig, "Developmental Communities on China's Coast: The Impact of Trade, Investment, and Transnational Alliance," *Comparative Politics* 27, no. 3 (April 1995).

9. "Jurisdictional competition places some limits on this system of patronage and spoils. So does competition in the international market," Gabriella Montinola, Yingyi Qian, and Barry Weingast, "Federalism, Chinese Style: The Political Basis for Economic Success in China," *World Politics* 48, no. 1 (October 1995), p. 81.

10. William P. Alford, "Tasseled Loafers for Barefoot Lawyers: Transformation and Tension in the World of Chinese Legal Workers," *China Quarterly* 141 (March 1995), pp. 22-38.

11. Jerome A. Cohen and John E. Lange, "The Chinese Legal System—A Primer for Investors," *Investment Opportunities in China*, (New York: Morgan Stanley & Co., January 1995), p.3.

12. World Bank, *The Emerging Asian Bond Market*, (June 1995) as cited in Jim Rohwer, *Asia Rising*, (New York: Simon and Schuster, 1995), p. 297.

13. Cohen and Lange, "The Chinese Legal System—A Primer for Investors," p.2.

14. As Jerome Cohen cautions, "The impediments to this transition [to financial disclosure] are all the more difficult in China, where much business information is still classified as "state secrets"—penalties for unauthorized disclosure being sometimes quite severe—and where public securities ownership and the concept of accountability of stockholders are very new phenomena" Cohen and Lange, "The Chinese Legal System—Primer for Investors," p. 17.

15. The Basic Law of the Hong Kong Special Administrative Region of the People's Republic of China, pp.9-14.

16. Susan Shirk, *The Political Logical of Economic Reform in China*, (Berkeley: University of California Press, 1993), p. 87.

17. China is not the only Asian country where Western expectations of corporate governance are unmet. The rule of law in Japan is extremely attenuated, at least in Western terms. The so-called Asian growth model generally delegates a great deal of authority to largely unaccountable bureaucrats, who work under conditions of minimal disclosure and dubious accountability. Moreover, the bureaucratic authority does not rest on a presumption of fairness, efficiency, and predictability.

18. Stanley Lubman, "The Future of Chinese Law," *China Quarterly* 141 (March 1995), p. 20.

19. The Administrative Litigation Law (ALL) is an excellent example of the stubborn obstacles to spillover from the commercial to the political realm. "Under the ALL, foreign business enterprises may challenge the legality of decisions by China's administrative organs [but] while it appears to subject the state to a modicum of judicial restraint, the ALL to a large degree reinforces the state's power to make arbitrary decisions that intrude on foreign business activities. The statute does not permit review of discretionary decisions. ALL does not extend to the lawfulness of the underlying regulations upon which administrative decisions are based . . . finally, it does not extend to party decisions, thus prohibiting scrutiny of the most fundamental sources of state intrusion," Pitman B. Potter, "Foreign Investment Law in the P.R.C.: Dilemmas of State Control," *China Quarterly* 141 (March 1995), p. 170. "More fundamentally, despite constitutional and legislative language that confers the power to decide cases independently,

the courts, like the other governmental institutions, are subject to tight political control." Jerome Cohen and John Lange, "The Chinese Legal System—A Primer for Investors," p. 5.

20. Minxin Pei, *From Reform to Revolution*, (Cambridge, Mass.: Harvard University Press, 1994), p. 155.

21. *China Statistical Yearbook*, pp. 462-465.

22. Shirk, *The Political Logic of Economic Reform in China*, p. 187.

23. Ibid. pp. 71-72.

24. Zang Xiaowei, "The Fourteenth Central Committee of the CCP: Technocracy of Political Technocracy?" *Asian Survey* 33 (August 1993), p. 787.

25. Todd M. Davis, *Open Doors 1994/1995: Report on International Eductional Exchange*, (New York: Institute of International Education, 1995), p. 31.

26. Thomas J. Bickford, "The Chinese Military and its Business Operations," *Asian Survey* 34, no. 5 (May 1994), p. 469.

27. To put this in perspective, in 1992, the PLA's estimated revenue was $6 billion, its official budget was $6.7 billion, and its estimated total expenditures were $22 billion. PLA revenues represent almost 25 percent of the military's total revenues.

28. Alastair Iain Johnston, "Learning Versus Adaptation: Explaining the Change in Chinese Arms Control Policy in the 1980s and 1990s," *The China Journal* 35 (January 1996), p. 20.

29. There are precedents for corporatism and rent seeking coexisting with high economic growth. Japan and Korea are two good examples; however, the scale of rent-seeking is generally smaller and its character is more discreet and less overtly nepotistic. A closer analogy for China may be Indonesia, where Jakarta's equivalent of Beijing's "princelings" are a major commercial force.

30. Swaine, *China: Domestic Change and Foreign Policy*, p. 29.

31. Mark Mason, "FDI in East Asia: Trends and Critical U.S. Policy Issues," *Asia Project Working Paper*, (New York: Council on Foreign Relations, 1994), p. 16.

4

Security Engagement

A POLICY OF SECURITY engagement is meant to complement economic engagement if things go well and hedge U.S. interests if they do not. Its prime function is to encourage China to comply with the ten principles by applying pressure wherever economic incentives prove inadequate. This will be particularly important with respect to the principles of military moderation, transparency, nonproliferation, and cooperative approaches to transnational problems. The moderating factors associated with China's economic integration will not be sufficient to guarantee China's compliance in these areas.

Security engagement's broader function is to build a diplomatic and military foundation in the region that will allow the United States and its Asian allies to defend vital interests, in the event that China were to violate the ten principles with belligerent conduct. This broader role is not equivalent to a policy of preemptive containment; there is no hostile or aggressive intent toward China. A defensive and loosely knit security structure among the sovereign states of Northeast and Southeast Asia is proposed, aimed at discouraging Chinese military adventurism by making the cost of such adventurism unacceptably high to the decisionmakers in Beijing. Security engagement raises several questions: Under what broad constraints should such a policy operate? How can such a policy encourage China to comply with the military principles of moderation, transparency, and nonproliferation and to cooperate in addressing transnational problems that are not solved by economic engagement? How should policymakers prepare for a possible breakdown of economic engagement brought on by persistent Chinese violations of the ten principles? Specifically, what does security engagement mean for long-term U.S. military planning in Asia?

CONSTRAINTS ON SECURITY ENGAGEMENT

A POLICY of security engagement must operate within broad constraints to avoid becoming a unilateral, dangerous, and ultimately futile strategy of neocontainment. It must be flexible enough to incorporate solutions for security threats throughout the region, not just those involving China. The most immediate security threat is the standoff on the Korean Peninsula; in the long run, Japan's military role in the region will be a source of risk. As Byung-joon Ahn stresses in Chapter 9, "An American leadership strategy should not be directed at China alone, but also designed to anchor Japan firmly in its bilateral security relationship with the United States so that it can remain free of nuclear weapons and defensively postured. The American military presence is the essential glue that holds Japan's and South Korea's bilateral security relationships with the United States together and that allows ASEAN countries to have some measure of confidence in America's balancing role."

A policy of security engagement must work within the limits of American resources and be consistent with the overall U.S. security strategy. Security engagement must therefore be designed as a multilateral undertaking from the ground up, with the United States taking an active and leading role in some respects, but with the full participation and economic support of Japan, South Korea, and ASEAN. This is not to say that there should be an Asian version of the North Atlantic Treaty Organization; a formal collective security system in Asia is not politically feasible, at least within the 10 to 15-year time horizon of conditional engagement. But there should be much more cooperation on security matters with the Asian states assuming more of the burden of regional defense and more of the responsibility for forging the regional security structure of conditional engagement.

SECURITY ENGAGEMENT AND COMPLIANCE

How CAN security engagement encourage China to comply with the military principles of moderation, transparency, and nonproliferation and to cooperate in addressing transnational problems? How can it serve as a hedge against the risks posed by noncompliance with the four national integrity principles?

The idea behind economic engagement is the use of carrots and sticks to encourage principled behavior on China's part. But the carrots and sticks employed must be appropriate to the principle in question: tariffs should be fought with tariffs, for example. Such symmetrical tactics are inappropriate to security engagement. It would be foolish to counter Chinese shipments of missiles with a breach of the Missile Technology

---

THE TEN PRINCIPLES OF CONDITIONAL ENGAGEMENT

1. No unilateral use of offensive military force
2. Peaceful resolution of territorial disputes
3. Respect for national sovereignty
4. Freedom of navigation
5. Moderation in military force buildup
6. Transparency of military forces
7. Nonproliferation of weapons of mass destruction
8. Market access for trade and investment
9. Cooperative solutions for transnational problems
10. Respect for basic human rights

Control Regime by the United States, or to counter Chinese military secrecy by dropping a curtain over the transparent confidence-building exercises of the ASEAN Regional Forum (ARF). It would be even more foolish to counter a lack of Chinese cooperation on loosening pollution and crime with those types of sanctions. Therefore, the United States should have a flexible response to serious breaches of the security principles, a response that rewards or punishes Chinese behavior with similar actions if possible, but is flexible enough to act on another if it is less dangerous, less expensive, or more effective.

There are not many carrots available to win Chinese cooperation on transnational problems and even fewer sticks. The problem is that the Chinese authorities understandably view the international spillover effects of crime, illegal migration, drug trafficking, and environmental pollution to be trivial in comparison with their domestic effects. There are few domestic repercussions in China, for example, from illegal emigration, which may even help matters by bringing in money or ridding the body politic of malcontents.

In any case, China's emigration is dwarfed by its internal migration. And although Chinese society suffers from rising crime rates, the government is penalized little, if at all, for the offshore depredations of the triads. As for environmental pollution, however, Chinese citizens certainly suffer from smog more than the Japanese or Koreans.

Still, with security engagement there are some ways to craft incentives for China to assist in comprehensive solutions to these problems. Such solutions generally involve a three-step process: limiting the scope of a problem, targeting its most objectionable and dangerous aspects, and reinforcing the process through cooperative efforts.

In the case of illegal migration, for example, it would make sense for the United States and perhaps Japan and South Korea to issue short-term work visas for Chinese migrants in cooperation with China and under the auspices of the Asia-Pacific

Economic Cooperation forum. The vast majority of Chinese migrants are economic refugees, not political refugees. If they had a legal and safe way to go to the United States or Japan, make money, and then return home, demand for the services of the snakeheads would plummet—particularly if the program combined effective law enforcement against the smugglers on both sides of the Pacific. One carrot to induce Chinese cooperation in enforcing a guest worker system would be for the United States to stop pressing Beijing on the issue of free emigration. It makes no sense whatsoever to badger China on this subject when neither the United States nor its Asian allies is willing to accept large numbers of Chinese immigrants.

The United States could also use carrots to elicit Beijing's cooperation in suppressing organized crime and drug trafficking. The demand for addictive drugs is fairly inelastic with regard to price, so capturing smugglers is not enough. A comprehensive program to partially legalize less dangerous drugs, combined with full-fledged preventive education and addiction treatment programs, is probably necessary to tackle the American drug problem. The interdiction of dangerous drug traffickers is just part of the solution. The United States and its Asian allies could offer technical assistance to help China deal with the triads and criminal allies around the world. This would help China address its homegrown drug abuse problem. Such cooperation might include the sharing of clinical data on the treatment of addictions, the exchange of data on criminal organizations and drug flows, restrictions on trade in chemicals posed to make narcotics transfer of surveillance and inspection technology, controls on money laundering, and reciprocal law enforcement, including the deportation of criminal suspects.

Arm-in-arm collaboration with Chinese law enforcement may prove to be distasteful in some cases. China's legal system is politicized and frequently corrupt, and some methods of Chinese law enforcement are brutal by Western standards. Inevitably, some Americans will become suspects and suffer the tender mercies of China's police and prison system. But there is evidence that this type of collaboration can work. The Hong Kong police have successfully worked with the police in Guangdong to crack down on the smuggling of automatic weapons into the colony—AK-47s were being used to rob jewelry stores—and to crack down on the smuggling of stolen vehicles out of the colony—Mercedes-Benzes were being snatched to order and shipped off to Shenzhen in cigarette boats. The success of this collaboration is all the more impressive since elements of the People's Liberation Army were allegedly involved in both the sale of the weapons and the shipment of the stolen vehicles.

Uncooperative behavior might be punished by imposing time-consuming inspections on Chinese imports if there is a suspicion of involvement with illicit narcotics, by blocking travel and visa applications for Chinese citizens and officials connected with drug trafficking, and by impounding funds related to suspected money-laundering schemes. The most effective stick, however, would be to publicly insist that Beijing honor its obligations under the U.N. narcotics regimes, although Washington might be called to account for its own lack of performance on this score.

There are fewer carrots with respect to the military principles of moderation, transparency, and nonproliferation; on the other hand, there are many more sticks. Cooperation in some areas of arms control and transparency can be to China's benefit.[2] This benefit can be explained to Beijing, but it cannot be proffered by the West as a reward for good behavior. Through cooperative behavior in the various international and regional fora where arms control regimes and transparency exchanges are negotiated, China could gain a measure of international prestige, and its negotiators a measure of personal prestige. There are already groups of PLA officers who see some value in transparency dialogues and other military-to-military contacts, if only for the purposes of intelligence-gathering.

The most appealing carrot to the PLA would be the transfer of advanced technology as a reward for conformance with transparency and arms-control regimes. The PLA would like to use Western advanced weapons technology to accelerate its modernization program and spend its money more efficiently by avoiding dead-end programs. It would make sense under conditional engagement to reinstate such technology exchanges, but limit them to defensive weapons systems, along the lines of the programs initiated by the Carter and Reagan administrations. All parties would clearly benefit if China were able to acquire technologies to reduce security risks such as the accidental launch of nuclear missiles or the theft of fissile materials.

A few diplomatic carrots could be dangled before Beijing to encourage compliance with the principle of nonproliferation. As China becomes increasingly dependent on Persian Gulf oil, its leadership will begin to recognize that China is hostage to the same Middle Eastern instabilities that the United States, Europe, and Japan face, and that the temptation to fish in troubled Gulf waters by exporting weapons of mass destruction is ultimately dangerous and self-defeating. As one of the Permanent Five members of the U.N. Security Council, China played a key, if reluctant, role in the Gulf War and participated in the subsequent sanctions against Iraq. It would be an excellent idea to resurrect the Permanent Five consultations on arms exports to the Middle East that were terminated in 1992, and to include missile and nuclear technologies in the U.N. arms registry and the notification procedures that were originally proposed in the talks.

Should China violate the nonproliferation principle, several asymmetrical tit-for-tats are available. Each of the multilateral arms control regimes has detailed procedures for determining whether sanctions will be applied and how they will be enforced. Multilateral sanctions can sting because Beijing may lose face and prestige, particularly when a sanctions regime falls under the U.N. umbrella. China has already been reproached for its dilatory tactics in the Comprehensive Test

Ban Treaty negotiations. While there is much to be gained from cajoling China on issues of nonproliferation, an asymmetric response can carry a much sharper sting. A shipment of Chinese missiles to Pakistan, for example, could be countered with a shipment of advanced fighter aircraft to Vietnam, if extreme measures were necessary.

There are no substantial carrots and only a few blunt sticks with which to encourage Beijing to moderate its buildup of conventional forces, particularly in the area of power-projection capabilities. If the outlook for restraining the PLA's conventional weapons buildup is bleak, it is even bleaker for restraining the expansion of the PLA's nuclear forces or discouraging a shift in Chinese nuclear strategy from minimal to limited deterrence. The American nuclear arsenal is far larger and more sophisticated than the PLA's, so it is difficult to concoct an equation for mutual arms reduction that would be even remotely acceptable to both parties. Even after current arms reduction agreements with the former Soviet Union are implemented, the United States will possess about 3,500 nuclear warheads, more than ten times China's current stock. The nuclear arsenals of France and the United Kingdom, which the PRC would attempt to include in any such arms reduction talks, add another layer of complexity to this problem.

The renewed American interest in anti-ballistic missiles systems, especially theater-missile defense systems, might force Beijing to be more cooperative, but it might also spur China to accelerate its move toward limited deterrence and the more sophisticated and destabilizing nuclear weapons such a doctrine requires. The cost of theater-missile defense systems is exorbitant, and there are doubts about the reliability of their performance, but if the Soviet response to the Reagan administration's Strategic Defense Initiative is any guide, these systems may be one of the few means of inducing China to the nuclear arms control table.[3]

BEING PREPARED

THE TACTICAL STICK for responding to Chinese violations of the principles of military moderation, transparency, and nonproliferation is the same stick that will ultimately deter China from violating the first four national integrity principles: the military forces of a loosely structured alliance of the United States, Japan, Korea, and ASEAN. The alliance would be built upon cooperative efforts toward proportional defense spending, a fair division of labor between the United States and its Asian allies, the interoperability of weapons and communications systems, and extensive joint training.[4]

To sustain proportional defense spending, the states of Northeast and Southeast Asia should be encouraged to maintain or increase the percentage of gross national product (GNP) they now allot to national defense. The same Asian economic dynamism that is enhancing China's military power should be harnessed to enhance the defensive forces of China's neighbors. The risk of any of these Asian states attacking each other is slim.

The current tactical division of labor, among the United States and its East Asian allies should be enlarged along the same lines to include the ASEAN region. As one strategist has observed, "the military posture of the host country is usually oriented to defending its air, land, and sea space through reactive means. In contrast, American military forces take primary responsibility for all *initiatory* military operations."[5] Although the distinction between offensive and defensive weapons is fuzzy, particularly for sophisticated aircraft and communications systems, it is still a useful starting point for coordinating the roles and missions of the United States and its Asian allies. The United States focuses on sea and air forces and advanced communications and intelligence functions; Asian states emphasize land forces and shorter-range air and sea power.

The United States and its Asian allies should move gradually toward similar military infrastructures such as airfields and naval bases, similar or identical weapons systems, and similar communications systems in order to establish a high degree of tactical interoperability. U.S. arms deliveries to East Asia totaled $1.3 billion in 1993 and $2.3 billion in 1994. This policy would require the United States to expand its efforts and improve its credibility as a reliable weapons supplier to Asian states. Thus weapons sales to key members of ASEAN, such as Indonesia, Thailand, and Vietnam should not be held hostage to excessively high standards of domestic political behavior.

Joint training would require a substantial expansion of field exercises to complement military coordination and education efforts. The more participants in these exercises, the better. By the same token, efforts such as the Pentagon's International Military Education and Training (IMET) program are very important, particularly to involve ASEAN closely in security engagement. The IMET program has been cut back for political and budgetary reasons; its funding amounted to only $4 million last year. This is a remarkably shortsighted decision.

Military infrastructure takes longer to build than any weapon, and is also the measure least likely to provoke China. Putting interoperable weapons systems in place is not as time-consuming as building bases, but it still takes years to plan, acquire, and integrate the necessary components. Joint training can be initiated with a relatively short lead time. Although these measures are expensive, spending money on them should be more politically palatable to Asian governments than paying more money to the U.S. government under the rubric of "burden-sharing."

Nevertheless, the need for increased burden-sharing by Asian nations is likely to be one of the troublesome if unavoidable aspects of security engagement. America's allies currently do not bear an equitable portion of the incremental costs of forward-deployed U.S. forces. Japan pays about $5 billion annually for the U.S. troops stationed on its soil, South Korea about $100 million, and both gripe about even those sums. It would cost both nations far more to field equivalent forces themselves. The ASEAN members pay nothing for their implicit U.S. security umbrella, and in fact are inclined to charge the U.S. government for such services as naval repairs.

Increased burden-sharing of expenditures should be placed near the top of the list of things in America's security relationships with South Korea and Japan to be renegotiated, as should increased burden-sharing of manpower and equipment requirements. There is no reason why these allies should not bear 100 percent of all local costs for U.S. troops and equipment. Ultimately, an appropriate division of labor would permit U.S. ground troops to be pulled back from South Korea and Japan so the United States can maximize its comparative advantage in air and naval forces.

The primary function of American ground forces in Asia and particularly those on the Korean peninsula, is a tripwire for American involvement if war breaks out in the region. However, a few thousand ground personnel will be as effective a tripwire as a hundred thousand if the underlying strategy is realistic and the bilateral security relationships are sound. There are few surer ways of undermining long term security engagement in Asia than allowing the current situation to persist indefinitely, with large numbers of U.S. troops in South Korea and Japan that are barely tolerated and often secretly despised by their host citizenry, as well as inequitable burden-sharing by the host governments. The response to the recent brutal rape in Okinawa allowed the resentment felt toward the "occupying forces" to be openly expressed. Pressure within Asian countries to expel these American forces will continue to mount, and the U.S. public's perception that Korea and Japan are ungrateful allies will grow in proportion. Polls suggest that less than 45 percent of the American public supports using American troops to defend South Korea in the face of a North Korean invasion. That number could easily dwindle in the face of repeated demonstrations against U.S. forces on the peninsula.[6]

Beyond the redeployment of American ground troops in Asia, security engagement would entail a greater flexibility for all U.S. military forces in Asia, regardless of their types or level.

For example, it makes no sense to shackle the U.S. government to a commitment to keep 100,000 troops deployed in the region, as recent Clinton administration statements have done. The evolving security environment in Asia may require more or fewer troops. Washington is unwise to mention specific numbers of troops because if the number of troops falls, Asian governments will take it as a sign that the United States is withdrawing from its commitments. If the troop total rises, China and North Korea will regard it as a provocative signal. It makes far more sense to focus public statements on the overall security strategy and relationship and make changes in the size of U.S. forces without fanfare.

Flexibility is also an important consideration when the roles and missions of U.S. forces in Asia are under discussion. In addition to investing time and energy in joint weapons planning and force training, Washington should emphasize military diplomacy in the region even more, in symbolic activities to "show the flag" and in humanitarian undertakings, especially with ASEAN. Policymakers must focus on the long-range goal of a loosely structured Asian alliance, not solely on current short-range contingencies such as winning the next Korean war. Without a clear long-term strategy such as security engagement, the United States is likely to find itself with neither the rationale nor the will to maintain a forward-deployed military force on a reunited Korean Peninsula, or anywhere else in Asia.

How do these rough guidelines for a long-term military posture in Asia apply to the region's two most likely flash points—Taiwan and the South China Sea—the two places where China might resort to force in the pursuit of political goals?

As noted earlier, the Taiwan case is troublesome because it is a conflict between the principle of national sovereignty (Chinese unification) and the principle of national self-determination (if the Taiwanese were to vote for independence). The invasion of Taiwan would be a tragic event, an immensely destructive conflict with no winners. The best preventive strategy for

Washington is to exert pressure on Taipei not to declare independence, quietly help it maintain a defensive military deterrent, and maintain a studied ambiguity about whether the United States would come to Taiwan's aid if it were attacked. This strategy of deliberate ambiguity has been encapsulated in the phrase, "If Taiwan declares independence, don't count on us; if the PRC invades Taiwan, don't count us out."[7]

The U.S. government should clearly express to the government and the people of Taiwan, both privately and publicly, that de jure independence might seriously harm the U.S. national interest and that it has no intention whatsoever of defending Taiwan should such a declaration invite an invasion by China. The Taiwanese desire for a badge of international prestige such as U.N. membership cannot be purchased by the U.S. Seventh Fleet.

Were Taiwan to insist on declaring de jure independence, and the PRC to react violently, the United States should not assist Taiwan militarily. A civil war between the PRC and Taiwan could not be won by Taiwan and would become a bloody clash of attrition. Taiwan would have no Asian allies in such a conflict, and it is doubtful that the U.S. public would support sending American soldiers to assist a state that has no formal diplomatic relations, much less any security treaty, with the United States.

Were Taiwan not to declare independence but provoke an invasion of PLA forces anyway, the United States should offer all assistance to it short of a direct military involvement of American forces. However, Taiwan still could not win such a conflict; American intervention could prolong the conflict but not resolve it. The risks of escalation would be very high. No Asian states would be on Taiwan's side, the United Nations would have no jurisdiction—certainly not through the Security Council, where China possesses veto power—and the American public's support for intervention would be marginally higher.

The PLA would win the battle for Taiwan—eventually—but both China and Taiwan would pay a terrible price, not just in human suffering, but in terms of economic disruption and political isolation. It would be a disaster of the highest order. Ironically, there would be no faster or surer way for Beijing to turn the loosely structured defensive alliance of security engagement in Asia into a hard cordon of neocontainment.

The policy of security engagement would approach conflict in the South China Sea much differently, however. The principles at stake—the peaceful resolution of territorial disputes and freedom of navigation—are crystal clear, although the competing claims for the reefs and islets of the South China Sea are certainly murky, and no one involved has a rock-solid claim.

An aggressive takeover of disputed areas by the PLA in the South China Sea would almost certainly precipitate a coordinated response by ASEAN, particularly if they were backed up by the United States. A military clash in the South China Sea involving the PLA would likely be small, limited to naval and air combat, and arguably winnable by the PLA's opponents, especially if they were benefiting from the interoperability, division of labor, and joint training exercises of security engagement. The degree of American public support for such an intervention would still be modest, but the strategic case for involvement would be far stronger than with Taiwan. And a successful limited conflict in the South China Sea would strengthen the loosely structured defensive alliance.

This discussion of military intervention raises lingering questions about the logical implications of conditional engagement. At what point is economic engagement deemed a failure, and a measured tit-for-tat response abandoned in favor of linking security to an economic carrots-and-sticks policy? When should wholesale military deterrence and an economic embargo—in effect, neocontainment—be used? Conditional engagement provides no secret key for making such a difficult decision. What it does provide is a clear progression as much as possible, a smooth escalation path from measured tit-for-tat to wholesale resistance to Chinese behavior.

If the point is reached at which the wall between economic tit-for-tat and security tit-for-tat can no longer be maintained, the PRC's security transgressions will be met by economic sanctions that "bite." The wall will most likely start to crumble when Japan cuts off direct aid, or the World Bank places China on hold because of its belligerence, or limited trade sanctions are triggered by some multilateral regime, the Nonproliferation Treaty, for example. However, the fallout from the private actors responsible for trade and investment decisions would have been felt by Beijing well before any official decisions to sanction China. Ultimately, the difficult decision to impose an official embargo against China might not mean a great deal; private markets would have made the decision already. By that point, conditional engagement would no longer be working; the uglier but simpler strategy of neocontainment would be defining the strategic environment in Asia, and the military foundation built under a policy of security engagement would not be directed toward reinforcing principled behavior, but instead to constraining a belligerent power.

NOTES

1. As Hisahiko Okazaki observes, "The best way to defend peace is to create an international environment in which there is no way to settle disputes except through peaceful means. Otherwise, the threat remains of alternatives that could endanger millions of lives with no clear prospects of victory. This does not mean a containment policy against China, still less a policy of encirclement. It means . . . a power balance allowing only peaceful solutions. In a nutshell, this is the basic condition for engagement," ("China: Function of Japan-U.S. Alliance," *Yomiuri Shimbun*, August 28, 1995).
2. See Alastair Iain Johnston, "Learning Versus Adaptation: Explaining Changes in Chinese Arms Control Policy in the 1980s and 1990s," *The China Journal* 35 (January 1996).
3. See David B.H. Denoon, *Ballistic Missile Defense in the Post-Cold War Era*, (Boulder, Colorado: Westview Press, 1995).
4. See Phillip C. Saunders, "Implementing Conditional Engagement," *Asia Project Working Paper*, (forthcoming), (New York: Council on

Foreign Relations).

5. Ashley J. Tellis, "Military Technology Acquisition and Regional Stability in East Asia," *East Asia's Potential for Instability and Crisis: Implications for the United States and Korea*, ed. Jonathan D. Pollack and Hyun-Dong Kim (Santa Monica, Ca.: RAND, 1995), p. 51.

6. Chicago Council on Foreign Relations, *American Public Opinion and U.S. Foreign Policy 1995*, p. 39.

7. See *Managing the Taiwan Issue: Key is Better U.S. Relations with China*, Report of an Independent Task Force, (New York: Council on Foreign Relations, 1995).

5

The Risks of Engagement

CONDITIONAL ENGAGEMENT must pass the litmus test of political reality, and it is not a strategy without risks. In constructing this or any other strategy for dealing with China, policymakers will have to face the problems presented by resurgent Chinese nationalism, by China's sheer size, and by the complexity of its political, social, and economic organization. Moreover, China's leadership is in transition, which adds another layer of uncertainty to strategic calculations.

The most daunting obstacle in some respects is the aggrieved Chinese nationalism reflected in the public and private attitudes of most Chinese leaders and many citizens as well. This nationalism rejects the notion that there should be any external constraints on China's behavior, and rejects international law as a barely disguised foreign attempt to keep China down and prevent the nation of the Han people from reasserting its position as a great power.[1] Expressions of this sentiment are partly tactical, used for effect by skilled diplomats, and partly real, reflecting deeply felt emotions. As Paul Godwin points out, "Chinese Communist representatives have shown extraordinary skill at the game of diplomacy. But skill and sophistication do not negate the likelihood that Beijing's leaders also sit at the bargaining table suspicious and resentful."[2]

This aggrieved nationalism is also behind the official characterization of "peaceful evolution" as a subversive plot. Not mere rhetoric, this is a useful political justification for resisting the moderating spillover effects of economic engagement. More dangerous still, however, is the neuralgic reaction of the government in Beijing to any countervailing structure in Asia that even remotely resembles containment. Again, this is partly tactical: Chinese diplomats frequently invoke the specter of containment for rhetorical effect to establish some tactical advantage. But internally among Beijing decision makers, the containment "threat" is a potent justification for higher military spending and for hard-line policy positions.

Because of this reaction, if the positive premises of conditional engagement are not communicated clearly and carefully to the Chinese leadership, the strategy will fail. Even if they are, the strategy may still fail. If resurgent Chinese nationalism leads Beijing to refuse to acknowledge that the international community, including the United States, has legitimate interests in Asia and a legitimate right to take steps to defend those interests if they are threatened, conditional engagement—or any other strategy short of preemptive capitulation—will deteriorate into neocontainment.

In addition to this prickly issue of Chinese nationalism, there is also the problem of scale in dealing with China, of the sheer size and complexity of the nation. Given China's matrix of dual party and administrative organs at multiple levels, with which units of the Chinese government should outside parties negotiate? Compounding this is the unsurprising fact that politics in China is largely inward-looking and self-absorbed. Foreign policy decisions in China are often part of a side deal—a tradeoff of domestic interests—in pursuit of narrow political advantage in a setting of factional infighting, partly or wholly opaque to the outside world. This self-absorption and opacity will immensely complicate the successful execution of conditional engagement.

The much debated leadership transition in China is problematic, not so much because of the inevitable consolidation after Deng Xiaoping's death but because there is no institutionalized mechanism for power transition. In their continuous jockeying for position, all contenders need to cover their flanks on the issue of national unity. For that matter, all contenders are likely to invoke nationalism as the wellspring of legitimacy, in place of the bankrupt ideology of Marxist-Leninist-Maoist thought. No serious contender for a position of power in Beijing can risk appearing to be an internationalist, to be accommodating to the outside world and in particular to the United States.[3]

The risks associated with conditional engagement will also vary from one Asian capital to another. Each state has its own unique history with China. In terms of economic power, the countries range from industrialized powerhouse democracies like Japan to desperately poor authoritarian states like Vietnam. From Washington's perspective, the Asian states fall into two camps: formal U.S. allies like Japan and South Korea, where the institutional foundation for participating in conditional engagement is already in place, and "partners of convenience" among the members of ASEAN, whose degree of participation in conditional engagement will depend on the degree of Chinese belligerence in ASEAN's South China Sea backyard.

The political calculus that pursuit of conditional engagement will involve is discussed from various national perspectives in chapters 7 through 10. However, the Asian states present some common challenges and risks. With respect to the ten principles, all the Asian nations assign a higher priority than the United States to compliance with national integrity and military principles. This is not surprising in light of the desire of China's Asian neighbors to keep the PLA out of their backyard. Their concern about the potential fallout from a China in chaos also leads them to make solving the transnational problems in the region a priority. When it comes to human rights, however, most Asian elites are sympathetic to so-called Asian values and believe that the United States has lost the moral high ground because of its own well-publicized social problems.

With respect to economic engagement, most Asian states are ambivalent about putting pressure on China to open up its markets because of their own protectionist policies. Having been the targets of American trade pressure to abandon or liberalize their trade practices, many Asian states are sympathetic to the Chinese position. Moreover, most government officials and many businesspeople in Japan and South Korea believe that industrial structure policies are essential to rapid economic development. Japan and China's official bilateral discussion frequently calls for "greater coordination of industrial policies" and "a complementary division of labor" between the two countries. Japanese bureaucrats press this model through such multilateral financial organizations as the Asian Development Bank, in which Japanese personnel play a central role and Japanese financial contributions are extremely important.

Ironically, to the degree that Asian firms encounter protectionist obstacles in China—or outright theft of software, for example, or trademark violations—they have been more than willing to allow the U.S. government to do the heavy lifting of negotiating with Beijing to clear those obstacles so they can exploit the commercial opportunities that result. For example, the Japanese game manufacturer Sega, by way of its American subsidiary, pressed China to halt illegal copies of its software through the office of the United States Trade Representative. As a general rule, the opportunity for economic free riding on the American commitment to the principle of market access principles is not lost on Asian corporations or Asian governments.

Private businesspeople throughout Asia are busy making

money in China markets, thereby furthering the process of economic engagement. But the leverage of economic integration works both ways. Many Asian firms have huge investments in China and depend on its markets to absorb a growing percentage of their exports. These firms are useful conduits for political pressure from the Chinese authorities. For example, while the *hua qiao*, or overseas Chinese, make up less than 5 percent of the population of the ASEAN states, they account for about 75 percent of their assets, and they dominate trade and investment between their countries and China. The *hua qiao* businesspeople have been assiduously courted by government officials in the PRC, principally provincial and local authorities but to some degree the leadership in Beijing as well. *Hua qiao* industrialists and bankers, despite their best intentions and personal integrity, may well be exploited by Beijing to exert subtle but effective pressure on ASEAN governments.

Asian domestic politics will also impinge on security engagement, the military version of the free-rider phenomenon, posing the biggest risk to the strategy's success. In theory, the Asian states could concentrate on profiting from the economic integration of China, paying only lip service to security engagement and engaging in minimal cooperation with their neighbors and the United States, so they could seek shelter were China to become clearly threatening.

If push comes to shove, individual states may be tempted to cut their own deals with China on security issues. Beijing has demonstrated its skill at divide-and-conquer diplomacy and at keeping China's neighbors off balance. Korea is a case in point. As Byung-joon Ahn points out in chapter 9, "Although Beijing has been busy expanding China's economic interdependence with South Korea and advocating peaceful solutions to the problems that divide the peninsula, it has endorsed North Korea's foreign policy by withdrawing its representative from the Military Armistice Commission at Panmunjom in November 1994, backing Pyongyang's quest for negotiating a peace agreement directly with the United States rather than with South Korea, and refusing to join the Korean Peninsula Energy Development Organization, which will provide substitute energy sources like heavy oil to North Korea."[4]

In the long run, the biggest risk to the success of security engagement in Asia will be the same as in the United States—the lack of political will to stay the course and to face up to the unpleasant possibility that China may have to be conditionally constrained, by force if necessary. Finance ministries will object to the cost. Businesspeople will object to the constraints it places on their ability to turn a profit. Journalists and politicians will object to the risks it poses. And as politics in Asia gradually become more pluralistic, many more opportunities to raise these objections will arise within the foreign policy decision-making debate all over Asia.

The risks U.S. domestic politics pose for conditional engagement are mirror images of those posed by Chinese politics. Like China, the United States has an inward-looking decision-making process in which foreign policy decisions are often made on the basis of short-term domestic considerations. The process is governed by the four-year presidential elections cycle. Mass media coverage of even the most complex foreign policy problems is simplified into sound bites. And the United States has its counterpart to resurgent Chinese nationalism, the "America as missionary" syndrome that has helped mold policy toward China for the better part of two centuries.

THE TEN PRINCIPLES OF CONDITIONAL ENGAGEMENT

1. No unilateral use of offensive military force
2. Peaceful resolution of territorial disputes
3. Respect for national sovereignty
4. Freedom of navigation
5. Moderation in military force buildup
6. Transparency of military forces
7. Nonproliferation of weapons of mass destruction
8. Market access for trade and investment
9. Cooperative solutions for transnational problems
10. Respect for basic human rights

American domestic politics present yet another complicating factor: a divided government. With the White House and Congress struggling over control of foreign policy, both sides speak to China, loudly and often with a different message. And both the White House and Congress are generally unwilling to recognize the limits of unilateral American power. American leaders do not like to be constrained by coalitions, but coalition politics and consensus building are essential to conditional engagement.

The question with respect to the ten principles is whether Washington can settle for rules of the road that are both realistic and modest enough to allow Chinese compliance. A deeply rooted Wilsonian idealism is intertwined with realpolitik in U.S. foreign policy formulation. Realpolitik is famously hard to sell domestically. Americans thirst for an ethically and morally just world; they are reluctant to make personal or financial sacrifices in the name of balance of power political expediency.

The tussle between the White House and Congress over foreign policy poses several other problems for economic engagement. Since no one group on the Hill has to worry about the overall relationship with China, decisions tend to be made in a vacuum.

Human rights advocates do a terrific job of lobbying Congress to help keep most-favored-nation status hostage to China's human rights record. Environmental groups exert similar pressure on China to modify its policies toward endangered species or the environment. Trade sanctions are the preferred instrument of pressure for these single-interest advocates, but the use of trade sanctions for short-term political objectives undermines conditional engagement.

If Congress succeeds in dismantling the bureaucratic apparatus for trade promotion and trade negotiations with China, it will hamper Washington's ability to manage the bilateral trade relationship and head off more serious commercial clashes with China. Beyond that, American trade protectionists look to Congress to get barriers erected against competitive imports from China. The traditional free trade bloc in the United States is already under siege. Booming Chinese exports to the United States, the persistent trade deficit, and tensions over security issues increase domestic protectionist pressures aimed at China, which will threaten economic integration

The biggest obstacle to a successful policy of security engagement is Americans' expectation of a "peace dividend" at the end of the Cold War. Few leaders want to face up to the fact that the United States may be in for several decades of difficult and possibly costly dealings with China as an emerging great power. Many Americans feel that the United States has for decades shouldered a disproportionate share of the burden of keeping Asia safe for democracy—or at least safe for business. Under these circumstances, the sustained American military presence in Asia that conditional engagement calls for is likely to be a hard sell.

If the perception widens among the American people and their elected representatives that Asians are getting wealthier without pulling their weight on defense, and if popular resentment against U.S. forces continue in South Korea and Japan, there will be enormous pressure to withdraw all U.S. units from Asia and garrison them in the United States—where their presence can benefit the local economy—or to disband them. Such a withdrawal would not only be precipitous and destabilizing, but possibly fatal to conditional engagement.

Vested interests in the U.S. military may also view conditional engagement as threatening. Large organizations anywhere suffer from inertia, and their budgets and programs take on a life of their own. The U.S. military may not enthusiastically take to the task of looking beyond the clear but narrow mission of fighting another Korean war, to entertain a new set of organizing principles for security in Asia, to undertake the time-consuming coalition building that security engagement would require, and to embrace a flexibility in force deployment that might affect its budget.

HEDGING THE RISKS

How CAN these risks to conditional engagement in China, elsewhere in Asia, and in the United States be overcome?

First, the U.S. government should engage China's leadership broadly and consistently, not only the officials in the central government in Beijing but also those in provincial and local government, and the PLA. This should be continued through good times and bad, and problems over one issue, even serious problems, should not be allowed to poison the relationship.

China's leaders should be dealt with on a basis of mutual respect and seriousness, keeping expectations about their behavior realistic. There will be fits and starts, and periods of tension. The government in Beijing will do bad and brutal things to the Chinese people; there will be disasters in China, natural and man-made, and CNN will be there. It is important that Washington not overreact to the *crise du jour*.

It is equally important that Washington react with tough measures when tit-for-tat is in order, particularly in the security realm but in commercial disputes as well. When Beijing successfully called the Clinton administration's bluff on most-favored-nation status, this not only damaged American credibility but led the Chinese to overreach in the subsequent WTO negotiations.

Engagement, mutual respect, and credibility should also guide Washington's behavior elsewhere in Asia. A wide range of governments must be dealt with in Asia under the umbrella of security engagement, and dealings with the democratic governments will not necessarily be easiest. Washington can discourage economic free riding by Asian governments through bilateral tactical pressure and through the WTO; it can discourage military free riding through flexible decision-making on troop deployments, weapons sales, and the locus of joint maneuvers. Ultimately, however, it is the behavior of the PLA that will make—or break—the case for Asian states to abandon their free-rider proclivities and pull their weight in security engagement.

These modest guidelines will also be helpful in managing the response in the United States to conditional engagement. The most important requirement is that the White House publicly states a clear and relatively simple strategy toward China and stick with it through shifting political winds. Such leadership should foreclose some meddling by Congress, although there will always be partisan sniping and second-guessing.

Stating and pursuing a clear strategy is a necessary first step in educating the American public to the potential rewards and real risks of dealing with China. Educating the mass media, particularly the broadcast media, in these risks and opportunities and in the complexities inherent in dealing with the government in Beijing is a key element of this public education process.

Under its system of division of powers, the United States is likely to have two China policies for some time to come, even if the same party controls Congress and the White House. As Congress will constantly be pressing for a say on China policy, it should be given more responsibility as well. Members of Congress should be involved in most aspects of negotiations with China as delegation members and in the extended policy-formulation process. It will take as much if not more congressional hand-holding to conditionally engage China as it did to manage negotiations with the former Soviet Union, since talks with the Soviets were largely limited to security and arms control, whereas negotiations with China will include commercial and transnational problems as well.

Several potential lobbies with a big stake in the success of conditional engagement should be harnessed to the effort of actively managing Congress to support conditional engagement. The most influential of these lobbies, and the one with the deepest pockets, represents firms with commercial interests in China. Many of these firms have been vocal in criticizing the administration for mismanaging the U.S.-China relationship, but they have not persuaded Congress to adopt a more responsible and farsighted stance toward the PRC. As U.S. exports to

China expand—assisted by aggressive trade promotion and trade negotiations—a growing and geographically diverse group of firms acquires a strong vested interest in keeping the relationship on an even keel.

Policy interest groups and other NGOs concerned with elements of foreign policy formulation, such as the arms control intelligentsia, environmentalists, drug policy advocates, parties to the birth and population control debate, and those interested in the overhaul of immigration policy, are also potential supporters of conditional engagement. China holds a key to a comprehensive solution for the problems that concern these groups. Since Chinese cooperation is more forthcoming when the overall relationship with the United States is stable, holding trade with China hostage to single interests is counterproductive in the long run.

The third potential lobby for conditional engagement is China itself. The government in Beijing is often its own worst enemy when it comes to public relations overseas, especially with the U.S. Congress. Beijing's occasional efforts to make its case on the Hill and justify its policies are usually clumsy and remarkably unsophisticated. The authorities in Beijing are understandably resistant to lobbying Congress; they do not understand the necessity of lobbying in a pluralistic democracy, and they are particularly indignant at the prospect of competing with Taiwan lobbyists for the hearts and minds of American politicians.

COMPREHENSIVE, CONSTRUCTIVE, OR CONDITIONAL?

How DOES the proposed strategy of conditional engagement differ from the current U.S. strategy toward China, sometimes termed comprehensive or constructive engagement? Conditional engagement recommends that Washington make clear to the Chinese leadership at the highest levels that the United States and its Asian allies wish to engage China on the basis of principles of acceptable behavior, while acknowledging China's claim to great-power status; that this strategy encourages economic integration and political cooperation with China; and that its security engagement component is essentially a fallback position, an undesirable fallback at that, in the unhappy event China were to behave belligerently.

However, a series of U.S. government actions has led to a widespread perception in China of American hostility—keeping China down as a political power and keeping China poor as an economic power. As Karen Elliott House pointed out in a *Wall Street Journal* editorial, "A combination of American ineptitude and Chinese paranoia are creating the fiction of a new U.S. containment strategy against China."[5]

Conditional engagement recommends that the U.S. government build on the October 1995 meeting between President Jiang Zemin and President Clinton in New York and embark on a regularly scheduled series of summit-level meetings with the Chinese leadership, maintaining this dialogue through thick and thin. Nothing is gained and much is risked by isolating or refusing to deal with the leadership in China.

Yet, Clinton administration policy appears to be to keep Chinese leaders at arm's length. Powerful figures in Washington, including members of Congress, continue to refer to the Chinese leadership in provocative terms more appropriate to a brutal totalitarian regime. To characterize, as some have, any engagement of China's leadership as coddling dictators is shortsighted and, in the long run, dangerous.

Conditional engagement recommends that the U.S. government be prepared to negotiate principles of reciprocal conduct with China, both bilaterally and through multilateral discussions under the aegis of both APEC and ARF. These principles should encompass modest and realistic expectations for Chinese conduct, while respecting the vital interests of the United States and its Asian allies. Under current U.S. policy, only limited progress has been made in working out additional formal agreements to accommodate the numerous changes that have taken place in U.S.-China relations in the 23 years since the Shanghai Communiqué and 17 years since the Normalization of U.S.-China Relations Agreement.

Conditional engagement recommends that economic integration of China into the global economy be supported as a key policy goal and that China be admitted to the WTO under reasonable phase-in requirements. Trade statistics should be harmonized to eliminate the accounting anomaly caused by the flow of Chinese goods destined for the United States through Hong Kong. The U.S. government must develop an even more activist and high-profile trade policy with China for the purposes of trade liberalization and trade promotion. China's persistent command economy interventions, industrial structure policy, and local corporatism will present a unique trade policy challenge, as difficult to fathom and hard to deal with as the one Japan has presented the last two decades.

As trade policy stands, however, China is treated as just another big emerging market. Multilateralism, including such weak vessels as APEC, is generally viewed as the policy instrument with the best odds of success; there is a distinct reluctance to become involved in any bilateral negotiations that "manage trade." The United States appears loath to face up to the scale and complexity of the trade problem with China.

Conditional engagement recommends that the U.S. government not subordinate the goal of China's economic integration to short-term attempts to force political change on Beijing. Pluralism and even democracy may come to China, but it will be a long-term, largely autonomous process. Universal values of human rights and political pluralism should be urged on China through multilateral forums, by NGO's, by private business operating under codes of conduct, and particularly by other Asian states.

Under current U.S. policy, by contrast, trade with China is hostage to a host of requirements concerning Chinese domestic political behavior.

Conditional engagement recommends enhancing the military strength and independence of Asian states on China's periphery in a measured and systematic way, to deter possible coercion by China.[6] This should be accomplished through a clear "division of labor" between the security forces of the United States and those forces of its Asian allies, and through more equitable burden sharing.

Current U.S. military strategy in Asia, in contrast, is based on a vague "balancing" rationale for a forward U.S. security deployment and on a short-sighted commitment that locks the United States into providing an arbitrary number of troops (100,000), despite budget pressures on the United States, increasing frictions between U.S. troops and host civilian populations, and the increasing wealth and military sophistication of America's Asian allies.

Conditional engagement recommends that current and potential allies in Asia, particularly the ASEAN states, be provided with expanded access to American military technology and training and engaged in a broad variety of military-to-military contacts.

In contrast, Washington has limited or terminated the supply of International Military Education and Training, weapons systems, and military-to-military contacts with key Asian nations, including ASEAN members Indonesia and Thailand, as a symbol of U.S. disapproval of their domestic policies.

Conditional engagement recommends engaging the Chinese government on transnational issues like illegal migration, drug smuggling, organized crime, and environmental degradation in a pragmatic fashion, before these problems escalate to crisis proportions.

Under current U.S. policy, in contrast, such problems are treated exclusively from a domestic point of view, virtually without reference to the Chinese element of the solution.

CONDITIONAL ENGAGEMENT
OR CONDITIONAL CONTAINMENT?

How DOES conditional engagement stack up against the alternative strategies of unconditional engagement and preemptive containment that are outlined briefly in chapter 1 and discussed in more detail by Jonathan Pollack in chapter 6?

To answer this question, one must first ask what the benefits and costs of these alternative strategies would be under the two widely divergent scenarios for China's political evolution: one in which things go well and China follows a moderate path, essentially keeping to the status quo, as it is integrated into the international community of nations; and one in which things go badly and China's internal political dynamics push it onto a belligerent, expansionist path.

The biggest reward of unconditional engagement under the first scenario is the savings that would be gained—at least at the outset—from reduced defense spending by the United States and China as well as the other Asian states. Under the second scenario, however, as the United States and China's neighbors scrambled to rearm in the face of a hostile China, defense would become a major drain. A crash program of rearmament would be more expensive and more dangerous than a measured and systematic security buildup, particularly since in the interim, interdependence will have afforded the PLA the opportunity to increase its power-projection capabilities. Moreover, this risk is compounded by two corollary costs of a pell-mell military buildup: the reasonably good chance that the PLA would prevail in any early test of power such as a conflict over Taiwan or the South China Sea, and the strong temptation for some Asian states to jump on the Chinese bandwagon by accommodating Beijing's desire to exercise regional hegemony.

By the same token, the most obvious cost of preemptive containment under the first scenario, in which Beijing chooses the path of moderation, is the "wasted" outlays for defense perceived by Asian countries and the United States. In addition, containment could spark an arm's race that would destabilize regional security. This would likely lead to a hardening of Chinese political attitudes toward the outside world, fueling an aggrieved Chinese nationalism and others' consequent distrust of China.

On the other hand, a strategy of preemptive containment offers several striking benefits under the second scenario, the inverse of the costs that would be incurred by unconditional engagement if things were to go badly: a measured security response would be safer and cheaper than a panicked buildup; the likelihood of early losses to Chinese expansionism would be much reduced; and the incentive for Asian states to jump on the Chinese bandwagon would be lower.

To return to the question of how conditional engagement compares with alternative strategies, it has the merit of being fully open to the possibility of China's peaceful economic and political integration into the global community while providing a fallback should the process not go smoothly. Under the first, optimistic scenario, conditional engagement would also lead to some wasted defense spending; possibly increase the likelihood of a military response to tensions between armed Asian states over issues unrelated to China; and most likely also cause a hardening of Chinese domestic politics, though certainly not to the degree that preemptive containment would do.

Under the second, more pessimistic scenario, conditional engagement would face Chinese belligerence with a countervailing security structure that can be expanded (or contracted) in proportion to Chinese military threats and military actions. As with preemptive containment, the risk under conditional engagement of incurring early losses or of pushing Asian states onto the Chinese bandwagon is low, although there is a higher risk of "losing" Taiwan.

Above all, conditional engagement has the cardinal virtue of flexibility in an uncertain world. This strategy would allow the United States and its Asian allies to ride out the inevitable downturns in their relationships with China while economic integration works its long-term magic. The leaders in Beijing have good historical reasons to be suspicious of foreigners, but the world cannot afford to accommodate a great power China that recognizes neither legitimate international rules nor the legitimate foreign interests in its behavior.

This conflict over principles is sharp enough today; it will be intolerable a decade from now. Thus it is far more prudent for the United States and China's neighbors to address these issues now by reaching a consensus on pragmatic principles, crafting incentives to encourage Beijing's compliance, and preparing to defend these principles if necessary. Otherwise, China's push for power will end in a slow spiral into containment, with its terrible risks and needless expense, rather than in a world enormously enriched by China's commerce and culture. In short, it is far wiser to weave a net than to pray for fish.

NOTES

1. The most pithy statement of this view is, "The Chinese have had a few bad centuries, but they're back."
2. Paul H. Godwin and John J. Schutz, "China and Arms Control: Transition in East Asia," *Arms Control Today* 24, no. 9 (November 1994), p. 11.
3. This posturing toward for the outside world has a cyclical character, paced by the internal clock of bureaucratic politics in *Zhongnanhai*. As a consequence, the risks associated with conditional engagement will wax and wane. When the leadership is strong and has consolidated its power, it has more room to maneuver with the West and is likely to be far more flexible than when it is new or challenged from within.
4. See Byung-joon Ahn, chapter 9, p. 202.
5. Karen Elliott House, "Drifting Toward Disaster in Asia," *Wall Street Journal*, July 26, 1995.
6. See Phillip C. Saunders, "Implementing Conditional Engagement," *Asia Project Working Paper*, (forthcoming), (New York: Council on Foreign Relations).

Perspectives on Conditional Engagement

臨淵羨魚不如退而結網

6

Designing a New American Security Strategy for Asia

Jonathan D. Pollack

As THE TWENTIETH CENTURY draws to a close, the United States confronts choices in its national security strategy unmatched since the Korean War and the decision to globalize containment. Despite the end of the Cold War and the collapse of the Soviet Union, there has yet to be a comprehensive reassessment of the goals of U.S. strategy and the role military power should play in realizing U.S. goals. To be sure, policy reviews in the Bush and Clinton administrations have resulted in a reduced and rationalized military establishment and led to a substantial reduction in the U.S. military presence overseas, especially in Europe. Both administrations have also reaffirmed the abiding American commitment to regional deterrence and defense, particularly with respect to contingencies in the Persian Gulf and Northeast Asia.[1]

The Clinton administration has embedded this commitment in its strategy of "engagement and enlargement," through which it seeks to enhance U.S. national security, promote domestic prosperity, and extend democratic processes and institutions abroad. The administration deems East Asia integral to the realization of all three of these goals: "Nowhere are the strands of our three-pronged strategy more intertwined, nor is the need for continued U.S. engagement more evident [than in East Asia]."[2]

Despite—or perhaps because of—the end of the Cold War and its global strategic competition between the superpowers, U.S. forces are engaged in a wide array of geographic settings. Indeed, the armed forces are more active currently than during the Cold War (except during the Korea, Vietnam, and Persian Gulf wars). Some observers see these involvements as part of a gestational process that will eventually lead to a new global security structure. Others, however, worry that they are simply a reaction to instability, violence, and disorder after the Cold War, entered into without any clear sense of whether vital U.S. interests are at risk. Although the Clinton administration has put forward criteria for deciding when and how to employ U.S. forces abroad, these afford only an approximation of the challenges to American interests.[3] This is not surprising at a time when international security does not lend itself to precise formulations. In the midst of the current upheaval and uncertainty, two fundamental questions are frequently obscured or ignored: Does the United States have a vision of the world that it seeks to realize? And, assuming there is such a vision, how does it propose to do so?

This chapter looks at some of the requisites of an American security strategy for Asia and the Pacific. In essence, it attempts to place the region in the context of long-term American interests and goals. Asia and the Pacific, especially Northeast Asia, is routinely deemed a vital interest of the United States. In recent decades the region has been a relative oasis of tranquility and stability. Despite mounting concern about the social and environmental consequences of the region's rapid modernization, leaders in most other regions of the world would gladly trade East Asia's problems for their own. An economic transformation of extraordinary scale and scope has continued, with occasional slowdowns, for four decades, encompassing an increasing number of countries and the development of multilateral arrangements for trade liberalization. Not only does this transformation show no sign of abating, but it has infused the entire region with self-confidence and the belief that East Asia's time has come.[4]

The United States has been an observer, participant, and beneficiary in this process. Since the early to mid-1970s, when the United States disentangled itself from vexing and costly involvements in revolutionary struggles in Asia, the region has been an extraordinary success story for American interests. Yet Asian intellectuals and governments and, to a somewhat lesser degree, American specialists on Asia now routinely express a feeling that the United States has lost its bearings in the region and that Washington has been unable to fashion a coherent plan that could work on both sides of the Pacific. This concern forms a leitmotif in innumerable reviews of U.S. policy toward Asia and the Pacific.

I regard as axiomatic an enduring American commitment to the well-being, stability, and security of Asia and the Pacific. But such a strategy cannot be undertaken as a favor to Asian states. It needs to be unambiguously rooted in a definition of vital American interests to which the regional security partners of the United States must pay heed and render appropriate contributions. Absent this commitment and a set of achievable goals, it is doubtful that any U.S. regional security strategy, including the forward presence of American forces, can be sustained over the long run, even though many in the region continue to assert that U.S. military power is indispensable in maintaining a viable security order.

A set of assumptions about the region, about American interests, and about the capacity of the United States to influence the strategic dispositions and policy calculations of regional actors underpins the discussion that follows. Particular attention is paid to the prospective emergence of China as a true major power—in contrast to China's long-standing status as a candidate superpower—and to ways to more fully incorporate China into a future regional security order. But China is only the most significant example of Asia's economic, political, and military emergence and of the strategic realignment this may portend. Indeed, one of the central challenges of the coming decade will be to avoid focusing exclusively on China. Such a strategy, besides failing to address the full array of American interests in the region, would imply that China's emergence as a genuine major power is a prima facie threat to America's regional security interests.

WHY DOES ASIA MATTER?

WHY INDEED? Although the answer may be blindingly obvious to specialists, it may not be to others. Many observers assert that in the absence of a singular threat to the physical security of the United States or a major ally there is no reason for the United States to maintain significant defense commitments or military assets in Asia. According to this approach, since no country in the region except North Korea presents an immediate threat to U.S. security interests, the cessation of the threat from Pyongyang would invalidate the U.S.'s regional security strategy.[5] This is clearly an insufficient foundation on which to plan long-term U.S. policy.

The United States' determination to maintain its present force levels and commitments in the region assumes an essentially static situation, particularly in Northeast Asia.[6] Longer-term U.S. security requirements, especially in the event of a diminished North Korean threat or the disintegration of the North Korean state, remain unexamined in policy documents.

A better rationale for long-term U.S. engagement is an integration-based logic, but one that acknowledges that a preferred strategy may not be achievable. The United States must seek to ensure that it remains a primary participant and stakeholder in the regional security order, its participation premised on a set of rules and security objectives that it and the states of the region have agreed upon. But policymakers must allow for the possibility that the United States and its principal partners may sometimes differ. There is no guarantee that the region's future direction will be wholly compatible with American interests. But U.S. readiness to help fashion a viable security order will measurably increase the likelihood that the future will be more to America's liking, whereas unwillingness will do the reverse. Moreover, the depth and seriousness of the U.S. commitment will be crucial to persuading regional partners to pursue an agreed-on strategy.

Regional security, therefore, must be embedded in a concept of American interests, of which national security is only one component, albeit a very important one. Specifying the components provides a means for evaluating the relevance of different instruments of American power and for keeping regional actors closely identified with U.S. policy goals. This concept encompasses the following considerations:

- East Asia's extraordinary economic growth, capital accumulation, and technological development make the region pivotal in the global equation and thus for U.S. strategic interests. Technological maturation will also have implications for weapons innovation. These trends will ultimately be reflected in the political and strategic importance accorded the region and specific countries within it in the global balance of power. The United States must ensure that it is fully engaged in this transition, or its security and well-being may be undermined.

- A central goal of U.S. strategy must be to ensure that America is able to participate fully and fairly in the economic and technological development of Asia and the Pacific. Particular attention must go to removing constraints or inhibitions that limit its opportunity to do so.

- Washington's ability to influence the behavior of regional states (and their incentives to collaborate with the United States) decreases as engagement decreases. This heightens the risk for American interests—particularly if the United States is excluded from regional policy deliberations or if regional actors become less attentive to core U.S. policy concerns. The United States must strive to avoid such possibilities.

- Despite the region's extraordinary dynamism, its political norms and structures lag seriously behind its economic development, especially in Northeast Asia. At the same time, there has been no major crisis in Asia for several decades, in part because U.S. security guarantees have been effective. But U.S. strategy has long assumed that the core regional actors would play secondary roles, either because of political constraints (as in Japan) or technological and military short-comings (as in China). As the region's principal powers come of age, the United States has an abiding interest in seeing that the transition to a new political and security order is a peaceful one. At the same time, it must ensure that its allies of long standing continue to conceptualize their security interests in terms compatible with U.S. strategy while ensuring that ascendant states do not undermine or unduly complicate the pursuit of U.S. regional policy goals.

- In the most basic sense, America's principal strategic interests in Asia and the Pacific encompass five objectives: (1) denying any single state or coalition of powers the ability to dominate the region; (2) ensuring that no state achieves the military means and will to pose a direct threat to its neighbors; (3) guaranteeing unimpeded movement of goods and resources within the region and between the region and the United States; (4) encouraging states committed to political openness and increased economic opportunity for their citizens; and (5) enhancing the incentives for the region's states to collaborate with the United States in pursuit of complementary political, economic, and security goals.

• The strategic directions of the region will be shaped principally by developments in Northeast Asia. This does not render Southeast Asia unimportant, but attention must be focused on the region's major powers. Given present and prospective trends, Japan and China each possess the resources to assume a larger regional role, but are otherwise dissimilar. Japan's current leadership, though aspiring to a more prominent international position that depends less directly on the U.S.-Japan relationship, continues to favor maintaining a high degree of security interdependence with the United States.[7] Though exceedingly unlikely, Tokyo's decision to chart a security course independent of the United States would entail a basic reconfiguration in the regional security structure, and the United States must work assiduously to avoid such a possibility. In China, which already enjoys substantial autonomy in determining its national security strategy, the looming issue is an appreciably more powerful and outwardly oriented Chinese state. In Japan or China or both, enhanced political or security identities could have global as well as regional ramifications. A unified Korea, though less powerful than its neighbors, would also aspire to increased influence; however, it would likely wish to preserve close relations with the United States.[8] Russia, a much diminished political and military actor, is also seeking to preserve and ultimately enhance its regional influence, with the hope of regaining its great power status within the region.[9]

• The United States must seek to calibrate its presence and role in relation to the ambitions, needs, and concerns of the region's major states. This is especially relevant to refashioning relations with long-standing political and security partners who are seeking to ensure their security and well-being under changed international circumstances. In the absence of an overt military threat, Washington's expectations of its traditional partners are shifting, causing its allies to feel uneasy about the U.S. commitment to their security.

• Although many states in the region genuflect before the altar of cooperative security, the behavior of the most important among them (especially in Northeast Asia) belies their commitment.[12] All powers are looking toward the long-term, and most are seeking to preserve as much freedom of action as possible. The absence of a regional security structure in the context of extraordinary economic and technological dynamism lends weight to the argument for a vigorous U.S. role. The United States enjoys mutually reinforcing relations with the major regional actors. It must be prepared to utilize this comparative advantage to help ensure its continued centrality in the policy calculations of the region's dominant powers.

• The major Asian powers will continue to pursue their long-term goals in relation to their perceptions of American power. This should prove an ongoing source of leverage for the United States. There is no need for Washington to be apologetic or squeamish about exercising its influence: American power in all its forms will be a decisive factor in shaping attitudes toward a future regional order, and must be used intelligently if regional actors are to accord serious attention to U.S. interests. Observers who doubt the efficacy of American military power as an instrument of U.S. influence are insufficiently attentive to the array of policy goals military capabilities may serve.

• Policymakers and the public should disabuse themselves of the notion that a given level of military capability will enable the United States to buy preferred policy outcomes such as reduced trade deficits or increased market access. Disruptive internal developments must also be expected in societies undergoing rapid economic and social change. However, in the absence of purposive American involvement and the continued commitment of American power in all its dimensions, the United States will be much less able to assert its core interests and will have fewer options should optimism about the region's direction prove misplaced.

• The United States must convince the nations of Asia and the Pacific of the credibility and durability of its commitment to the region. It is, therefore, imperative that Washington impart a far clearer sense of its regional goals and how it will use its power to reach these goals than it has done so far.

THE STRATEGIC ALTERNATIVES

THE UNITED STATES appears to have four strategic options with respect to Asia and the Pacific: strategic autonomy; liberal internationalism; preemptive containment; and conditional engagement. Each has its limitations, but those associated with strategic autonomy are especially glaring.

Strategic autonomy assumes that the United States can mobilize sufficient resources within its immediate sphere of influence to avoid dependence on or commitment to any other region of the world. While earlier versions of this doctrine were frequently identified with Asia-firsters in the United States, the current incarnation appears to be premised on holding both Europe and Asia at bay. This option is neither credible nor realistic in the face of America's economic, technological, and policy interdependence with both regions; the United States cannot expect to regain its economic vitality through autarky. But it still resonates with some domestic audiences, and it is, therefore, incumbent on proponents of alternatives to demonstrate why it is not a realistic basis for securing long-term American interests.

The second option, liberal internationalism, rests on the assumption that states can ameliorate their differences and keep their competitive instincts in check by making a more determined commitment to interdependence and by forgoing a measure of national sovereignty. It assumes the development and maturation of multilateral institutions that create interdependence and clear incentives for states to move toward shared goals—assumes, in fact, that the United States and its regional interlocutors will succeed in building a community of like-minded states whose common interests far outweigh their differences. Coercion or the threat of it is a residual (and highly undesirable) category within this construct. The results of this approach are presumed to be cumulative: success will beget success, ultimately leading to a systemic transformation that will sharply diminish or eliminate the pursuit of national security by unilateral means.

The principal limitation of a liberal internationalist strategy is that it makes assumptions about collaboration that skeptics deem heroic, or at least premature. As I have observed elsewhere:

> Strategists and policymakers remain stymied by the unresolved status of current regional arrangements and the inability to move toward a preferred future. On the one hand, it is possible to hypothesize a set of nonantagonistic relations among a united Korea, China, Japan, and Russia, with each simultaneously maintaining collaborative, mutually beneficial ties with the United States. This would presume military forces configured defensively; an array of collaborative security relations that included regular dealings and information exchanges among armed forces; and increasing regional integration, with security cooperation as an integral component.
>
> But this vision remains unfulfilled, and many observers deem it unattainable over the next decade or more. At a minimum,

it would require: first, resolution of the half-century division of the Korean Peninsula; second, formal understandings between China and Taiwan that would permit longer-term amicable relations; third, the emergence of a sustainable consensus within Japan on its longer-term international roles and responsibilities that is fully acceptable to Japan's neighbors; fourth, the emergence of a political and institutional system within China capable of genuine integration with its neighbors and long-term accommodation with the United States; and, fifth, a successful transition to a postimperial Russian system able to define a regional role commensurate with its geographic position and legitimate security needs.[11]

This is a daunting set of requirements. Even if liberal internationalism is seen as a vision to which the region should aspire over the long-term, how—except through incremental steps or building blocks—to proceed from here to there is not addressed. Moreover, although its proponents believe such a path can be found, its route is not discernible in the shifting landscape of Asia's major power relationships over the coming decade. Asia and the United States cannot simply leapfrog into a less competitive security order. If states are to move successfully from one era to another, liberal internationalism remains more aspiration than practical strategy.

The third strategic option, preemptive containment, assumes a much more antagonistic world. In the regional context, this focuses attention on China, the only state with the ambition, long-term potential, national autonomy, and prospective military power that would make it an even remotely possible strategic challenger to the United States. The worries of those who advocate this option are reinforced by the fact that China's ambitions are nuclear, and maritime as well as continental; by the degree to which Beijing's territorial claims in Asia and the Pacific appear to conflict with those of its neighbors; by the extraordinary obscurity of its long-run security objectives and defense plans; and by its lack of fidelity or accountability to legal and institutional constraints.

Advocates of a containment strategy assert that we must prepare now for the inevitable day when China arrives militarily. Its military power and its ambitions and interests will be such that America and its regional security partners will need countervailing capabilities to preclude Chinese domination or coercion of neighboring states. Those who favor this strategic option argue that there is still sufficient time to build a coalition of states against China. Some proponents believe that the United States can quietly construct such a coalition step by step, without provoking Beijing. Proponents assume that there is no alternative to careful military preparations if the United States is to ensure that it never finds itself at a disadvantage in a crisis entailing potential strategic consequences; the United States, they say, needs to maintain or even supplement its military power now.

There are many reasons to be wary of a containment strategy. Even in the absence of appreciable Chinese power-projection capabilities, such a course of action would have an inherently self-fulfilling character.[12] It assumes a China almost mechanistically proceeding not only toward great power status but toward conflict with its neighbors as well as the United States, failing to ask whether there is sufficient regional support for such a strategy. It also disregards China's burgeoning economic links with its neighbors, which will enormously complicate any effort to curtail China's geographic reach and inhibit it from pursuing highly coercive strategies toward its neighbors. Perhaps most ironically, it gives China's military forces far more weight than they deserve. To be sure, as some strategists assert, we should look beyond China's present capabilities. But linear projections of the aggregate and relative increases in defense capabilities over the next two decades could prove vastly overstated. Moreover, a containment strategy fails to consider regional states' ability to compensate for increases in China's military power with augmented capabilities of their own. And it fails to address the societal and institutional transitions looming for China, which are at least as likely to affect the character of the Chinese state as the inevitable development of China's military power.

By assuming China's emergence as a hegemonic power and Chinese-American hostility, a containment doctrine would do much to guarantee such an outcome. Threat shopping may appeal to some strategic analysts, and China appears to be the biggest game in town. But it is a poor substitute for strategic thinking.

A variant of the third strategic option is more akin to the classic realist formulation of what a strategically mature Asia-Pacific region might look like. Proponents of this alternative describe a balance of power system, presumably tied to a still-powerful United States, an ascendant China, a normal Japan, a unified Korea, and a revived Russia. Australia, and potentially Vietnam and Indonesia, would also possess significant military assets, and Taiwan would remain an important special case. Stability and security would presumably be maintained through shifting alignments among various regional powers, with no one state achieving dominance. Some analysts argue that the United States would have a comparative advantage in this context if it maintained power projection capabilities that regional states would not possess that could be brought to bear in a crisis, since it would likely enjoy closer relations with each of the key actors than any two would enjoy with one another. Although some actors would occupy a higher rung than others in the regional hierarchy, none would achieve primacy; the region would achieve a position in the global system commensurate with Asia's growing economic, technological, and military resources; and the United States would enjoy pride of place at the Asia-Pacific table.

This alternative assumes the need for continued military preparation and prudence on the part of the United States. But the focus of U.S. strategy would be on ensuring strategic equilibrium rather than countering Chinese power per se. (However, given China's disproportionate size and weight relative to its neighbors, this may be a distinction without a difference.) Some exponents of this strategy think there would be little need to maintain bilateral security alliances, since Japan, Korea, and Australia would all presumably be cut loose from their American moorings. Indeed, the pure realist would not preclude major strategic challenges from erstwhile U.S. allies. This vision of the future presents a disturbing picture of a world prone to nationalized defense policies, recurrent realignment, open-ended suspicion and rivalry, and unregulated military competition, including the prospect of nuclear proliferation. Under such conditions, the United States would have no recourse but to maintain appreciable military assets in Asia and the Pacific. However, given the increase and spread of military capabilities in the region, maintaining large forces in the area will become progressively less realistic for the United States. As with a more focused containment strategy, however, there appear to be no means, other than resource constraints and the enlightened self-interest of all involved powers, to regulate or diminish political-military competition. A China-oriented containment strategy at least has the virtue of specificity and a definable goal, whereas a balance of power system (in theory) does not. It dwells on the means of strategy but not the ends, thereby falling short in both concept and practice.

The fourth strategic option is conditional engagement. This is a hedging strategy. Assuming neither a Kantian world of perpetual peace, nor a hegemonic China, nor an endlessly shifting balance of power, it rests on uncertainty about the ultimate configuration of power within the region. Since a variety of outcomes are possible, this strategic option can only offer signposts along an indeterminate path, but it can provide clear incentives for all the major actors to engage in collaborative, long-term relations with the United States. And it encompasses a preferred set of outcomes for the United States over the coming decade:

• The appreciable enhancement of open, rule-based regional and global trading regimes;

• A prosperous, internally stable, and more tolerant Chinese state, secure enough to interact amicably and credibly with its neighbors and with the United States;

• A more self-assured Japan better able to contribute to regional peace and stability but still committed to the primacy of collaboration with the United States;

• The realization of a unified, democratic, non-nuclear Korea, able to defend itself while also contributing to regional security, with both goals realized through continued close association with the United States;

• The development of viable political and economic institutions in a democratically inclined Russia able to resolve the lingering territorial disputes with its Asian neighbors, especially Japan;

• Enhanced consultation and collaboration between the United States and ASEAN, including in the area of security issues;

• The maintenance of mutually advantageous political and defense ties between the United States and Australia.

American power should be applied to bring about these preferred outcomes, but they cannot be guaranteed. The proponents of a strategy of conditional engagement acknowledge these considerations, but they contend that how the United States acts and what signals it sends in the near-term will shape, perhaps in decisive ways, the prospects for regional stability and security and the readiness of regional states to work closely with the United States toward shared ends. If the United States is unwilling to participate vigorously in Asia's looming transition, its capacity to fashion regional ties congruent with its interests will diminish. A strategy of conditional engagement assumes neither a benign nor a malign outcome: it hopes for the best but prepares for the worst. Aimed at creating a regional order in which collaboration and accommodation are maximized, it presumes the retention of core military capabilities in the event that optimistic visions of the future are not realized. No matter what the circumstance, the United States would retain ample latitude for action.

The difficulty with this option is that it runs the risk of being all of the above and hence none of the above. The United States can ill afford to dissipate its resources through multiple courses of action that may be conceivable but not sustainable in actual policy terms, especially in relation to regional security partners whose policy calculations and interests may diverge from its own. A more conditional strategy could also prove inertial, as bureaucracies latched onto self-perpetuating rationales. Misapplied, this could lead to passivity and become self-defeating.

How can such a strategic dead-end be avoided? The answer lies in part in how effectively the United States articulates its long-term preferences. But the real challenge is maximizing America's strategic leverage in a manner that makes sense to the American people, is comprehensible and credible to those in the region expected to contribute to its realization, and is flexible enough to deal with adverse regional developments or outright policy failures.

A fully developed strategy of conditional engagement, therefore, must possess an internally consistent logic, a specified set of requirements, signposts to measure its degree of success (or failure), and a list of requisite actions. To be successful, such a strategy must impart a sense of direction.

Although the future is assumed to be uncertain, everyone must understand what the United States hopes to achieve in the region, what resources it is prepared to commit to realize particular ends, and what America in turn requires of its regional partners. Otherwise, the policy will always be seen as too little too late by the states of the region. Should these states as a result opt to pursue their primary interests independent of U.S. preferences and needs, this strategy will have failed.

Conditional engagement may be seen less as a hedge against an uncertain future and more as a bridge—among the present and the next century; between the political, economic, technological, and security components of American policy; across different parts of the region; and for two-way traffic between America and Asia. It is the means of getting from here to there temporally and conceptually, with the scale of the U.S. effort conveying the idea that America's stake in Asia's future is neither ephemeral nor opportunistic.

CONDITIONAL ENGAGEMENT

THE ASSUMPTIONS and requirements that underlie this bridge-building strategy derive from the challenges an Asia in transition presents. These challenges include maintaining the military capability to address the threats to regional stability that persist in the post–Cold War era; redefining alliance

---

THE TEN PRINCIPLES OF CONDITIONAL ENGAGEMENT

1. No unilateral use of offensive military force
2. Peaceful resolution of territorial disputes
3. Respect for national sovereignty
4. Freedom of navigation
5. Moderation in military force buildup
6. Transparency of military forces
7. Nonproliferation of weapons of mass destruction
8. Market access for trade and investment
9. Cooperative solutions for transnational problems
10. Respect for basic human rights

arrangements and redistributing alliance burdens and responsibilities in a manner appropriate to changed circumstances;
and engaging emergent regional powers more effectively and
incorporating them in any new regional security structure. If
the United States is to meet these challenges, it must:

- Maintain in the near to mid-term a forward-deployed military posture appropriate to persistent security threats,
especially in Korea;

- Retain, though in significantly modified form, existing
bilateral alliances, in particular those with Japan, Korea, and
Australia;

- Move toward a more equitable and mutually agreed on distribution of roles and responsibilities with its security partners;

- Negotiate political and security agreements elsewhere in the
region that will permit access in the event of an abrupt
regional crisis or destabilizing event;

- Make a far greater effort to achieve bilateral political and
strategic understandings (for example, on U.S. and Chinese
regional security policies) with the successors to Deng
Xiaoping, supplanting or augmenting those dating back to
the Nixon, Carter, and Reagan administrations;

- Accelerate its efforts to promote China's political and economic integration within global and regional institutions;

- Support, beginning immediately, more regular interactions
between states, like Japan and Korea, that have had little
experience in security cooperation with one other. And create, over the long run, multilateral military and diplomatic
arrangements to underpin a new security structure.

These seven components of a strategy of conditional engagement are explicitly linked to the present uncertainties of the regional security setting, which could increase measurably under certain scenarios. In descending order of importance, these uncertainties include:

- A wide range of possibilities for China's internal political evolution, institutional arrangements, strategic orientation, and military capabilities, any of which could be relatively benign or genuinely worrisome;

- The indeterminate future of the Korean Peninsula, with the possibilities ranging from undiminished hostility between North and South and protracted uncertainty with respect to North Korea's nuclear weapons and missile development, to modest changes in the status quo (assuming a North-South accommodation), to severe instability and unification, whether by implosion or explosion;

- Japan's continuing pursuit of internal political realignment and the effects of this on the scope and character of external responsibilities that Japan might be prepared to assume;

- Russia's wrenching transition to a market-oriented, quasi-democratic state, and its resultant effects on Russia's presence and policies in East Asia, especially in relation to China but extending to other major powers as well;

- The continued absence of a viable, broadly legitimized intraregional security structure commensurate with the economic and political transition underway in the region, particularly in Northeast Asia.

Among these uncertainties, the consequences of destabilizing change would be greatest with respect to China and the Koreas. Assertiveness fueled by its dynamic economic growth and heightened political-diplomatic involvement in East Asia combines with a sense of vulnerability, if not outright weakness, as the death of Deng Xiaoping nears. China is widely characterized as a nation moving decisively in a range of areas, particularly those related to military development, but a more accurate characterization would highlight the mix of often highly contradictory behaviors and attitudes that reflect the diversity of views in China today.[13] The other principal uncertainty concerns the feasibility, affordability, and sustainability of China's defense modernization effort—that is, do the Chinese have an agreed-on strategy and the wherewithal for narrowing the large technological gap between their armed forces and those of more developed countries? At the same time, where and how might the Chinese be prepared to put any new capabilities to political or military use?[14]

These are very difficult questions to answer conclusively. On the one hand, China would appear (especially in the near to mid-term) to have an incentive to avoid overt hostilities, particularly if these created the prospect of a regional coalition to oppose the extension of Chinese power. Beijing is also keenly aware of the risks to its interests should Chinese actions prompt a major response from the United States. The Chinese are masters of the indirect approach: they are inclined to avoid any high-visibility military operations that would draw widespread attention to their regional ambitions or that would run the risk of military failure.

China's maneuverings over contested claims in the South China Sea offer an instructive example of the indirect approach. China has carried out a careful, periodic probing of an "island-hopping" or "reef-occupying" sort. These actions indicate to many observers a worrisome pattern of accretion and aggrandizement, but looked at singly (for example, the moves in early 1995 to establish a Chinese presence on reefs in the declared territorial waters of the Philippines) they appear less consequential, given that they did not entail escalation into highly coercive strategies. To be sure, China is not alone in staking claims and pursuing "planting-the-flag" options in the South China Sea. Moreover, such low-risk activities do not require sustained military operations, although they quietly underscore China's ability to assert its claims and to deny opportunities to others. But the precedent of heightening territorial disputes with an ASEAN member state is nonetheless disquieting. Such behavior is likely to represent one of the principal ongoing challenges to regional security and to efforts to induce self-restraint on the part of China and other claimants.

If one assumes that a more powerful Chinese state is inevitable, the need to engage with the modernists in Chinese military circles increases. Concern over China's growing naval activities is widespread. But there is also evidence that the more conservative (that is, continentalist) military leaders are wary of China's reach exceeding its grasp. This conflates the usual "hardliners versus moderates" characterization of the Chinese military. These leaders worry that an overextended China seeking to enhance its military reach could increase the vulnerabilities among ethnic minority populations in lightly populated areas of the interior, or along its northern and western borders. However, there is also in Chinese military thinking a pronounced pessimistic strain that depicts the United States as overtly antagonistic to the enhancement of Chinese military power and determined to frustrate the realization of China's longer-term national security goals. U.S. and Chinese security interests are no longer presumed to be complementary, as they were during much of the 1970s and 1980s. The pessimists argue that China must steadily seek to limit or erode America's military role in the region and build capabilities that deny the United States the ability to restrain the exercise of Chinese military power. In the view of these strategists, the viability of the Chinese state in a hostile world can only be ensured through a steady augmentation of China's military power in every dimension.[15]

Unfortunately, our knowledge of the internal dynamic that shapes Chinese military policymaking is extremely limited. This underscores the relevance of the Clinton administration's efforts to reengage the Chinese military establishment. The administration has been careful not to oversell the prospects of such ties since they offer an admittedly limited window into Chinese thinking and policy deliberations, but they are preferable to having no window at all. At least as important, such engagement would enable Washington to impart its concerns at a very high level in Beijing about Chinese behavior that may undermine U.S. regional security interests.[16] Following up on these preliminary steps will be crucial to realizing more positive outcomes from conditional engagement, since this strategy presumes the simultaneous retention of significant U.S. military capabilities in the region and development of a wider range of ties to the leaders who will shape China's political destiny in the post-Deng era. But such steps do not represent a policy "lock-in," nor do they assume a benign outcome.

The other major uncertainty in East Asia is the Korean Peninsula. The possibility of destabilization is in all likelihood much higher there than anywhere else in the region. But opinions on Korea's future vary widely. Many observers assert that the signing in October 1994 of the U.S.–North Korean Agreed Framework, freezing and (if fully implemented) dismantling North Korea's nuclear weapons program, points to signs of change and accommodation in Pyongyang. But the United States has no way of knowing whether this is true today, or whether it will be true in another few years. The extremely protracted timetable for clarification of the history of North Korean nuclear weapons activities and Pyongyang's efforts to delegitimize the Korean War armistice agreements are hardly reassuring. Given the level of military confrontation on the peninsula and the outside world's ignorance of leadership arrangements in North Korea (and even assuming a reformist leadership in Pyongyang), the prospects for the North Korean system are problematic indeed. Internal changes in North Korea could unleash events on the peninsula that would affect the interests not only of both Koreas but of China, Japan, Russia and the United States. Indeed, even a relatively painless unification scenario—an highly unlikely possibility—will engender major political and strategic repercussions throughout Northeast Asia. The peninsular logic that has defined South Korea's security requirements and the expectations of the United States for more than 40 years would lose much of its relevance. If the Republic of Korea no longer faces a threat from North Korea, the U.S.-R.O.K alliance would have to be supplanted or at least supplemented by a broader regional concept in which Korea, Japan, and the United States would endeavor to build on the successes of bilateral security cooperation.[17]

In the case of Korea, however, the maintenance of deterrence and defense capabilities appears to be the prudent option for the near to middle-term. At the same time, the United States must be prepared to engage all affected powers far more fully to address the implications of increased instability in North Korea or the breakdown of the Agreed Framework intended to freeze and ultimately eliminate Pyongyang's nuclear weapons potential. The effective management of a future unification process is a vital interest of all the states of Northeast Asia, and now is the time to address this concern. Working on the assumption that the North Korean threat will diminish or disappear, the United States and others should heighten their efforts to incorporate Korea into a new set of regional security arrangements. Such steps would be wholly appropriate with respect to a unified Korean state in search of normal relations with its much more powerful neighbors but still integrally linked to the United States by security ties. This would be especially true in a protracted, messy unification process.

Japan presents different challenges. The Kobe earthquake in 1995 revealed the failures of the existing system. The search for a more adaptable and modern political structure appropri-

ate to an economic actor of global stature continues to bedevil
the country's political leadership. As long as the Japanese
remain unwilling to address the deficiencies of their system, a
mature security order in Asia will remain elusive. The Japanese
themselves must deal with these issues, but American policymakers can and should encourage this internal debate. Such
encouragement, however, must be deftly offered, lest it fuel
fears in Japan that it is a precursor to American disengagement
from U.S.-Japanese security arrangements or engender anxi-
eties elsewhere in the region that the United States is intent on
bequeathing its regional security obligations to Japan. Future
U.S. policy must enable a more self-confident Japan to assume
a regional role commensurate with its latent political capabilities without posing a fundamental challenge to the close ties
between the United States and Japan. Short of a major new
threat in the region, however, it is doubtful that the United
States will in the long run continue to carry as much of the
weight in the security relationship. The issue here is not burden
sharing but genuine responsibility sharing. The highly asymmetrical relationship between Japan and the United States cannot be sustained indefinitely.

The challenges presented by Korea and Japan underline
the fact that a strategy of conditional engagement bears cen-
trally on America's alliances, not simply on its relations with
China. The principal regional challenges for the United States
are those of alliance transition (so that the United States continues to reap political, security, and economic benefits and
avoids malign outcomes) and of forming a more defined and
desirable relationship with China commensurate with that
country's rapid political and economic development and the
prospective enhancement of its military capabilities. Ensuring
credible and amicable relations with other states in the region
(especially with ASEAN members, where there are sources of
genuine strain with the United States, primarily for reasons
deriving from the internal politics of the Southeast Asian coun-

tries), though an important policy objective, must be a subsidiary one. Effecting a meaningful transition in Northeast Asia is the challenge on which the creation of a viable security order ultimately depends. This transformation becomes the indispensable means to longer-term ends, although—unlike either the unadorned realist position or the liberal internationalist perspective—it does not presume a specific outcome.

A strategy exclusively oriented toward (or, rather, against) China would be transparent in its focus and intent and be all but certain to elicit an adverse response across a broad spectrum of Chinese leadership opinion. A more diversified and artful approach—and one that addresses a wider array of U.S. regional interests—is far more likely to gain acceptance across the region, including among some Chinese officials. It is also far more likely to permit a level of U.S. military activity that diminishes the possibility that U.S. allies and security partners will opt for autonomous strategies, while simultaneously giving the Chinese pause with respect to political-diplomatic conduct or military activities that could undermine the development of a stable regional security order.[18] Without an appropriate level of U.S. military capabilities and political-military engagement, both regional allies and the Chinese will see a strategy of conditional engagement as toothless and therefore not credible.

A more robust presence, however, will enable the United States to prevent untoward developments while seeking to shape preferred ones. It will also clearly signal the conditions that will govern security cooperation between the United States and the region. The pursuit of a unilateralist regional security strategy is not a viable American option. The United States can only expect to maintain and nurture a regional security coalition if it makes explicit what it expects from others while also making clear its intention to retain core capabilities in the region over the longer term. Under some circumstances, this could lead to a divergence between the United States and its regional partners, who might well prefer to maximize their economic opportunities with continental Asia while the United States continued to shoulder the primary security responsibilities. But there is no inherent contradiction here since the United States also seeks to expand its economic involvement throughout the region. The difference between past policies and future policy under conditional engagement is that while America will retain a singular capacity to help shape the longer-term security order, it will expect its security partners to participate meaningfully and responsibly in pursuit of complementary goals. However, if the United States wants to design a new set of security arrangements in which U.S. interests will be fully addressed, America's voice must be heard, and therefore American power must remain visible. Without such a presence, the United States will find itself increasingly disadvantaged in a region of genuine import to American strategic interests. The states of Asia understand and acknowledge this; so too must the United States.

THE CHINA CHALLENGE

EVEN ACCEPTING this logic, the problems of transition with respect to China are certain to prove particularly challenging. The United States cannot expect to anticipate internal political outcomes in China, and it should not delude itself that a highly calibrated American policy is likely to strengthen the hand of a given leadership group in Beijing—even assuming Washington could identify accurately those of appropriate disposition. Indeed, it stands to reason that any conscious effort to tilt toward particular leaders could undermine them domestically; none would wish to be seen as backed by the United States or any other foreign power.

But this in no way invalidates the need for clarity and consistency in America's dealings with China. A clearly articulated U.S. policy that is presented fully and fairly to China's leaders is far more likely to elicit a considered response from them than one that obscures American policy preferences. The United States will have to specify areas of potential divergence or conflicting interest to the Chinese, but even so, sustained high-level attention from Washington will in itself make a difference to leaders in Beijing, who will take this as evidence that the United States views China as a major power.

U.S. policy should seek to specify its expectations about Chinese leaders' behavior in the regional arena and to convey to the Chinese a clearer sense of the benefits that would accrue under enhanced cooperation (for example, ongoing senior leadership consultations and greater access to American high technology). Although any such rules of acceptable behavior would have to be presented judiciously, it is vital that the effort be made and that they be discussed with the Chinese at senior levels. Given the Chinese predilection for principles, it may be more appropriate to cast proposed norms in such terms. Indeed, quite apart from what U.S. officials choose to convey to a post-Deng leadership, the United States must determine whether Chinese behavior comports with American expectations of a legitimate Chinese political-security role. Some tests of China's behavior might include the following:

- Refraining from the unilateral use of force against any of its neighbors;

- Avoidance of the pursuit of irredentist claims, especially those that would challenge stated U.S. regional security objectives (such as ensuring the security of sea lines of communication);

- A readiness to work collaboratively with the United States and South Korea to manage any "endgame" crisis in North Korea;

- A measured pattern of military acquisition that does not exceed China's legitimate defense needs (an issue that could prove highly contentious between China and its neighbors);

• A willingness to refrain from destabilizing actions outside East Asia (such as facilitating ballistic missile development programs that could undermine regional military balances elsewhere in the developing world);

• A willingness to be more forthcoming about the purposes, dimensions, and ancillary activities underlying its defense modernization effort, including fuller dissemination of defense data similar to that published by Japan and Korea;

• An increased willingness over time to move toward the building of a collaborative security structure in East Asia with its neighbors and with the United States.

Many in China would object to moralistic or preachy proffering of such goals. At the same time, the Chinese will continue to go to appreciable lengths to maintain "wiggle room" and ambiguity in their diplomatic conduct and military activities. Leaders in Beijing demonstrate a knack for actions that skirt the edges of what others would deem objectionable or that leave unresolved China's longer-range intentions.

Nonetheless, establishing such criteria is a necessary first step in understanding and evaluating Chinese actions. If China is to allay the suspicions of its neighbors and the United States about its longer-term political-military ambitions, it must present a more candid and clear-cut explanation of its strategic goals. However, rather than see China's future defense development only in terms of an intrinsic threat to American and regional interests, Washington must try to empathize, if not necessarily sympathize with Chinese hopes and fears. At the same time, China's leaders must ensure that the emergence of a more powerful Chinese state does not engender serious instability or tempt them to try to unilaterally redefine the character of the East Asian security order.

These issues go well beyond a rule-based conception of China's defense strategy and foreign policy. They speak even more profoundly to the character of the future Chinese political and institutional system and the processes that will attend the transition. Even if this is fundamentally an internal question, the United States and the other regional powers are deeply interested parties. This message must be imparted to those defining China's strategic directions. Conveyed clearly but not in an overbearing fashion, such a message could draw Beijing into discussions about the region's future.

The need for an enhanced strategic dialogue between the United States and China is self-evident. Such discussions will in no way preclude the need for interactions between China and its neighbors, but given that American military power continues to assume a central managerial role in East Asia, strategic understandings must begin with the United States. Sustained high-level interaction between Washington and Beijing would unambiguously convey America's strategic stake in the region and signal Beijing that a viable longer-term security order in Asia and the Pacific is not possible without the full and constructive participation of both powers.

Thus, Washington must seek to engage China more fully in the creation of a post–Cold War strategic framework. Leaving China out of the process will only lead to increased uncertainty and instability in the region. Making Beijing a stakeholder will not guarantee a complete congruence of interests between China and the United States or between China and its neighbors, but it will appreciably improve the likelihood of a peaceful transition to a new regional security structure.

The United States and China should begin where past negotiations left off. In the 1970s and early 1980s, the public enunciation of principles for U.S.-Chinese relations led to private understandings between senior officials in both governments, including on the difficult issue of Taiwan.[19] At bottom, those understandings recognized the benefits to both countries

Weaving the Net

of restraint toward each other and the region as a whole. A post-Cold War framework must reflect the profound political, economic, and strategic changes since the heyday of the "strategic triangle." It should reinforce previous commitments by both governments not to undertake any unilateral alterations of the status quo. It should acknowledge China's growing power and presence. It should also acknowledge that American interests in East Asia are enduring, and not simply a consequence of a now-defunct global rivalry. And it should obligate both leaderships to initiate an ongoing process of interaction.

In the absence of such an understanding, neither Washington nor Beijing will be able to craft stable policies toward the other; with such an understanding, they will be able to plan for the long-term. Neither the United States nor China can expect to dictate the region's future. They have no credible alternative except to begin a serious effort to engage one another in a discussion of rules of the road for the long-term.

THE NEXT STEPS

IT SHOULD NOT BE especially difficult to define conditional engagement in operational terms. At base, the strategy would entail America's allies assuming a full or near-full range of responsibilities for their own defense. The United States would retain power-projection forces in the region to be deployed in military emergencies. Such forces would also convey visibly American commitment and presence. However, such forces should not be China configured, since this would undoubtedly undermine any larger effort to engage a successor leadership in Beijing. The retention of such capabilities would make unmistakably clear the broader abiding American commitment to a stable regional order.

An appropriately designed and executed conditional engagement strategy would be neither the precursor of U.S. military disengagement nor a slippery slope to an explicit containment doctrine with respect to China. It represents a prudent, evolutionary approach to the region, leaving open responses to developments that at present cannot be foreseen or predicted with confidence. Such a strategy admits that Washington cannot know the ultimate configuration of political and military forces within the region. But it recognizes a continuing American ability to shape the regional future in a manner that serves U.S. interests and plays to America's comparative advantage. A strategy that affords the United States latitude and flexibility in its regional security interactions under conditions of dynamic change and potential realignment is preferable to any of the alternative strategies discussed.

That said, a credible transition strategy in East Asia will entail commitment and expenditure. Short of a major amelioration of regional rivalries and rapid development of new region-wide understandings and arrangements, U.S. military power will remain deployed in East Asia for some time to come. As I have noted elsewhere, America's security engagement, though an incomplete and imperfect policy instrument, "is both an insurance [policy] (diminishing the risks and consequences of adverse security developments) and an investment strategy (committing American resources to the longer-term development of a stable and secure regional order). This security role, however, must be tailored to affordability, feasibility, and reciprocity."[20] Reciprocity could well prove the most important factor. America will remain in the region so long as it is welcome and so long as its military presence is seen as serving larger American interests; it cannot be otherwise. Again, as I have observed elsewhere, "There are clearly promising avenues between the extremes of dominance and disengagement; it is in these realms that a creative long-term American regional strategy must endeavor to operate, and in which the United States still enjoys distinctive opportunities and advantages to participate fully in the shaping of Asia's future."[21] It is to this challenge that American policymakers must now turn in earnest.

The opinions expressed in this chapter are my own, and should not be attributed to RAND or any of its government sponsors.

NOTES

1. For the current formulations of official U.S. policy, see the White House, *A National Security Strategy of Engagement and Enlargement*, February 1995; and the Department of Defense, *National Military Strategy of the United States of America*, February 1995.
2. *A National Security Strategy of Engagement and Enlargement*, p. 28.
3. Ibid., pp. 12-13.
4. For an especially vigorous presentation of this view, see Kishore Mahbubani, "The Pacific Impulse," *Survival* 37, no. 1 (Spring 1995), pp. 105-120.
5. This conclusion is amply demonstrated in Department of Defense, *United States Security Strategy for the East Asia-Pacific Region*, February 1995.
6. Ibid., especially pp. 23-29.
7. See Patrick M. Cronin and Michael J. Green, "Redefining the U.S.-Japan Alliance: Tokyo's National Defense Program," *McNair Paper* 31, (Washington, D.C.: Institute for National Strategy Studies, National Defense University, November 1994); and Mike M. Mochizuki, Japan: *Domestic Change and Foreign Policy* (Santa Monica, Ca.: RAND, 1995).
8. For an exploration of possible alternatives, see Jonathan D. Pollack and Young Koo Cha, *A New Alliance for the Next Century: The Future of U.S.-Korean Security Cooperation* (Santa Monica, Ca.: RAND, 1995).
9. See Hannes Adomeit, "Russia as a 'Great Power' in World Affairs: Images and Reality," *International Affairs* (London) 71, no. 1 (January 1995), pp. 35-68; see also Peggy Falkenheim Meyer, "Russia's Post-Cold War Security Policy in Northeast Asia," *Pacific Affairs* 67, no. 4 (Winter 1994-95), pp. 495-512.
10. See Harry Harding, "Prospects for Cooperative Security Arrangements in the Asia-Pacific Region," *Journal of Northeast Asian Studies* 13, no. 3 (Fall 1994), pp. 31-41.
11. Jonathan D. Pollack, "Sources of Instability and Conflict in Northeast Asia," *Arms Control Today* 24, no. 9 (November 1994), p. 4.
12. Chinese sensitivities (at least in certain leadership circles) remain highly acute in this regard. For example, the February 1995 Department of Defense report on East Asian strategy (which seeks

primarily to reassert the relevance of current U.S. policy and forward deployments) was described in a Chinese-controlled Hong Kong newspaper as "biased and untrue in evaluating Chinese defense capabilities. The report reveals an undisguised attempt to pose confrontation against China. Beginning last year, the United States gradually changed its security guarantee policy in Asia, promoted military modernization in Taiwan and the Southeast Asian countries, upgraded diplomatic relations with Taiwan, and strengthened relations with Vietnam and India. All of this could not but arouse misgivings in China. Does this constitute containment of China?" "Analysis of Report on U.S. Asian Strategy," *Wen Wei Po*, March 4, 1995, cited in *Foreign Broadcast Information Service* report, CHI-95-043, pp. 4-5.

13. For a discerning analysis, see Michael D. Swaine, *China: Domestic Change and Foreign Policy* (Santa Monica, Ca.: RAND, 1995).

14. A burgeoning cottage industry presupposes the inexorable emergence of an appreciably more powerful and externally oriented Chinese defense establishment. Although these assessments point to growing evidence of such an orientation, it is important not to overstate its dimensions and achievements. The Chinese military remains unsettled and internally inconsistent, suggesting continued and possibly growing internal debate over these issues. For representative examples of recent analyses, emphasizing the likely emergence of a more militarily robust Chinese state, consult Chong-pin Lin, "Chinese Military Modernization: Perceptions, Progress, and Prospects," *Security Studies* 3, no. 4 (Summer 1994), pp. 718-53; David Shambaugh, "Growing Strong: China's Challenge to Asian Security," *Survival* 36, no. 2 (Summer 1994), pp. 43-59. For a more cautious and skeptical assessment of China's military modernization prospects, see Kenneth W. Allen, Glenn Krumel, and Jonathan D. Pollack, *China's Air Force Enters the 21st Century* (Santa Monica, Ca.: RAND, 1995), especially chaps. 8 and 9.

15. For a detailed discussion of this viewpoint, see Swaine.

16. For an especially cogent example of such opportunities put to effective use, see the remarks Secretary of Defense William Perry delivered before the Chinese National Defense University, Beijing, October 18, 1994, reprinted in *Defense Issues* 9, no. 81.

17. For further discussion, see Pollack and Cha.

18. Defense Secretary William Perry's October 1994 speech in Beijing is an exemplary example of how to air U.S. differences with China without eliciting predictable, stylized Chinese reactions. This extended to the most explicit statement to date of U.S. policy toward

the use of force in the South China Sea. As Perry observed: "This situation has been a source of tension for years, and it creates anxiety about the future. If disputed territorial claims to the Spratly Islands erupt into conflict, it could be a devastating blow to regional stability and threaten sea lines of communication vital to the United States and to other countries of the world." To the author's knowledge, no Chinese official took exception to Perry's remarks.

19. For an insightful and detailed treatment of these issues, see Richard H. Solomon, *Chinese Political Negotiating Behavior, 1967-1984 (Santa Monica, Ca.: RAND, 1995). This publication is a declassified version of a study prepared for the U.S. government in 1985.

20. Jonathan D. Pollack, "The United States in East Asia: Holding the Ring," in *America's International Role in the Post-Cold War Era*, Adelphi Paper no. 275, part I (London: International Institute for Strategic Studies, March 1993), p. 79.

21. Ibid., pp. 81-82.

7

Coping with China
as a Rising Power

Jianwei Wang

AMERICAN PERCEPTIONS of China have shifted dramatically in the last five years. After the 1989 Tiananmen tragedy, China was perceived as a villain. It appeared to have lost most of its internal legitimacy and external credibility, and its system seemed on the verge of collapse. Then came the dramatic disintegration of the Soviet empire and the consequent change in the world balance of power of 1990-91, and almost overnight China lost its importance as a strategic partner in the post–Cold War international order. A year later, however, the talk was of a rising China, whose growing economic and military power posed a potential threat to world peace and stability. These striking perceptual changes—a collapsing China became a rising China, and China the paper tiger became China the threat—reflected actual changes taking place in China. The American perception of China, however, tends to shift faster than the reality.

A U.S. strategy toward China must be based on a realistic assessment of the country. The situation in China is rarely either as bad or as good as Americans think it is. And although there is no doubt that China is emerging as a major player in world politics, its rise so far has been asymmetrical: visible economically, hypothetical militarily, and inconsequential politically.

For the first time in 100 years, China has an opportunity to become a major power. Yet the road ahead is replete with difficulties that will consume most of China's energy; thus the threat to the existing international system should not be exaggerated. This process is long overdue—and probably inevitable—irrespective of what the United States does. However, the United States can influence what kind of power China becomes.

The challenges China will pose for American policymakers and to U.S. national interests in the coming decades are largely those any emerging power would pose. Attributing them exclusively to China's authoritarian political system is misleading. It is also naive to assume that the "China problem" will disappear as soon as China becomes a democratic country.

Therefore, the objective of U.S. strategy should not be to obstruct China's development as a major power but to facilitate its integration into the international system. Moreover, policymakers should avoid looking at China's international behavior solely as the product of domestic politics.

The utility of a strategy of conditional engagement, or a hedging strategy, as outlined by Jonathan Pollack in chapter 6 of this volume, should be viewed in a broad historical context.[1] In this chapter, I will try to elaborate on some variables that might affect China's reaction to this strategy by answering the following questions: How does China perceive the United States? What is the relationship between China's domestic politics and foreign policy? How has China's strategic culture evolved? What rules of behavior would be acceptable to China? What combination of integration and containment is desirable in dealing with China?

CHINESE IMAGES OF THE UNITED STATES

THREE DISCERNIBLE images of the United States and its role in the post-Cold War era coexist in China. The first deriving from an ideological perspective, casts the United States as a rival value system; the second, which comes out of a realist perspective, casts the United States as a hegemonic power; and the last, the product of an interdependence perspective, sees the United States as a necessary and even preferable world leader.[2]

Those who view the United States through ideological lenses believe that the ultimate goal of U.S. foreign policy is the elimination of communism from the earth. This goal, they believe, has not changed since the end of World War II and will not change so as long as socialism exists. Chinese who hold this view tend to regard American policy toward their country as inherently hostile, characterized by a grand strategy of "peaceful evolution," in which Western democracy, with its emphasis on individual freedom and human rights, will conquer the world. With the collapse of communism in the Soviet Union and Eastern Europe, China is naturally the next target. An article internally circulated among the Chinese leadership declared: "We realized quite early that (after the Gulf War and the disintegration of the Soviet Union) the United States certainly will change its direction toward the East (*huishi dongxian*) to use all means at its disposal to deal with China . . . Because China refuses to give up socialism, the United States is very likely to shift its focal point of peaceful evolution to China."[3] The United States is seen to be waging another cold war or anticommunist crusade, this time against China. Since 1989 the real purpose of Washington's policy, the ideologues say, has been to topple the communist government and change the socialist system in China.

Chinese realists view the United States in traditional realpolitik terms: power and interest still drive world politics. Through this lens, and given the superior aggregate national power (*zongheguoli*) of the United States, America's post-Cold War strategy looks expansionist. The motivation behind the American global strategy is not abstract values such as democracy and human rights. Rather, the strategy seeks to maintain U.S. superiority and avoid being squeezed in competition with other major powers. Those who look at the United States from the realist perspective disagree, however, in their estimates of American power. Radical realists argue that the United States will take full advantage of its unique position as the sole superpower and create a world empire. Moderate realists believe that instead of pursuing an all-around strategy of expansion, the United States may choose to pursue a more moderate foreign policy so as to give more attention to its domestic problems. Ironically, some realists do not see the main thrust of America's global strategy as being aimed at China, given China's relatively weak power position. More likely, they believe, American policy is designed to deal with the economic and political competition with fellow developed countries.

Those who look at the United States from an interdependence perspective argue that, in view of increasing global economic interdependence, international affairs should not be viewed solely from the standpoint of nation states. They do not see post–Cold War American foreign policy in terms of pure ideology or power. Instead, they rate American leadership in international affairs a necessity in a world of transition and interdependence. As one well-known scholar notes, "The United States is not necessarily a hegemonic country by nature. The United States is the best major power compared with Britain, France, and Japan. The style of its international behavior is similar to China's rule of the East in history. Before the Industrial Revolution, China was the most benign power, whereas the United States is the most benign power since the Industrial Revolution."[4]

These three perspectives hold different implications for policy toward the United States. Those in China who look at

America from an ideological perspective advocate "a campaign of anti-evolution, anti-penetration, anti-sabotage, anti-sanction, and anti-interference." Specifically, they call for tit-for-tat tactics in the areas of trade, human rights and arms control. Those in China who have adopted a radical realist perspective share this confrontational attitude toward the United States. They also favor the traditional strategy of exploiting differences between the major powers in dealing with the United States. Those who view the United States from a more moderate realist perspective, however, hold that China should steer a pragmatic course and avoid confrontation, since the United States is still the most powerful country in the world and will remain so for a long time. They believe China should refrain from ideological polemics against the United States, concentrating instead on developing its own national power. Those in China who argue from an interdependence perspective emphasize that China and the United States have a common interest in addressing transnational issues and maintaining stability in both East Asia and the world. They hope that China's leadership will refrain from emotional responses that could damage the fragile but gradually improving Sino-American relationship. Moreover, they believe that China must abide by international rules and practices if it wants to be a full member of the international community.

China's leaders look at the world, and the United States in particular, from all these perspectives at once. They believe that America's fussiness over China in recent years is ultimately a reflection of an instinctive dislike of China's political and social system. So long as China remains even a nominally socialist country, as a senior Chinese leader put it, America will not cease its efforts to "Westernize" (*xihua*) and "split up" (*fenhua*) China. The People's Republic of China must be prepared to contend with the United States for a long time to come.[5] However, China's leaders also see competition with the United States in economic rather than ideological terms. As they often declare, in order to secure a favorable position for the country in world politics for the next century, enhancing "aggregate national strength" is China's top priority, not engaging in an ideological cold war.

China can achieve this strategic goal more easily by integrating into the world economic system than by rejecting it. Therefore, while China should stick to its own course politically, economically it must both take advantage of and meet the challenges of complex interdependence. China's economy should be "connected" (*jiegui*) to the world economy; no matter how uncomfortable it is in doing so, China must adapt its economic structure and practices to international regimes and norms. The country should never again close its doors to the outside world.

The relative weight of the three perspectives in Chinese thinking changes with events. Immediately after the Tiananmen incident, for example, the rhetoric coming out of Beijing was markedly ideological. But it soon became apparent that the moderate version of the realist perspective was driving policy toward the United States. Yet U.S. diplomacy in recent years — from the high-handed treatment of the *Yin He* container ship[6] to the annual torture over most-favored-nation status; from opposition to China's bid to host the Olympic Games in the year 2000 to the pursuit of a Chinese nuclear submarine in international waters; from the blocking of China's entry into the World Trade Organization (WTO) to ordering China to close its own factories, to upgrading America's relations with Taiwan—has served to push China's leadership to adopt a more radical realist/nationalist perspective. Policies, such as the Clinton administration decision to grant Taiwan's President Lee Teng-hui a U.S. entry visa, put the liberals among the Chinese elites on the defensive and boost the more nationalistic elements.

At this moment, the notion that the United States is the best candidate for world leader or that it does not necessarily see China as one of its biggest enemies can hardly be expected to be viewed sympathetically by mainstream Chinese elites. Many have come to the conclusion that despite its protestations the United States does not really want to see a strong, stable, prosperous China. When China rejected the world system in the 1950s and 1960s, the United States declared that its policy goal was to bring China back into the family of nations. Now that China is ready to join, the United States seems unwilling to allow this to happen. U.S. policy is perceived as aimed at keeping China weak, divided, and at arm's length from the Western-dominated world economic system. Some Chinese scholars describe the American mentality as a "professed love of what one really fears" (*yegonghaolong*).

Thus, China, as it strives to take its place among the major powers, has increasingly, though reluctantly, come to see the United States as a potential adversary. As one Chinese diplomat told me, "The tree may prefer calm, but the wind will not subside. China sincerely hopes to have stable relations with the United States and to avoid confrontation. But the troublesome relations in recent years proved that this is just wishful thinking on China's part. The United States will not let you sit in peace." If one thing is certain about China, it is that nationalism is on the rise. The military and political hard-liners are riding this wave, advocating tougher policies toward the United States. More noteworthy, however, is that the traditionally pro-Western intellectuals are becoming more and more disillusioned with American policy, and their indignation is echoed by ordinary people who think their government is not strong enough in dealing with the United States.

In this psychological environment, it will be difficult to sell conditional engagement to the Chinese, who will naturally look at such a strategy with great suspicion. One of the main challenges for American policymakers, therefore, is figuring out how to reverse the ominous buildup of nationalistic sentiment in China and to encourage the reemergence of the interdependence and moderate realist viewpoints. Washington must convince the Chinese that it aims at peacefully integrating China into the world system and that containment is not its policy of choice.

POST-DENG POLITICAL SUCCESSION AND FOREIGN POLICY

THE AMERICAN media tend to attribute China's rising nation-alism and its hardened positions on the WTO, property rights, human rights, and Taiwan exclusively to the intensified power struggle within the leadership in anticipation of Deng Xiaoping's imminent death. This interpretation overlooks other factors that may have a more lasting impact.

It is true that in the past Deng Xiaoping played a pivotal role in Chinese foreign policymaking and that his physical decline has caused China's diplomacy to stagnate. The current leadership basically follows the principles he laid down. When facing a tough policy choice that presents significant political or economic risks, no single member in the current leadership team can speak with Deng's authority: no one has enough nerve to strike a deal and say yes or no. A consensus must be reached among the foreign policy elites. Policy preferences and public opinion at the lower levels of the bureaucracy exert much more influence than they did during the Mao and Deng eras. As a result, decision making is a more piecemeal process.

However, to describe the Chinese leadership as paralyzed by power struggle and to say that everything is frozen in China is overdoing it. There is little hard evidence that China's current leaders are so deeply involved in a fierce power struggle that they do not care about foreign policy issues or are unable to take any policy initiatives. To the contrary, there is evidence that the current team is functioning as it is supposed to. On the occasion of the 1995 Lunar New Year, for example, General Secretary of the Chinese Communist Party Jiang Zemin announced an eight-point policy initiative toward Taiwan.[7] In his speech, he proposed an agreement to formally end the hostility between Beijing and Taipei and another agreement to guarantee the interests of Taiwanese investors. While this initiative was widely interpreted by the Western media as an effort on Jiang's part to consolidate his power, such a policy announcement would have been inconceivable if the leadership were split. The arrests on suspicion of corruption of Zhou Beifang, the chairman of Shougang (Hong Kong), who is widely perceived as a close associate of the Deng family, and the purge of the hard-line Beijing mayor Chen Xitong also indicate that senior leaders are more or less united behind Jiang.[8] It is unlikely that a paralyzed leadership could agree on such moves while Deng was still alive.

The struggle for succession is therefore an incomplete explanation of the dynamics of China's foreign policy. Chinese leaders and their constituencies are fed-up with American pressure on one issue after another. On issues such as intellectual property rights and Taiwan independence, the leadership had to decide whether China should once again "swallow the bitter fruit." The last-minute concession by the Chinese on the intellectual property rights issue demonstrated the leadership's ability to control the rising tide of nationalism and make a deal with the United States. However, the crisis over Lee Teng-hui's recent visit to the United States pushed the leadership's political endurance to its limit. Yet, overall, China's diplomacy has been phased and well-calculated. It can be said that while the new leadership is slow in making decisions, it is also less likely to take drastic measures that would seriously damage Chinese-U.S. relations. Indeed, if Deng were still active in foreign policymaking, his "no" to the Americans might have done just that.

Although the current Chinese leadership is holding to Deng's basic pattern in foreign policy, predicting what will happen after the paramount leader's death is tenuous business. There are too many variables, and our understanding of the relationships among them is speculative rather than empirical. If we take the intensity of the power struggle at the top as the primary independent variable and the degree of political and social chaos as the main dependent variable, several scenarios present themselves. (And even here, we should realize that certain unpredictable low-level social variables—such as the Tiananmen incident—may touch off a political showdown at the top.)

In the no-chaos scenario, there is a smooth power transition from the Deng-system to the Jiang-system. Deng's death is almost a non-issue, and everything is business as usual. The so-called third generation of collective leadership installed by Deng and the surviving first-generation veterans remain united and functioning. Jiang Zemin's position as the "core" of leadership is not seriously challenged. The team continues to enjoy the support of the military, whose political role remains marginal. Concurrently, although economic and social problems are rampant, general political and economic conditions remain stable and there is no significant social unrest. Consequently, China's current domestic and foreign policy does not change very much.

In a low-chaos scenario, there is some reshuffling of personnel at the top. For instance, one or two of the four "magnates"—Jiang Zemin, Li Peng, Qiao Shi, and Li Ruihuan—leave the scene peacefully or switch positions with each other. Some leaders at the second level, such as Zhu Rongji and Hu Jintao, move up. However, the basic structure of the current leadership remains unchanged. Jiang's core position is not seriously challenged. The military remains politically neutral, but its influence on some policy issues closely related to its interests, such as arms sales and military expenditure, may increase due to a weaker political leadership. Some small-scale social protests erupt, but they do not have nationwide significance and are soon brought under control. There may be some foreign policy changes on specific issues, but an overall directional shift is unlikely.

In a medium-chaos scenario, there is either a serious power struggle at the top or turmoil at the societal level gets out of hand. The Jiang leadership is unable to remain unified and rival coalitions form around key leaders. As a result, Jiang may lose one or all of his titles. If a balance of power cannot be maintained within the leadership team, surviving first or second-generation leaders such as Yang Shangkun and Wan Li, as well as the military, may intervene to control the damage. The possibility of a palace coup, in which some leaders are ousted by force, also exists. However, the power struggle at the top does not immediately spill over onto the societal level, as when the Gang of Four was arrested in 1976. In a variation on this scenario, large-scale social turmoil breaks out as a result of acute economic and political problems, such as corruption, high inflation, unemployment, and widespread crime. Yet the top leadership remains united and effectively mobilizes the coercive mechanisms of the state to put down social unrest. Chaos is visible and consequential, but because chaos does not occur simultaneously at both levels, things return to normal relatively quickly. Under the second variation, it is China's domestic rather than its foreign policy that is affected. Under the first variation, some foreign policy adjustments are plausible, but so long as the change occurs within the system rather than transforming it, the basic direction of current foreign policy survives.

In a high-chaos scenario, fierce political struggle at the top and large-scale social unrest echo each other—as in 1989—and produce national upheaval. Civil war or national disintegration is possible. However, the outcome of such a scenario is highly unpredictable. If the central government still survives, four prospects can be envisaged: (1) the extreme ideologues or nationalists capture power; (2) more liberal communist leaders, such as Zhao Ziyang, are rehabilitated; (3) a popularly elected government is established; or (4) in the absence of political control, the military takes over the government. Needless to say, such a scenario implies profound change in China's policy both at home and abroad.

The probability of either the first or fourth scenarios occurring is low. In the short term—that is, in the period immediately after Deng's death—the second scenario is the most plausible. In the medium term, the third scenario is more likely. To better understand the dynamics of the situation, it is useful to compare some aspects of the post-Deng succession with those of the post-Mao succession.

First, when Mao was on his deathbed, China's economy was in ruins and the living standards of ordinary people were steadily deteriorating. Today, China's economy is booming and the quality of life has significantly improved over the last decade.

Second, although Deng has been the paramount leader since 1978, he does not enjoy Mao's god-like status. So, while Mao's death meant the fall of heaven for many Chinese, Deng's death will not cause anything close to the social repercussions that Mao's did. Moreover, Mao's illness was kept secret and everyone was shocked when his demise was announced. Now the Chinese people know that Deng is going to die soon, so psychologically they are much more prepared.

Third, in Mao's last days, he did not have the time or energy to arrange his succession. Hua Guofeng was hastily designated as Mao's successor just a few months before Mao's death and was virtually unknown both at home and abroad. Although Deng suffered the same setbacks as Mao in choosing his heir apparent, he was able to choose an entire team of new leaders while he was still relatively healthy. This new leadership has been in place for more than five years. Time equals legitimacy in China: the longer a leader holds power, the more difficult it is to delegitimize him unless he makes gross mistakes.

Jiang Zemin is a case in point. Jiang is often described in the West as a conservative, incompetent, and colorless leader who is bound to be a transitional figure.[9] It might be true that Jiang is not a leader with vision and talent, but he is a smart politician who knows how to balance relations with various interest groups in the party and how to make compromises. That is where he is different from Hu Yaobang and Zhao Ziyang, the two previous Chinese Communist Party general secretaries who were purged in 1986 and 1989 respectively. Jiang's record since he came to power, and especially in the last year, shows that he is steadily consolidating his power base, with the "Shanghai Gang" at the center. We have to measure his prestige and ability in terms of his potential competitors. The other members of the current team are not much better than Jiang overall. The only two figures who could justifiably replace Jiang are Yang Shangkun, a senior official who was once the standing vice chairman of the Military Commission of the Central Committee of the Chinese Communist Party, and Zhao Ziyang. While Yang's prestige and seniority are indisputable, he is in his late eighties, and it is by no means certain that he has ever had the desire to be the supreme leader. Zhao Ziyang is recognized as a capable administrator, and his resistance to the Tiananmen military crackdown won him great respect among liberal intellectuals. However, while he was hailed as a reformer overseas, he is not nearly as popular among the Chinese. Moreover, his rehabilitation would likely threaten the vested interests of the whole team, since they all benefited from his fall.

Fourth, before Mao's death, the Chinese leadership was fatally paralyzed by different ideological orientations, policy preferences, and personal animosities. Among the current leadership, ideological and policy disagreements are apparently not that deep. Indeed, it is difficult to group leaders meaningfully into "conservatives" and "reformers." The main sources of possible internal strife stem from the lust for power. However, the current crop of leaders has a much clearer sense than Mao's successors did of the suicidal risks that are attached to an excessive desire for power.

Several unfavorable factors are also associated with the impending succession. First, the Chinese people are no longer as politically submissive as during the Cultural Revolution. They are much more independent and dynamic in choosing their way of life and more receptive to non-Marxist ideologies and values. Second, in Mao's China the centralization of political, economic, and social life was extremely effective. In contrast, Deng's China is much more decentralized and the central government has much less control over provincial governments and society. Third, Chinese society in the Mao era was closed and isolated. The government controlled all sources of information, and it did not have to take world opinion into consideration.

Chinese society today has integrated itself into the world to a great extent. The Chinese people are better informed, and what happens in China is closely monitored by the international media. The Chinese government, therefore, does not have a free hand in ruling the country. Finally, while life was much harder during the Mao era, people also had fewer expectations. Now people are in much better shape, but economic and political expectations are growing faster than they can be met. As a result, society is restless and agitated.

In balance, the transition after Deng's death should be easier than the one after Mao's—if Deng's successors can control their lust for absolute power. When Mao was dying, no one could even imagine what would happen after his death. Now, while uncertainty is still pervasive, there are at least some scenarios to chew on. In any case, we all have to live with some uncertainty: can anybody accurately predict who is going to win the 1996 U.S. presidential elections? Even the post-Mao succession was not as bloody and chaotic as people expected it to be.

The way the succession plays out will have implications for U.S. strategy. Unless large-scale political turmoil erupts in China and seriously upsets the existing political system, the primary goals of Chinese foreign policy and the basic patterns of its international behavior will remain more or less the same. Compared to the past, China's diplomacy is relatively independent of domestic politics, thus domestic political change should not unduly influence China's foreign policy commitments, obligations, or standards of behavior. The regime's handling of the Tiananmen incident showed that it has the desire and ability to decouple domestic politics and foreign policy. After Tiananmen, the traditional wisdom that domestic turmoil and repression would lead to external belligerence and assertiveness proved false. Instead, China's overall diplomacy became more flexible and accommodating.

Viewing China simply as a rising power, one can see that many features of its foreign policy would remain constant even if a democratic system was in place: China would still take back Hong Kong and Macao; it would not recognize the independence of Taiwan or Tibet; it would not easily give up its claim over the Spratly Islands; and it would modernize its military — just as a democratizing Taiwan still claims sovereignty over Outer Mongolia and the Spratlys, a democratic India would not hesitate to fight for Kashmir, and a nonsocialist Russia assaulted secessionist Chechnya.

What does this mean for U.S. policy? First, Washington should not be unduly concerned about China's domestic politics. It should take China's external behavior at face value rather than viewing it as a mechanical extension of its political system. If U.S. policymakers follow the simplistic logic that "governments behave internationally as they behave toward their own citizens,"[10] there is no rationale for conditional engagement. U.S. strategy should be based on the assumption that although China will have an authoritarian regime for the foreseeable future it is still possible to integrate China into the world system as a responsible player. Without such a conceptual breakthrough, any strategy is doomed to failure.

China may experience a period of uncertainty and instability after Deng's death. However, the United States would be wise to refrain from overexploiting the regime's weakness for its own benefit. While such opportunism might yield some short-term gains, it could well have a negative effect on the future direction of China's policy toward the United States. The Chinese dislike people who take advantage of someone in a precarious position (*chengrenzhiwei*).

THE EVOLVING CHINESE STRATEGIC CULTURE

IN CULTURAL TERMS, a strategy of conditional engagement should not alienate the Chinese because it is largely consistent with China's custom of "taking strong measures only after courteous ones fail" (*xianlihoubing*) and "gaining mastery by striking only after the enemy has struck" (*houfazhiren*). Of course, while China's strategic culture has many enduring features, it is evolving along with China's internal and external environments. The United States could be well off target if it were to judge China's current diplomatic strategy by its strategic culture of the 1950s to 1970s.

For instance, the strategy of "using barbarians against barbarians," which dominated China's diplomacy in the 1970s, apparently is no longer so appealing to Chinese leaders. Immediately after the Tiananmen incident, more conservative elements of the realist camp once again advocated this strategy. He Xin, widely perceived as an ultra-nationalist, was explicit: "China should pay close attention to those countries which are either at odds with American interests or could be potential strategic adversaries of the United States. We must understand that our enemy's enemy is our ally. We should try to help and warn those countries not to be divided and destroyed by the United States like the former Soviet Union and Eastern bloc countries were. For that purpose, China should try its best to find allies among countries and regions which could become the potential strategic adversaries of the United States [Germany and Japan]."[11]

Western scholars suspected that Beijing would employ this traditional strategy in countering the U.S. attempt to isolate China after Tiananmen. However, China resisted the temptation to play the Russian card or the Japanese card while suffering through its post-Tiananmen isolation.[12] China has followed a strict line of "neither confrontation nor alliance" in improving its relations with Russia, the leadership having concluded that China now has sufficient weight in international relations to pursue an independent diplomacy without relying on a stronger partner. China's leaders have also realized that alliance has its costs. If China was disillusioned by the Sino-Soviet alliance's collapse in the early 1960s, it felt betrayed by the United States after the 1989 events in Tiananmen Square.

The dramatic reconfiguration of post–Cold War Sino-American relations sent a chill through the ranks of China's foreign policy elites. They bitterly resented the way the United States downgraded China from a strategic asset to a political liability overnight when the Soviet Union collapsed.

American policymakers, therefore, should not worry too much about the prospect of a Sino-Japanese or Sino-Russian alliance against the United States. The Chinese have not lost their traditional suspicions of the Japanese.[13] The last decade has witnessed several bursts of anti-Japanese sentiment in China. Japan's permitting a high-ranking Taiwanese official to attend the Asian Games in September 1994 and its recent expressions of unhappiness over China's nuclear testing program have not allayed this suspicion. Many Chinese analysts believe that Japan will not be content to remain solely an economic power but will gradually strive to become a political and regional military power as well. China is worried that the United States is actually encouraging Japan to become a military superpower.[14] China is also alert to any attempt by the United States to explicitly adopt an alliance strategy against China, by lining up other Asian countries to "contain" the PRC A strategy of conditional engagement should not be based on an anti-Chinese Asian coalition. Unless China turns to an alliance strategy first, the United States should not be responsible for once again plunging Asia into an era of pro and anti-Chinese blocs.

Another example of China's evolving strategic culture is its abandonment of the policy of befriending distant states while attacking those nearby (*yuanjiaojingong*). China's relations with almost all its neighbors before the 1980s were turbulent. Mao's grand strategy of "befriending" the United States while "attacking" the Soviet Union was in part a response to historical legacies and to the East-West confrontation of the time, but it also reflected the country's diplomatic flaws. Mao was obsessed with projecting China's diplomatic influence globally. He cared less about China's relations with its neighbors than about its friendships with remote countries like Albania and Cuba. This global-oriented diplomacy had serious consequences. While Beijing concerned itself with events in far-off places, it paid inadequate attention to its peripheral interests and regional affairs. To a certain extent, China was "a regional power without a regional policy."[15]

This has changed significantly in recent years. Interestingly, China's isolation after Tiananmen facilitated the formulation of a real regional policy. The innovative implementation of a "good neighbor" policy enabled China to normalize relations with almost all the surrounding states. As Beijing proudly declares, China's "peripheral environment" has never been better. It can be argued that this is a strategic reorientation and not simply a tactical adjustment, the result of a realistic redefinition of China's national interest.

This change in China's strategic culture means that the goals of a strategy of conditional engagement and China's national interest converge to a degree. One objective of China's post–Cold War foreign policy has been to maintain a peaceful and stable surrounding environment. At least for the time being, Beijing does not want to get into any serious trouble with neighboring countries. China's willingness to engage in cooperative diplomacy to resolve the Cambodian conflict was telling, as is Jiang Zemin's new policy on Taiwan, which rules out the prospect of imminent military action against the island. Moreover, China has substantially improved its relations with its three historical adversaries—Russia, India, and Vietnam. The only apparent exception to this policy is China's creeping assertiveness in the South China Sea. But even there, Beijing's strategy is to "expand its presence" without risking open armed conflict. It engages in preventive diplomacy to minimize the side effects of its activities there and to avoid military clashes with Vietnam and the Philippines. It is also by no means clear whether the 1995 occupation of Mischief Reef in the South China Sea was part of a master plan endorsed by the top leadership.

However, there are some Chinese cultural or psychological constraints that may complicate the projection of a strategy of conditional engagement. For instance, the Chinese tend to see things from a historical perspective, believing themselves to have been deprived of many historical opportunities either by their own blunders or by foreign forces. Like other rising powers, China tends to see its actions and desires in light of the past deeds of the major powers. For this reason, the Chinese have a hard time understanding why they should not test nuclear weapons, sell arms, recover lost territories, or pollute the environment. Why should China be accused of being "irresponsible" and "disruptive" when it is merely following the example of other major powers? Similarly, the Chinese were stunned that the Clinton administration justified Lee Teng-hui's visit to the United States on the grounds that Taiwan is democratizing, disregarding the historical evolution of the U.S.-Chinese relationship and the commitments of previous U.S. administrations. By the same token, they are upset by the tendency of some Western observers to judge the question of the ownership of the Spratlys on the basis of the islands' geographic distance from China, ignoring the historical backdrop of the issue.

Another variation on this historical perspective is China's "inferiority complex." The Chinese have never been more aware of the gap in economic and political power between China and the developed countries, even though the gap is narrowing. For many Chinese, including the educated elites, the difference between China and the United States is not so much that between a totalitarian society and a democratic one as that between a poor country and a rich one. They believe the rich and the strong have a natural tendency to bully the poor and the weak. The existing international system and its regimes are largely defined by the Western powers and based on Western values and standards. In the past, China saw itself as a victim rather than a beneficiary of this system and as a result denied its legitimacy and rejected its norms and principles. Since the 1980s, however, with its open-door policy and market-oriented reforms, China has been seeking to benefit from the established international system. At first, Beijing thought that China could be a "free rider" on the system, bearing little of the costs. As soon as the Cold War was over, however, the deal changed. Recent experience has convinced the Chinese that more powerful countries, such as the United States, will ask China to pay a high price in exchange for its participation in the world economic system. Many Chinese feel that China must "endure humiliation in order to realize a historical mission in the future (*renrufuzhong*)."[16] It will not be easy for Washington to make Beijing believe that it sincerely wants to draw China into the international system without wishing to turn the country into its "dependent" (*fuyong*).

A deep-rooted element in the Chinese historical perspective and China's so-called inferiority complex is the Confucian creed: do not do unto others what you would not wish them to do unto you (*jisuobuyu, wushiyuren*).[17] The logic is simple: if the United States is unable to behave itself, it should not ask China and other countries to behave better. In contrast, the Western mentality is, even though I am not perfect myself, I still have the right to criticize your bad behavior. These philosophical and psychological differences may also affect China's understanding of a strategy of conditional engagement. The Chinese may respond to this strategy by saying that if the United States wants to draft a set of "rules of acceptable behavior" for China, it should first demonstrate that it is bound by these rules. It is futile to tell the Chinese that the United States is selling arms for peace while China is selling arms for war or that the United States is using force for a noble cause while China is using force for evil purposes.

In sum, China's strategic culture suggests that a credible U.S. strategy must meet three requirements. First, China's legitimate interests and aspirations as a rising power must be recognized. Second, the price for China's integration into the existing international system should not be too high. Third, the United States must set an example for China by America's own behavior.

RULES OF ACCEPTABLE BEHAVIOR

A SUCCESSFUL U.S. strategy toward China should be based on a balanced understanding of mutual national interests. While it is important to clearly define the U.S. national interest in the region, it is equally important to define China's national interest there, as well as in the world. Recognition of these interests should be the foundation on which "rules of acceptable behavior" are based. Needless to say, China's national interest may not be compatible with that of the United States. However, an incompatible Chinese interest is not necessarily an illegitimate one. For instance, Hong Kong's return to China may not be in the U.S. interest, yet it is a legitimate interest of China. From the point of view of U.S. strategy, it is necessary to recognize China's legitimate interests and not to make American interests the sole criteria for defining rules of acceptable behavior for China. China's legitimate interests may converge, partially converge, or be incompatible with American interests. Briefly, China's national interest may entail the following:

- Safeguarding its sovereignty and territorial integrity, and eventually achieving national unification;

- Securing peaceful and nonhostile borders to promote economic development and social stability;

- Preventing the Asia-Pacific from falling under the domination of a hostile power, be it the United States, Japan, Russia, Vietnam, or Korea;

- Ensuring the country's full participation in regional and world affairs so that it cannot be excluded from any bilateral or multilateral arrangements that may affect its national interests;

- Maintaining a defense capability equal to that of other major powers in the region and maintaining the credibility of its limited nuclear deterrence capability;

- Securing access to world markets and resources necessary for its economic well-being, and the right to engage in trade, investment, finance, and other economic activities.

In light of these interests, overall the rules of Chinese behavior set forth by Jonathan Pollack in chapter 6 with respect to China's use of unilateral force against its neighbors, its pursuit of irredentist claims, the management of the Korean problem, its military buildup, destabilizing activities outside East Asia, and its willingness to build a collaborative regional security structure, should be acceptable to the Chinese. In fact, China can claim that it has not seriously violated these rules since the 1980s. However, it may well suggest some modifications.

First, the term "irredentist claims" needs clarification. Does it also include China's existing territorial disputes with its neighbors? If this is the case, China would have to accept all its neighbors' territorial claims, and that would obviously be unacceptable. The term should be redefined with the following qualifications: China's efforts to recover Hong Kong, Macao, and Taiwan should not be regarded as irredentist claims; China should not make any new territorial claims on historical grounds, such as to Outer Mongolia or territories taken by Russia under unequal treaties; and China should commit itself to the peaceful resolution of outstanding territorial disputes with its neighbors, especially over areas in the South China Sea.

Second, the level of military expenditure appropriate to China's legitimate self-defense needs is a complicated issue. On what criteria should its defense spending be based? On a per capita basis, Chinese military expenditure is very low. It appears that the growing concern over this issue stems from continued increases in military spending when there is no visible threat to China's security. But the Chinese can point out that Japan's military budget increased more than China's from 1990 to 1993.[18] Do Japan's military expenditures exceed its defense needs? Is Taiwan's high military spending within the scope of its legitimate defense needs? The Chinese can also argue that to modernize their defense structure they have to spend more than others do. This does not necessarily prove that they have an expansionist agenda. China simply wants to build a military capability commensurate with its increasing economic might. As Admiral Richard C. Macke has pointed out, China is "a large nation and a growing military and world power. So to tell them [they] can't have aircraft carriers when we have aircraft carriers I'm not sure makes a lot of logical sense."[19] In fact, despite a marked increase in China's defense budget appropriations in recent years, the military can hardly make ends meet. Roaring inflation resulting from the ongoing economic reforms has reduced the actual value of the increase.[20] The military reportedly does not even have the funds necessary to fully equip itself with some of the advanced weapons China already produces.[21]

Third, perhaps the only thing China does that might be seen as destabilizing is to occasionally sell arms in critical regions outside East Asia. China long ago stopped supporting radical revolutionary or terrorist movements, like the Khmer Rouge in Cambodia. In the domain of arms sales, China is more likely to accept multilateral norms than criteria dictated by the United States. So far, there is no international consensus on the definition of destabilizing arms.[22] Nor is the United States innocent of selling arms that may have a destabilizing effect. The Clinton administration's policy of permitting American conventional arms sales to allies and friendly nations for purely economic interests give the Chinese additional reasons to seek their fair share of the world arms markets, especially since, China's arms sales have dropped significantly in recent years, while American arms sales have soared in the wake of Russia's decline.[23] Some would insist that the United States sells arms to good guys while China sells weapons to bad guys. But China would argue that you either sell or don't sell weapons, and that what kind of weapons sold to whom will have stabilizing or destabilizing consequences is a subjective matter.

Fourth, China is not yet ready to significantly increase its defense transparency or to fully integrate itself into a regional security regime. Beijing does not see a need for an institutionalized regional security structure. It prefers bilateral consultations or security discussions within the context of economic forums. As Jonathan Pollack points out, so long as China is still a militarily backward actor with respect to the other major powers, it does not want to expose its vulnerability to foreign countries and make it easier for a potential adversary to guess its strength.[24] Nor does China want to "internationalize" its "internal affairs" (Taiwan) or its disputed territorial claims (Spratly Islands) through a regional security regime. In other words, as a rising power, China is not very confident about its future position in the international system and therefore wants to keep its options open. So these two rules (military transparency and participation in a multilateral security regime) can only be presented as goals—similar to the U.S. commitment to gradually reduce its arms sales to Taiwan. Indeed, how far the United States is willing to go to further a regional security structure at the cost of its bilateral alliances remains to be seen.

If the United States asks China to accept certain rules of behavior, it is only natural that China will demand reciprocity. The Chinese believe that "one should return as much as one receives" (*laierbuwangfeiliye*). The point of departure is what China terms the "Five Principles of Peaceful Coexistence," among which respect for China's sovereignty and territorial integrity and noninterference in its internal affairs are fundamental. Specifically, China may expect the United States to:

• Encourage and support a dialogue and negotiations between Beijing and Taipei, and discourage any effort to create "two Chinas" or to make Taiwan independent;[25]

• Facilitate China's full participation in international economic and trade regimes at a reasonable price while resisting the temptation to push China to change its domestic economic and trade structures and practices overnight;

• Exercise restraint in supporting political dissidents inside and outside China and in attempting to influence the course of China's domestic political development;

• Take China's international behavior at face value and do not make Sino-American relations hostage to China's political system and related issues such as human rights.

Taking both American and Chinese national interests into consideration, the following set of rules should be reasonably acceptable to the United States and China, as well as other Asian countries.

• The United States recognizes the legitimacy of China's goal of national unification. It neither encourages nor supports the "internationalization" of Hong Kong and Macao, the separation of Tibet from China, or the independence of Taiwan. In turn, China promises to pursue reunification through peaceful means and to respect the political and economic systems and cultural heritage of these areas. Any attempt to impose its social system on Hong Kong and Macao against the will of their people, to launch a military attack on Taiwan without provocation (in the absence of Taiwan's de jure independence or foreign intervention), or to systematically "Sinologize" Tibet will be seen as a threat to stability, prosperity, and humanity in the region, and hence a threat to U.S. interests.

• The United States, recognizing that China has suffered from many unequal treaties in the modern period, does not automatically support the territorial claims of China's neighbors. However, the United States makes it clear that it will oppose any attempt on China's part to change its existing borders. China should commit itself to the peaceful resolution of outstanding territorial disputes with its neighbors. On such issues as the Spratlys, where any action would have direct implications for the security of the region as a whole, any effort to force a change in the status quo is unacceptable.

• The United States acknowledges China's right to modernize its defense structure and military forces, so long as the increase in military spending does not exceed the rate of China's economic growth and inflation. China also should exercise restraint in forward power projection. Actions such as constructing military bases in Burma, which are not consistent with China's repeatedly declared principle of a defensive military, will be considered destabilizing since they arouse concerns about China's intentions.

• The United States shows itself willing to consult and cooperate with China and other powers in creating and strengthening multilateral regimes on nuclear nonproliferation and the proliferation of weapons of mass destruction. It does not try to monopolize the world market in arms sales. In return, China should not under any circumstances assist other countries in establishing nuclear weapons programs. It should assume more responsibility for nuclear nonproliferation in such regional hot spots as the Korean Peninsula. It should also refrain from exporting weapons of mass destruction to countries that have a tendency to engage in military aggression and terrorism.

• The United States supports and facilitates China's full participation in the global economic and trade system. It does not block China's access to foreign capital, markets, and raw materials that are necessary for China's economic development. Meanwhile, China should adjust its domestic economic structures and practices to meet the norms and standards of international business. It should improve legal mechanisms to protect foreign business interests and minimize arbitrary regulations and practices. While the United States recognizes that China is still a developing country, China should (as its economy develops) move toward playing by the rules of the game that advanced countries follow.

• The United States offers no support to political forces either inside or outside China that wish to overthrow or subvert the existing Chinese government. It does not assume China to be an expansionist and menacing power simply because of its political system. However, the United States makes it clear that it wants to see further improvement in human rights and the legal system in China and modification in the authoritarian nature of its political system. The United States cannot maintain normal relations with China if serious human rights violations are pervasive. On the other hand, U.S.-Chinese relations will be strengthened if China

---

THE TEN PRINCIPLES OF CONDITIONAL ENGAGEMENT

1. No unilateral use of offensive military force
2. Peaceful resolution of territorial disputes
3. Respect for national sovereignty
4. Freedom of navigation
5. Moderation in military force buildup
6. Transparency of military forces
7. Nonproliferation of weapons of mass destruction
8. Market access for trade and investment
9. Cooperative solutions for transnational problems
10. Respect for basic human rights

can begin to treat political dissidents more leniently and eventually stop imprisoning people for their political beliefs.

In short, rules of acceptable behavior will be more palatable to China if they are based on empathy and reciprocity rather than on inequality and unilateral interest. The key to a successful U.S. strategy is recognition of China's legitimate interests as a major power. Only then can there be meaningful dialogues to address legitimate issues of Chinese national interest that are incompatible with American interests. When China feels that the United States and other Western countries are denying its legitimate interests, it tends, consciously or unconsciously, to cultivate its potentially illegitimate interests.

THE IMPLEMENTATION OF CONDITIONAL ENGAGEMENT

CHINA HAS NO reason to reject a strategy of conditional engagement providing that it is not a containment strategy in disguise; it does not single out China as its only target; and China's legitimate interests and rights are not denied. After all, Deng Xiaoping himself once said that if China one day became a superpower, the people of the world should work together to topple it. Yet the Chinese may be skeptical of conditional engagement because of its ambiguous nature. It may be perceived as either too soft a deterrent or too tough an inducement.

Washington would have to set out the integration and containment components of such a strategy and make its priorities clear. The goal ought to be to fully integrate China into the world system; military means should only be resorted to if China becomes bellicose. Specifically, a strategy of conditional engagement should consist of economic incentives, diplomatic persuasion, political encouragement, and military deterrence (but not threats).

The United States should continue to encourage economic and other kinds of interaction between China and the outside world. The important thing is to institutionalize such interaction within the international system so as to secure China's ties with the international community. A number of concrete steps can be taken in this direction:

- Accept China into the WTO at a reasonable price. Asking China to meet some basic requirements of the world trade regime is legitimate, but indefinite postponement of China's membership will become counterproductive, especially if the idea is to encourage further reform of China's economic structure and institutions. A better strategy would be to accept China under clear-cut, binding commitments on market access, currency convertibility, and deregulation of trade. Insistence that China, as a developing country, cannot be admitted and that, in any case, it must first drastically change its domestic economic structure, is unacceptable to China, as well as to other Asian countries.[26]

- Another step might be to consider China for membership in the Group of Seven. At the moment, China appears not to be interested in joining, and as a developing country, it is technically not qualified for membership. Yet to invite China to join the G-7 would signal to Beijing that the Western countries think of China as an important and equal partner, and this would be an important message for China. Indeed, if the G-7 is defined as an economic organization, China, with the third largest economy in the world, is a stronger candidate for membership than Russia.

- More effort should be made to engage influential interest groups in China through bilateral and multilateral economic, scholarly, cultural, and military exchanges.

With respect to the last step, balance must be maintained. It is not enough to cultivate the private and more liberal sectors in

China; their stakes in the international system are self-evident. It is more important to draw conservative and insular elements into the international community. For instance, efforts should be made to draw China's state-run enterprises into the international business cycle. While many of them are in bad shape, they are still the backbone of China's economy. If this sector develops significant stakes in foreign economic relations, China's integration into the world system may reach the point of no return. To this end, the United States might offer to provide technical, managerial, or even financial assistance to the bankrupt state enterprises.

Another important candidate is the Chinese military. The People's Liberation Army should be engaged at the strategic, technical, and economic levels. The U.S. military could come together with senior Chinese military leaders in regular discussions on broad regional and global security issues. At the working level, matters such as regional crisis management, confidence building, and preventive diplomacy could be discussed and practical mechanisms established. The United States should also encourage Chinese army entrepreneurs to enter world markets by offering technical assistance (on defense conversion, for example), establishing joint ventures, and the like. Finally, the United States could promote communication on security issues between the Chinese military, the Foreign Ministry, and other nonmilitary elite communities, thus guaranteeing that neither the military nor the Foreign Ministry apparatus have a monopoly on security policy.

In addition to official contacts, the United States should encourage international nongovernmental organizations to establish extensive contacts with the emerging Chinese NGOs. Although it may be argued that there are no genuine NGOs in China, there are about 200,000 nonofficial organizations and associations, many of which grew spontaneously and are financially supported by entrepreneurs and private funders, albeit with government approval. So far their ties with the outside world have been negligible and sporadic.

Since many policymaking prerogatives in China have been shifted to localities, the United States should balance its interaction with the central government by establishing regular ties with provincial, city, and even county authorities. This would also involve striking a balance between coastal areas and inland regions. However, in doing so, the United States should avoid being perceived as purposely cultivating "localism."

Integration will further political modification. Businesspeople, managers, scholars, and intellectuals can promote human rights and democracy in China better than governmental officials. They can learn from the American missionaries who worked in China in the past and advocated their own values without imposing them on people. In fact, many Chinese elites privately endorse democracy and human rights but do not like the way the United States pushes them on China. A Chinese diplomat noted, "Even the best food turns sour if you stuff it into people's mouth."

While taking China's domestic politics into consideration, a strategy of conditional engagement should not be primarily contingent on the situation in the PRC. Rather, it should be based on two premises. First, for the foreseeable future, China will remain a politically authoritarian state. As distasteful as this may be, the United States can only promote change, not dictate it. Second, having said this, a domestically authoritarian China does not necessarily mean an expansionist China. Domestic factors will no doubt shape China's international behavior, but so will foreign responses.

China's diplomacy in the wake of the Tiananmen crisis demonstrates that the efforts of the United States and others in the international community to integrate China into the global system will pay dividends. Even while facing the world's condemnation and Western sanctions, the stakes were too high for China to simply retreat into the "glorious isolation" or "self-reliance" of the 1960s. Foreign trade accounts for more than 40

percent of China's GNP, and more than half its consumer industrial capacity depends on exports for growth.[27] This also explains
why China is relatively willing to make concessions in negotiating with the United States. The senior leadership believes that
China must minimize confrontation with the United States to
maintain the dynamics of its economic development. China's
initially moderate response to the visit of Taiwan's president to
the United States was a reflection of this thinking, it was Lee's
assertiveness in his speech and the pressure building from below
that pushed the government to react more strongly. Even so,
Beijing was careful not to let the incident affect economic ties.[28]

Of course, because China is such a large country, the
impact of economic integration should never be overestimated.
It will be slow to be felt and in most cases will be reversible.
Often it can be a double-edged sword, creating stakes as well as
leverage. More important, the Chinese leadership still puts
regime survival and national sovereignty above everything else.
As Chinese leaders are fond of saying, China can survive without most-favored-nation status and other social and economic
relations with the West if necessary. Even during the 1950s,
when China was heavily dependent economically and militarily on the Soviet Union, Mao valued political autonomy over
good Sino-Soviet relations. Beijing is not merely bluffing when
it declares that it is willing to sacrifice good relations with the
United States to defend China's sovereignty and esteem it is
willing to sacrifice good relations with the United States.[29] Yet
the stakes are much higher now than they were in Mao's day.
The current Chinese leaders cannot offer the Chinese people
mere survival and hope to maintain a viable social order. The
people want a far better life than that. So although integration
does not guarantee a benign China, a China with a web of
interests in the existing international system will likely be less
willing to upset the international economic and political order.

Given the uncertainty surrounding the future orientation
of China, Japan, and Korea, it is understandable that the Unit-

ed States would wish to back a strategy of conditional engagement with a credible countervailing structure. With respect to China, this structure should enable Washington to deal effectively with the following contingencies: the fallout from large-scale social turmoil, such as a huge flow of refugees and weapons; military conflict across the Taiwan Strait; military clashes in the South China Sea; a border war with India or Vietnam; forward force deployment in foreign countries such as Burma and Pakistan; and hegemonic wars with Japan, Russia, or the United States. Among these, military conflict across the Taiwan Strait and in the South China Sea is considered the most likely. The components of such a countervailing structure may include: a strategic deterrent for coping with nuclear threats from China and other nuclear powers; a rapid deployment capability for dealing with a conventional domestic or an international crisis; permanent bilateral alliances to increase the risk for China of waging a local war; and ad hoc bilateral or multilateral coalitions to counter China's thrusts in any direction.

The construction of such a countervailing structure risks setting in motion a deadly game of action and reaction that would create the atmosphere of confrontation that a strategy of conditional engagement is intended to prevent. The art is to exercise "containment without confrontation"[30] and to establish a "security community" rather than a "defense community." To reduce the risks, some preventive measures are necessary. First, a countervailing structure should not be erected with China alone in mind. Rather, it should be designed and deployed in such a manner that it can be used against other potential threats. One way to do this is to make China itself a part of the countervailing structure by establishing military contacts, security dialogues, confidence-building mechanisms in bilateral and multilateral settings (joint exercises, intelligence sharing, training programs, port visits) and by collaborating with China on such issues as nuclear nonproliferation on the Korean Peninsula. Another method is relying more on building ad hoc coalitions than permanent alliances to contain possible Chinese assertiveness. For instance, in the South China Sea dispute, the United States can strengthen its consultations with the members of the Association of Southeast Asian Nations (ASEAN). If China's recent maneuvers there were the result of a general policy shift toward belligerence (which unlikely to be the case), America's echoing of the unified protests of ASEAN members made China pause.

Second, the negative impact of building countervailing forces can be offset by good bilateral relations. China's attitude toward the American military presence in Asia is ambivalent. With the cessation of the Soviet threat, there is no compelling reason for China to endorse the continued presence or strengthening of U.S. forces. On the other hand, China is aware of the stabilizing role U.S. forces play in the region, in checking the remilitarization of Japan and deterring military adventures by North Korea. So long as Sino-American relations are stable, China can live with this legacy of the Cold War, albeit uncomfortably. As some Chinese scholars have pointed out, the state of these relations influences the Chinese view of the U.S. force in Asia: if the relationship is in bad shape, China tends to regard the force as a threat.[31] Moreover, Lee Teng-hui's visit to the United States convinced the Chinese that Washington is willing once again to play the Taiwan card as part of its strategy of containing China around its periphery.[32]

Third, the United States should also exercise restraint in talking about the "China threat" or taking such talk by any of China's neighbors at face value. As Jonathan Pollack points out, China's capacity to project military power has been vastly overstated. The wolf-at-the door warning tends to be a self-fulfilling prophecy. It also annoys the Chinese. As one senior Chinese official put it, "I think the so-called China threat originated from a faraway place. We are tired of all these allegations. For the last 100 years, we have been hearing the same story. When China was poor, we were a threat and when China is rich, we are a threat. But history is history. We have been the victim of aggression and occupation. We are tired of all these allegations. Enough is enough."[33] Other actors in the region, such as the Philippines and Taiwan, harp on the China threat for their own geopolitical purposes. The United States does not have to join their chorus, and should avoid being dragged into confrontation with China when its interests are not at stake.[34]

To further reduce China's alarm over the creation of a countervailing structure, a strategy of conditional engagement should take an issue-oriented approach in implementing its containment elements. If China's behavior is unsatisfactory in one area, the United States should activate the appropriate checks. However, containment should not automatically spread to areas where China's behavior is acceptable. In other words, the integration and containment mechanisms of the strategy can function at the same time. The purpose of containment should be to push China back onto the right track so that the integration process can resume. Moreover, the United States should pick its issues carefully. Giving the Chinese the impression that Washington will exert pressure on one issue after another is undesirable, and reinforces the belief of the Chinese leadership that "if you give in an inch, they will ask for a yard" (*decunlinchi*). Such statements as that by former Under Secretary of Commerce Jeffrey E. Garten, who proclaimed that Washington will put Beijing "under tremendous pressure wherever we find it," alarm the Chinese and serve no useful purpose.[35]

Finally, while constructing a countervailing structure, the United States should avoid taking actions that the Chinese could view as irreversible and threatening. For instance, by entering into official relations with Taiwan or providing Taiwan with a large quantity of offensive weaponry, Washington would likely convince the Chinese that the United States was determined to maintain China's division. Beijing was close to drawing this conclusion from Lee Teng-hui's visit. The proposed theater missile defense system that Washington is considering deploying to protect American forces and allies has aroused great concern in China, where it is feared that the move will negate the Chinese nuclear deterrence capability.[36] Rearming Japan or eliminating the North Korean regime might also be taken as "irreversible" threats in Beijing.

The implementation of a strategy of conditional engagement will not be easy, particularly in light of current U.S. policy toward China. China policy lacks a clearly defined and achievable object. Does the United States want to turn China into a democratic society, or is its goal a less ambitious one of integrating China into the world system? Or is it bent on containing China? Washington's signals to Beijing are often contradictory. Nor is it clear how China fits into the Clinton administration's post-Cold War strategy of "enlargement." While uncertainty and instability in Chinese domestic politics may have adverse effects, the instability of U.S.-Chinese relations in recent years derives largely from U.S. policy. To some extent, this is because Congress, in the absence of a clearly defined policy, has set the policy agenda for the Clinton administration.

The administration's ill-defined policy goals have led to astonishing inconsistency and poor coordination in policy implementation. This is not to say that Washington's demands on China are unreasonable. American concerns over China's copyright piracy, trade surplus, arms transfers, and human rights violations are legitimate. Rather, it is the inconsistency in U.S. policy that has sickened the Chinese, who hold that good faith in the traditional sense is the highest standard for interstate relations. The Chinese watched with amazement as Washington exploited China's desire to become a founding member of the WTO to obtain seemingly endless concessions from Beijing, from the memorandum on market access in 1992 to the agreement on intellectual property rights in early 1995. Washington no sooner promised to support China's bid than it reneged in the hope of gaining further concessions. The administration's bowing to congressional pressure on Lee Teng-hui's visa further convinced the Chinese that the United States does not take them seriously.[37] The disarray in U.S. policy also results from lack of interest and attention on President Clinton's part. Since announcing the delinking of most-favored-nation status from human rights in June 1994, Clinton has paid little heed to China except for the half-hearted meeting with Jiang Zemin at the end of 1995, acting as if the problem of U.S.-Chinese relations was resolved once and for all.

The United States still tends to treat China as a special case. In the 1970s and 1980s, China received favorable special treatment because of its strategic importance in the conflict with the Soviet Union. Today, China receives special treatment of another kind because of its domestic social system. The United States tends to demand a higher standard of behavior from China than from other countries. Consequently, as one congressman observes, "Whatever the Chinese do, they do not get credit." The Chinese have yet to see a clear reward or incentive mechanism in U.S. policy. While they should be penalized for their bad behavior, they should also be rewarded for their good behavior.

For the past year or so, U.S. policy seems to have turned the logic of a conditional engagement strategy on its head, putting economic pressure on China while devoting insufficient attention to the building of a countervailing structure.[38] Some U.S. officials justify this on the grounds that it is important to prevent China from becoming a "second Japan."[39] But they have learned the wrong lesson from history. American policy toward Japan has been, on balance, a success story showing how a hegemonic power should deal with a rising power. To protect its strategic interests against the Soviet Union and Communist China, the United States offered Japan economic assistance and market access and instituted preferential trade and monetary policies to facilitate Japan's economic recovery and modernization. While this benign U.S. policy inevitably had some costs, it in large measure preempted the emergence of a resentful and vengeful Japan after World War II. Although there are serious economic frictions between the two countries, Japan is far from being the strategic adversary its economic capability might permit it to be. In this sense, if China becomes "another Japan," posing an economic challenge rather than a strategic threat to the United States, it will be a blessing for the United States.

Washington's most important task will be to make the logic of conditional engagement and reciprocal rules of acceptable behavior crystal clear to the Chinese. The objective of U.S. policy must be to engage a rising China in order to integrate it into the world system. Unfortunately, the Chinese perceive the essence of American policy to be to contain China, both geopolitically and economically, and to block its emergence as a world power. This misperception can only be corrected through high-level political dialogue. To this end, the United States and China need a second Shanghai Communiqué. The Communiqué of 1972 which marked President Nixon's opening to China after two decades of U.S.-imposed diplomatic isolation, served as a sound foundation for the relationship for more than a decade. While the basic principles of this document are still valid, post–Cold War international circumstances require some new ones. The United States and China need a similar document in which convergences and disagreements regarding bilateral and international issues should be enumerated so that neither side is uncertain about the other side's goals and intentions. The Clinton administration's policy of comprehensive engagement requires such an overarching strategic anchor.[40]

How China behaves on the world stage in the next century will be largely determined by how it is treated now by the United States and the other major powers. It cannot be in the U.S. interest to have a resentful and hostile China. The Japanese experience shows how to avoid this pitfall and a future confrontation. Washington should heed the advice of Admiral Richard C. Macke: "What we have to do is make China one of our friends. We can't confront the Chinese, we can't isolate them . . . We just need to work with them, to stay engaged in a dialogue."[41]

NOTES

1. Advocates of this strategy argue that, given the uncertain future of the security environment in Asia, the United States should avoid both a policy of containment—which by assuming that China will become an aggressive power will become a self-fulfilling prophecy—and one premature liberal internationalism. Instead, it should "hope for the best but prepare for the worst" by maintaining a credible capability for containing possible security threats, as well as by committing itself to engaging emergent actors in the region.

2. Jianwei Wang and Zhimin Lin, "Chinese Perceptions in the Post-Cold War Era: Three Images of the United States," *Asian Survey*, October 1992, pp. 902-17.

3. Ibid, p. 905.

4. Personal interview, Beijing, August 1991.

5. *Reference Materials for Social Sciences*, no. 22, November 21, 1994, p. 1.

6. The *Yin He* was inspected by U.S. and Saudi officials in September 1993 on the suspicion that it was transporting chemical weapons materials to Iran. The inspection revealed none of the suspected substances and Beijing demanded an apology. See *Far Eastern Economic Review*, September 9, 1993, p.9.

7. Jiang Zemin, "To Continue Our Struggle for the Course of the Unification of Our Motherland," *People's Daily*, January 31, 1995.

8. Simon Holberton and Tony Walker, "Chill through Ranks of the 'Red Princelings'," *Financial Times*, February 20, 1995.

9. See Gerald Segal, "China after Deng," *Jane's Intelligence Review*, November 1994, p. 516; and Lincoln Kaye, "Slippery Succession," *Far Eastern Economic Review*, August 4, 1994, p. 23; and Lincoln Kaye, "Leadership Crossroads," *Far Eastern Economic Review*, September 1, 1994 , p. 42.

10. Jim Hoagland, "Simply China," *Washington Post: National Weekly Edition*, June 12-18, 1995, p. 28.

11. He Xin, *China and the World at the Conjunction of Two Centuries* (Chengdu: Sichuan People's Publishing House, 1991), pp. 403-04.

12. Deng Xiaoping played a key role in this strategic orientation. He emphasized that China should refrain from forming an alliance or bloc. It should not, he insisted, join the Soviet Union in combating the United States, nor should it become pro-American.

13. Steven Mufson, "At the Marco Polo Bridge, China-Japan War Wounds Still Ache," *International Herald Tribune*, May 6, 1995.

14. Hu Yang, "Summary of Symposium with the U.S. National Defense

University," *Beijing Review*, December 14-20, 1992, p. 31.

15. Samuel S. Kim, *China In and Out of the Changing World Order* (Princeton, N.J.: Princeton University Press, 1993), p. 84.

16. "We will never forget how the United States treated us when we were in difficulty and one day when China becomes powerful, we will . . ." is a typical expression of this "inferiority complex."

17. Foreign Minister Qian Qichen quoted this saying in his speech in an international forum on May 14, 1995, as reported in "Chinese Minister Assures Neighbors," *International Herald Tribune*, May 15, 1995.

18. Richard K. Betts, "Wealth, Power, and Instability," *International Security* 18, no. 3 (1993/94), p. 42.

19. Michael Richard, "U.S. Warns of China's Big New Navy,"*International Herald Tribune*, March 8, 1995.

20. In real terms, China's 1994 defense budget was lower than the 1978 budget. Of course, it can be argued that China has "hidden sources" of military expenditure, but there is no evidence that the magnitude of hidden expenditures has been on the rise compared to the base year of 1978. See Shaoguang Wang, "China's Military Expenditure," forthcoming in *China Quarterly*.

21. Yang Kong, "China's Arms Trade Bureaucracy," *Jane's Intelligence Review*, February 1994, p. 83.

22. John Sislin and David Mussington, "Destabilizing Arms Acquisitions," *Jane's Intelligence Review* 7, no. 2 (1995), p. 88.

23. Yang Kong, "China's Arms Trade Bureaucracy," *Jane's Intelligence Review*, February 1994, p. 83; and *International Herald Tribune*, February 18-19, 1994, p. 83.

24. Jonathan D. Pollack, "Sources of Instability and Conflict in Northeast Asia," *Arms Control Today*, November 1994, p. 5.

25. The paragraph on Taiwan in last year's Department of Defense review of U.S. security strategy in the East Asia-Pacific region is particularly brief and lacks imagination. It names "contributing to maintaining peace in the Taiwan Strait" as one security objective (Department of Defense, *United States Strategy for the East Asia-Pacific Region*, Washington, D.C.: Office of International Security Affairs, February 1995, pp. 4, 20). But the question is how to do this. There must be measures other than selling arms to Taiwan. Many Americans think that the most the United States can do is to stay out of cross-straits relations. However, the most effective way to defuse China's suspicions that the United States intends to perpetuate China's division is to take a more clear and positive stand on cross-straits reconciliation. As the Chinese often say, "Let him who tied the bell on the tiger take it off." During the late 1970s and early 1980s, China hoped that the United

States could do something to facilitate its unification. Technically, I do not see any compelling reason why the United States cannot play a similar role between the mainland and Taiwan as it did between Israel and the Palestinians. For instance, Jiang Zemin's call for an end to the state of war between the two shores should be more forcefully endorsed by the United States. If formal reunification is still a remote prospect, it is plausible that China can make a deal with Taiwan by offering to renounce the use of force in return for Taiwan's promise not to declare independence. The United States will be better off if it can play a role in this process rather than being left out.

26. Peter Montagnon, "Dispute Timing A Setback for WTO," *Financial Times*, February 16, 1995.

27. Foreign trade accounts for about 10 percent of American's and Russia's. Even for export-oriented Japan, the figure is only 20 percent (Liu Li-qun, "The Strains that Chinese Manufacture Is In and the Way Out," *Strategy and Management*, no. 3 (1994), p. 64).

28. A Chinese Foreign Ministry spokesman said that China will not artificially link politics and economics (Li Binhua, "China Emphasizing Unification over Sino-American Relations," *Tao Kung Pao*, June 17, 1995).

29. The same spokesman asserted that compared with Sino-American relations, China's sovereignty and territorial integrity are much more important (*Ta Kung Pao*, June 17, 1995).

30. Richard Betts, "Wealth, Power, and Instability," p. 54.

31. Hu Yang, "Summary of Symposium with U.S. National Defense University," *Beijing Review*, December 14-20, 1992, pp. 31.

32. "China is Prepared for Any Challenges," *Tao Kung Pao*, May 24, 1995

33. Patrick E. Tyler, "China Warns U.S. Against Developing Asian Missile Shield," *International Herald Tribune*, February 18, 1995.

34. For instance, the Philippines suggested that its mutual defense treaty with Washington can be invoked to demand U.S. support in its dispute with China over the Spratlys. See Keith B. Richburg, "Saber-Rattling on Spratlys Raises Risk of Asian Conflict," *International Herald Tribune*, June 6, 1995.

35. Jonathan Gage, "U.S. Threatens China Over Import Barriers," *International Herald Tribune*, April 10, 1995.

36. Patrick E. Tyler, "China Warns U.S. Against Developing Asian Missile Shield," *International Herald Tribune*, February 18, 1995.

37. The prevailing American belief that China needs the United States more than the United States needs China obviously contributes to policy inconsistency, since policymakers and politicians may consider that reneging on China policy will have fewer consequences than

reneging on policy toward others. See Russell Watson, "A Little Fight Music," *Newsweek*, February 13, 1995, p. 39; and Nayan Chanda, "Winds of Change," *Far Eastern Economic Review*, June 22, 1995, p. 22. The Chinese, however, believe that the relationship is equally important to both sides.

38. The American media also tends to be too quick to assume that the pressure tactics used in the intellectual property rights negotiations can be applied to other issues, such as human rights ("A Welcome Outcome," *International Herald Tribune*, March 1, 1995).

39. David E. Sanger, "In Struggle with China Over Trade, U.S. Wins Skirmish," *International Herald Tribune*, February 28, 1995.

40. As Qian Qichen has asserted, if comprehensive engagement facilitates the improvement of the relationship, China endorses it. Otherwise it is not necessarily a positive thing (Xinhua News Agency, "Qian Qichen Meets U.S. Assistant Secretary of State Winston Lord," *People's Daily*, March 3, 1995).

41. Michael Richardson, "U.S. Admiral Warns of China's Big New Navy," *International Herald Tribune*, March 8, 1995.

8

Japan's Receptivity to Conditional Engagement

Masashi Nishihara

IT IS DIFFICULT to predict how Japan would react were the United States to adopt the strategy of conditional engagement because the Japanese government has yet to come to terms with the international security environment of the post–Cold War era. On its face, the strategy seems to fit Japanese national interests by encouraging a dialogue with China on political and security issues as well as on better economic, cultural, and scientific cooperation. China has shown many indications of moving in this direction, although it is equally possible that it will elect to pursue hegemonic power. Japan would discourage, and if necessary, deter a politically and militarily, if not economically, dominant China. Japan essentially wants a China—and a united Korea—that will seek stable and cooperative economic and political relations with Japan and the United States.

JAPAN'S OFFICIAL SECURITY OUTLOOK

THE PREVIOUS Japanese government, under the leadership of Tomiichi Murayama, had no uniform, integrated security policy. The prime minister himself underwent a dramatic conversion from the Socialist to the Liberal Democratic party line when he assumed office in July 1994. In an dramatic turnaround, the prime minister, who was and still is also chairman of the Democratic Socialist Party, announced that he now considered Japan's Self-Defense Forces (SDF) to be constitutional and spoke of the importance his government attached to the "firm continuation" of the Japanese-U.S. security treaty.

However, he stated on several occasions that he sees the post-Cold War era as a period of world disarmament, arguing that Japan should therefore reduce its defense budget. However, as the United States, Russia, and most western European nations have cut their defense budgets and military deployments, East Asia has moved in the opposite direction. North Korea's nuclear program, the defense buildups of China and Taiwan, and the arms modernization programs of most Southeast Asian countries are cases in point. Mr. Murayama appeared to be unwilling to take a hard look at the situation in East Asia. The Liberal Democratic Party (LDP), which dominated Japanese politics from its founding in 1955 until 1993, returned to the center of Japanese politics in January 1996, when its President Ryutaro Hashimoto formed a coalition government with the Democratic Socialists and the Sakigake (Forerunners) Party. Hashimoto's party has a different security outlook. In 1992, the LDP's Policy Research Council identified five possible threats to Japanese security: Russia's large and well-armed forces in the Far East, heightened tension between North Korea and South Korea, the weapons buildups of China and Taiwan, political succession conflicts in North Korea and China, and clashes over competing claims to islands and natural resources beneath Asia-Pacific waters. The Japan Defense Agency shares these worries. In its 1995 white paper on security issues, the agency estimated that, combining the figures for both Koreas, as many as 1.5 million battle-ready soldiers are stationed throughout the Korean peninsula. The large number of Russian troops in the Far East, the report said, is a source of regional instability, as is Beijing's determined rush to improve its navy and air force. In addition, it noted the efforts of many Southeast Asian nations to upgrade their arms.

The differing views of Prime Minister Hashimoto and his coalition partners lead to a confused, disintegrated outlook on the part of the Japanese government, which is not helpful in formulating a clear security policy. Although there has been consensus in the Japanese government about the importance of the security alliance with the United States, there is a lack of consensus about Japan's role within the alliance. In preparing the defense budget for FY1995 (¥4,723.6 billion, or about $55.6 billion [$1 = ¥85]), former Prime Minister Murayama reduced the rate of increase over the previous year's budget to 0.86 percent (compared with a 6.1 percent increase in the FY1990 budget, for example). This had the effect of lowering the defense budget's share of GDP, which dropped from 0.997 percent in FY1990 to 0.959 percent for FY1995. This raised a serious possibility that the Japanese share of the cost of basing U.S. troops in Japan might be squeezed. That this did not happen was due to the resistance of the U.S. government and the Japan Defense Agency, which managed to persuade the prime minister to appropriate ¥452.7 billion ($5.3 billion), or 9.6 percent of the defense budget.

Traditionally, the Democratic Socialist Party opposed the U.S. bases in Japan, and although it now officially supports the alliance with the United States, its lower echelons are less supportive. Among other things they know that the party's position will not help their electoral chances. By the same token, the Liberal Democrats below prefectural levels are also less enthusiastic about supporting the U.S. bases than before. Japanese who reside near the bases feel that, with the end of the Cold War, the number and size of the bases could be reduced.

Since the September 1995 sexual assault of a young Japanese girl by American servicemen in Okinawa, the Japanese public has been increasingly demanding a reduction in the number of U.S. bases. A target of their frustration is the group of U.S. bases on Okinawa, which are home to about 75 percent of the

45,000 American personnel in Japan. A linchpin for the projection of U.S. power in Asia and the Middle East, the bases cover about 18 percent of Okinawa's island. Developers are interested in turning some of the bases into tourist areas, although Tokyo officials would like the installations to stay indefinitely. Strong local opposition has prevented them from constructing a new airport at Miyake Island, 125 miles south of Tokyo, for U.S. naval pilots to practice night landings. The new airport was to replace Atsugi Airport near Yokosuka, where there is a U.S. naval base. Atsugi has been a target of citizens' ire because of the noise caused by the frequent night landings of pilots in training. As a result, an airbase developed at Iwojima, 750 miles south of Tokyo, as a temporary practice site appears to have become a permanent site.

During the Cold War, the central office and the prefectural branches of the ruling Liberal Democratic Party worked assiduously to promote the Japanese-U.S. alliance at the local level. Today, the gap between the central government and the ruling parties at the prefectural and local levels makes it difficult to formulate a clear alliance policy. Local allergies to the U.S. military presence have not yet had a serious impact on the security treaty. However, unless the issues surrounding the U.S. bases are managed properly by both Tokyo and Washington, they may impede security relations in the future and hamper the execution of a conditional engagement strategy.

JAPAN'S STRATEGIC INTERESTS AND OPTIONS

DESPITE THE confusion surrounding Tokyo's security policy, Japan's strategic interests remain clearly defined by its geostrategic position and national history. They are: to ensure Japan's economic and military survival through a close alliance with the United States; to prevent the emergence of a dominant power in East Asia (other than the United States); to ensure political openness and open market economies, thereby fostering economic interdependence throughout the region; and to secure the sea lanes through the western Pacific and the Indian Ocean by befriending countries in those regions.

The strategic interests of Japan are basically consistent with those of the United States, and that is why their alliance has endured. For Japan, this strategic option is far better than the alternatives: to go it alone or to form new bilateral or multilateral alliances with some combination of China, Russia, the United States, and the Association of Southeast Asian Nations (ASEAN).

Japan by itself cannot handle the major security issues presented by two Koreas, China, Russia, or the Middle East. The recent confrontation between the United States and North Korea demonstrated this well. Given its lack of military means, unwillingness to use force or a threat of force to resolve diplomatic problems, and the Koreans' historical animosity toward the Japanese, Tokyo could not have negotiated with Pyongyang as well as the United States did to achieve the Agreed Framework of October 1994, which seeks to provide North Korea with light-water nuclear reactors in return for the termination of its nuclear weapons program. Japan cannot and should not confront China, a rising power, by itself. China is becoming increasingly self-assertive, as evidenced by its unilateral decision to construct "shelters" on the Spratly Islands, its defiance in continuing nuclear testing, and its assertive reaction to the West's criticism of its human rights record. Nor could Japan tackle the Taiwan question alone

---

THE TEN PRINCIPLES OF CONDITIONAL ENGAGEMENT

1. No unilateral use of offensive military force
2. Peaceful resolution of territorial disputes
3. Respect for national sovereignty
4. Freedom of navigation
5. Moderation in military force buildup
6. Transparency of military forces
7. Nonproliferation of weapons of mass destruction
8. Market access for trade and investment
9. Cooperative solutions for transnational problems
10. Respect for basic human rights

because any official expression of support for a higher international political or economic status for Taiwan is likely to be misinterpreted by Beijing. Japan, which once colonized Taiwan, would be seen as advocating Taiwan's full-fledged independence.

Japanese-Russian relations are also problematic. Russia's high-handed attitude over disputed territories and fishing rights and its dumping of nuclear waste into the Sea of Japan are annoying to the Japanese. Moreover, the Russian military arsenal and troops stationed in the Far East remain formidable, despite reductions. Washington's support of Japan on all of these issues is extremely helpful. The heavy Japanese dependence on imported oil also underscores the importance of Japan's alliance with the United States, since Tokyo carries very little diplomatic weight in the Middle East. Japan cannot protect the global sea lanes upon which its export as well as import economy depends. Its defense perimeter is 1,000 miles from its shores, and it has neither nuclear-powered ships and submarines nor overseas naval bases. The presence of the U.S. Seventh Fleet, which operates in the Indian Ocean as well as the western Pacific, gives enormous assurance to Japan.

For these reasons, Japan's alliance with the United States protects its basic interests better than any other strategic option. Were it to choose another strategy it would forfeit U.S. assistance. None of the other strategic options—alliances with the United States and China; Russia and China; Russia and the United States; or ASEAN—are feasible. The bitter lesson Japan learned form World War II was that it should not disregard the immense strength of the United States and its allies; incurring their hostility was a fatal mistake.

JAPANESE INTERESTS AND CONDITIONAL ENGAGEMENT

FROM JAPAN'S perspective, conditional engagement is the most acceptable of the four theoretical U.S. strategic options discussed by Jonathan Pollack in chapter 6. Were the United States to adopt the first option, strategic autonomy—which is essentially a nonalignment strategy—Japan would have to build up its military capabilities to meet a possible crisis on the Korean Peninsula, cope with a China harboring hegemonic ambitions, and ensure the security of vital sea lanes. Such a strategy would lead to a Sino-Japanese rivalry and a highly unstable region.

The second option, a strategy of liberal internationalism or economic interdependence, is as Pollack argues, "more aspiration than strategy." The United States may elect to focus on promoting liberal economic institutions and strengthening economic interdependence between the United States and East Asian countries, but such a strategy assumes that all the major countries concerned, including China, will follow internationally accepted codes of conduct. The United States should encourage China to move in this direction, but relying entirely on their strategy would be too lenient toward China, which may simply take advantage of American capital and technology to become a military power of prohibitive strength.

The third option, a containment strategy, would be too harsh. It assumes the emergence of a formidable imperialist China requiring preemptive encirclement by the United States and like-minded countries. Although there are many signs that China harbors hegemonic ambitions, there are also signs that it wishes to participate in international economic institutions, such as the World Trade Organization. A containment strategy would simply compound Beijing's suspicions that the United States is intent on destroying China.

Thus, the last option, conditional engagement, seems to be the most promising for both Japan and the United States. The United States should be flexible in its China policy and, with like-minded nations, engage it in a security dialogue and dialogue on codes of international economic behavior. At the same time, Washington should keep a vigilant watch on China's assertive behavior in the diplomatic and military arenas. There is no doubt that Japan would benefit a great deal from China's acceptance as a politically and economically stable member of the international community, able to interact with the outside world in a constructive manner. A U.S. policy of engaging China in a security dialogue and encouraging economic and scientific cooperation would meet Japanese interests as well. In return, Japan would diplomatically support U.S. moves to check China's political and military power were China to begin to show signs of assertiveness on regional security issues such as the status of Taiwan. However, an agreed-upon fallback policy—were the strategy of conditional engagement to fail—would be imperative.

COPING WITH CHINA

CHINA HAS the potential to develop into a formidable power. Its economy is growing so rapidly that its GNP is expected to double in ten years. If the World Bank's projections are correct, the GNP of the "greater Chinese economic sphere" (China, Taiwan, and Hong Kong) in the year 2002 will be greater than that of France, Italy, and Great Britain combined. In terms of purchasing power, the greater Chinese economic sphere in the year 2002 is likely to surpass Japan and possibly the United States. If the Chinese economy performs as anticipated, China may well become an awesome military power. But its progress could be stunted by the widespread corruption, the absence of the rule of law, the gap between rich and poor, the mismanagement of state enterprises, and other internal weaknesses.

The China of today shows the world three faces: the first is the face of a constructive partner; the second is that of a hegemonic power; the third, a frustrated power. Sometimes, depending on the issues concerned, China wears more than one face at a time. The Foreign Ministry puts on the face of a constructive partner, whereas the military wears the face of a hegemon. The Communist Party appears uncertain which to wear, reflecting the relatively weak leadership of Secretary General Jiang Zemin.

As a constructive partner, China willingly participated in multilateral consultations and decisions. It accepted the U.N. peace plan for Cambodia and sent troops for U.N. peacekeeping operations there. It has joined the Asia Pacific Economic Cooperation (APEC) forum and the ASEAN Regional Forum (ARF). In its bid to join the World Trade Organization, it has made economic concessions, acceding, for instance, to U.S. demands that it enforce intellectual property rights. China's willingness to join international trade regimes stems from its recognition that a peaceful international environment is vital to its economic growth. By joining ARF, it signaled that it is willing to work with other nations to promote regional peace and security.

At the same time, however, China has displayed its second face. It has capitalized on the end of the U.S.-Soviet rivalry by expanding its political and military clout in East Asia. Its behavior in the South China Sea, where it has declared that territorial disputes are bilateral issues not amenable to multilateral frameworks, amounts to creeping expansionism. It has continued nuclear testing, alarming its neighbors, particularly Japan. The Japanese are also concerned that China may take unilateral action against the disputed Senkaku Islands, over which Japan currently has effective control.

The increase in China's defense capabilities is also alarming. China's defense budgets have been increasing at double-digit rates for the last seven years. Although high rates of inflation have slowed defense spending in real terms, China's official defense budget includes only a portion of what other countries consider to be defense expenditures, omitting, for example, arms procurement and R&D. China's official defense budget for FY1995 was $7.5 billion, but actual defense expenditures are estimated to be at least three times greater.

China's third face is that of a frustrated rising power, one that, despite economic success, is not unified. Sovereignty over Hong Kong will revert from Britain to China in 1997, but the reversion process has been a thorny one, exacerbated by Britain's last minute attempts to leave democratic (and anticommunist) institutions behind. The process promises to remain difficult after 1997. In addition, China faces continuing difficulties over the integration of Taiwan and, perhaps to a lesser extent, Tibet. Internal tensions flare up periodically, as Inner Mongolians, ethnic Koreans, the Muslims in Xinjiang, and other minority and separatist groups resist Beijing's control. Given China's long history of interventions by foreigners, the Chinese are particularly sensitive to issues of national sovereignty. This accounts for their belief that the status of Taiwan is a domestic issue.

On the subject of Taiwan, China wears its second and third faces simultaneously. Revealing its frustration, it resists every attempt to place Taiwan on the agenda of any multilateral forum. At the same time, it retaliates against any party that acts to strengthen Taiwan's international status. In November 1992, for example, China ordered France to close its consulate in Guangzhou after the French government authorized the sale of 60 Mirage fighters and 1,500 air-to-surface missiles to Taiwan. An intimidated France later promised not to sell any more arms to Taipei. In June 1995, China recalled its ambassador to the United States in response to the U.S. Government's decision to allow Taiwan's president, Lee Teng-hui, to enter the United States as a "private citizen." Relations between Washington and Beijing quickly soured. It is clear that China's increasing economic clout has contributed to Beijing's new assertiveness.

A strategy of conditional engagement would permit the United States to deal with China no matter which face it wears. Washington should continue to encourage China to become a constructive partner by promoting economic and cultural interaction and by broadening its contacts with the People's Liberation Army. China's desire for capital and technology from the United States gives Washington a bargaining chip, but the United States must carefully watch China's behavior toward its neighbors in Northeast and Southeast Asia and move to deter, by diplomatic means, any destabilizing actions on the part of Beijing.

Japan has used its economic clout to play a significant role in the past and can play an even more important role in encouraging China to become a constructive partner. Japan has been the largest supplier of development aid to China, contributing an estimated $19 billion for the period 1979-95. In 1993 alone, Japan provided China with $1.35 billion in aid. Since 1993, Japan has also been China's largest trading partner, surpassing Hong Kong. Total trade between both countries for 1993 amounted to $39 billion, compared to $32.5 billion between China and Hong Kong, and $27.7 billion between China and the United States. In 1994, total trade between both countries increased to $46 billion. Japan is also the third largest investor in China, behind the United States and Hong Kong.

In November 1990, Japan became the first country to break the international economic sanctions imposed on China after the Tiananmen Square incident. Visits by Prime Minister Toshiki Kaifu in August 1991 and Japan's emperor in October 1992 also demonstrate that Japan has been practicing an engagement strategy toward China for some time. A major reason for Japan's substantial economic assistance to China is the guilt the Japanese feel over World War II. However, Japan has long believed that one way to protect its national interests is to help stabilize Chinese political conditions through economic assistance.

While the United States and Japan share a common interest in helping China build a viable economy, there may be areas of incongruence between the two countries in the long run. First, they are both competitors for the Chinese market, which means that China can play one off the other. Second, Japan would like to treat sensitive issues such as China's poor human rights record quietly, whereas the United States tends to try to force improvement by public confrontation. Third, if the United States chooses to enhance the international status of Taiwan to a greater degree than Japan likes, the disparity may lead to diplomatic friction. Fourth, the two countries maintain different paces in engaging China in the military arena.

Although the current chill in U.S.-Chinese relations may slow military cooperation, in the past Washington has promoted exchanges of military personnel and technology and ship visits with China at a pace that made Tokyo nervous.

More recently, Japan has been considering using developmental aid to discourage China's military buildup and its nuclear arms programs, arguing that the military spending is "unnecessary." After China conducted a nuclear test in May 1995, for example, Tokyo decided to reduce its aid for this year. This first small but significant step to check Chinese moves demonstrates how Japan can contribute to a strategy of conditional engagement.

COPING WITH KOREA

A CONDITIONAL engagement strategy should be targeted not only at China but also the Korean Peninsula, where there are major security issues such as nuclear proliferation and Korean unification.

The United States should continue to engage North Korea under the Agreed Framework of October 1994. Negotiations with the North Koreans, no matter how difficult and slow, will decrease the likelihood of a military showdown and perhaps convince them of the economic and technological benefits of working with the Americans and international agencies. However, Washington should be prepared to take tough measures, such as multilateral sanctions, against North Korea if a clandestine program to develop nuclear weapons is uncovered.

The process of Korean unification is likely to involve China, Russia, and Japan more directly than the nonproliferation talks under the Agreed Framework. China would certainly like to see a united Korea that is friendly to Beijing, since it does not want to share a border with a hostile power. However, Chinese efforts to guarantee a pro-Beijing government in a new Korea would most likely make Russia and Japan nervous. Under such circumstances it would be in Washington's interest to retain its influence over the process of unification and over a post-unification Korea in order to ensure that neither China nor Russia felt threatened. Washington could retain its influence in a new unified Korea by extending to it the current bilateral security agreement with South Korea—with some modifications—and by assisting in the process of reducing North Korean troop levels and integrating the two Korean armies. A small U.S. troop presence would reassure all Koreans, who may fear that other regional powers will interfere and destabilize the political process. This will be a challenging task for the United States since a unified Korea may well be highly nationalistic and thus anti-American.

Japan has been able to exert little direct influence over North Korea with respect to nuclear proliferation. Negotiations between Pyongyang and Tokyo over the normalization of relations, which began in Beijing in January 1991, broke down in November 1992. One of the reasons for the failure was Japan's insistence that North Korea agree to an inspection by the International Atomic Energy Agency. When North Korea initially agreed to the bilateral talks, it was believed in Japan that North Korea's main interest was in obtaining war reparations to be used for national development. However, Tokyo thought it could engage North Korea economically as well as broaden bilateral political contacts. Amid the limited progress being made in May 1995 between Washington and Pyongyang on the issue of light-water nuclear reactors, North Korea turned to Japan with a request for an emergency supply of 1 million tons of rice. Japan responded that summer by sending 30 tons of rice in the hope of rekindling a bilateral dialogue.

The historical enmity between the Koreans and the Japanese discourages Japan from taking diplomatic initiatives. Yet, whatever form Korean unification takes, it will be in Japan's interest to remain engaged in the process. Japan seeks a united Korea that is friendly to Tokyo and Washington, that is economically viable and politically open, and that will allow a token U.S. military presence to remain. A U.S. presence in a new Korea would not only reduce friction between China and Russia but would help stabilize relations between Japan and Korea. This is another reason why the United States and Japan should conduct a conditional engagement strategy in concert.

CONDITIONAL ENGAGEMENT
AND THE JAPANESE-U.S. ALLIANCE

SINCE THE United States and Japan have common strategic interests in East Asia and the western Pacific, it is imperative for them to coordinate their regional strategies within the framework of the Japanese-U.S. alliance. The United States should not try to go it alone as the balancer in the region. Rather, the U.S.-Japanese alliance itself should serve as a balancer.

For the strategy of conditional engagement to be effective, the United States must maintain close relations with its formal allies—Japan, South Korea, Australia, the Philippines, and Thailand—and establish fuller security dialogues with the ASEAN countries. However, Japan will remain the most important of America's friends in the region because of its economic clout and geopolitical significance.

Without its military bases in Japan, the United States could hardly carry out a conditional engagement strategy. Such a strategy will be credible to the Chinese, the North Koreans, and other Asian nations only if the United States maintains its military presence in the region. By maintaining its bases, the United States will look serious in its attempts to integrate China and North Korea into the regional and international community and reinforce the U.S. commitment to interdependence with those countries. And should the United States be compelled to confront an aggressive China or North Korea, forces stationed in Japan will allow it to respond quickly in a crisis. This fact would give additional weight to a strategy of conditional engagement.

Since it is in Japan's interest that a U.S. strategy of conditional engagement succeeds and the success of this strategy depends on a healthy Japanese-U.S. alliance, Japan should increase its burden-sharing in operational terms. Under an agreement concluded in January 1991, Japan agreed that by 1995 it would cover all costs of maintaining the bases except U.S. operating costs, military pay, and related personnel expenses. The Japan Defense Agency allocated $5.3 billion in FY 1995 for the support of the 47,000 U.S. soldiers stationed in Japan. This amounted to about $113,000 per U.S. soldier, certainly an indication of the Japanese government's strong desire to help sustain the U.S. presence in the western Pacific. Japan has gradually moved to improve its operational support system, agreeing to provide fuel and other necessary materials for the U.S. and Japanese forces, for instance, under the Acquisition and Cross-Servicing Agreement, which is likely to become effective in 1996. Japan still needs to modify some of its laws so that its support of U.S. operations will become more effective.

Perhaps more fundamental are the questions of what kind of international security role Japan is likely to seek in the future and how that role will be related to a strategy of conditional engagement. The Gulf War had a significant impact on Japan's view of its international role. Japan's Self-Defense Forces (SDF) are now permitted to participate in U.N. peacekeeping operations, for instance. While there is widespread support for this in Japan, debate continues over what security role Japan should play beyond supporting U.N. activities. A growing number of Japanese security specialists and politicians, of whom Ichiro Ozawa, president of the New Frontier Party is representative, argue that Japan should become "a normal state," a state that can seek its international role unconstrained by a pacifist mentality. In contrast, liberals, such as Masayoshi Takemura, head of the Forerunner Party and the author of *A Small But Shining Country*, argue that Japan should be a small but noticeable power. The former advocate a more active security role, the latter a limited security role.

In order to support a U.S. strategy of conditional engagement, Japan needs to become a better ally, by establishing more adequate night landing practice sites for U.S. naval pilots, for instance, and changing the law so that the SDF will be able to cooperate fully with U.S. forces, in case maritime interdiction is required for economic sanctions against North Korea, for example. The government should also rethink its interpretation of the Japanese constitution and related laws that prevent the SDF from participating in the collective use of force or international peace enforcement operations, so long as the Japanese role is limited to noncombat military missions, such as disarming hostile forces, patrolling demilitarized zones, removing mines, and transporting medical and food supplies to friendly troops. Such actions will strengthen the bilateral alliance and make a strategy of conditional engagement possible.

9

The United States in Asia: Searching for a New Role

Byung-joon Ahn

THE END of the Cold War left American foreign policy in a drift that now appears to be ending as the United States feels its way toward a new role in the world. This process includes devising a new strategy for its relations with Asia, one that will integrate China into the global system and protect America's vital interests by checking the ambitions of any would-be hegemon. The core concepts of this strategy are engagement and leadership—reflecting the belief that the United States should be engaged in Asia militarily, economically, and politically, and should lead efforts to promote security, interdependence, and democracy in the region. Only the United States, it is argued, can constrain, if not contain, the hegemonic ambitions—whether military or political—of China, Japan, or any other Asian power. However, the United States can only take on such a role if it is consistent with America's vital interests. The professed goals of the Clinton administration's engagement and leadership strategy are to enhance U.S. security, promote domestic prosperity, and extend democracy abroad. And as Clinton administration officials have

stated, "nowhere are the strands of [the] three-prolonged strategy more intertwined, nor is the need for continued U.S.
engagement more evident" than in Asia.[1]

Despite such rhetoric, the conduct of American foreign
policy by the Clinton administration has been incoherent, reactive, and occasionally waffling. For example, by hosting the 1993
Asia-Pacific Cooperation forum (APEC) summit in Seattle,
President Clinton led observers to expect an enhanced U.S.
interest in Asia. But he failed to follow up on this initiative. In
1994, he made only one visit to Asia, in contrast to four trips to
Europe. In 1995, after initially turning down a request from Taiwan's President Lee Teng-hui for a visa to make an unofficial
visit to the United States, Clinton bowed to congressional pressure and granted the visa. This reversal caused perhaps the
worst crisis in Sino-American relations since the United States
granted the diplomatic normalization in 1979.

The fact that the United States faces no direct threat in the
post–Cold War world has blurred the focus of American foreign policy and resulted in international deregulation, with
containment yielding to confusion. As one analyst notes, "Public statements by Clinton administration officials about the
purpose of U.S. foreign policy have been inconsistent or simply
ambiguous."[2] The primacy given domestic politics over foreign
policy by both President Clinton and the Republican-con-
trolled Congress have only exacerbated this inconsistency and
lack of strategic direction.

Perhaps in an effort to respond to those concerns, the U.S.
Department of Defense issued a new East Asian Strategy Report
last year that reaffirmed Washington's policy of engagement: "In
thinking about the Asia-Pacific region, security comes first, and
a continued United States military presence will continue to
serve as a bedrock for America's security role in this dynamic area
of the world."[3] Moreover, the report noted, "U.S. interests in Asia
have been remarkably consistent over the past two centuries:
peace and security; commercial access to the region; freedom of

navigation; and the prevention of the rise of any hegemonic power or coalition."[4] There is little doubt, therefore, that the United States recognizes the importance of Asia to its vital interests and appreciates the fact that the world's center of strategic and economic gravity—and indeed even the center of cultural gravity according to some Asians—is shifting from the Atlantic to the Pacific.[5] This is a welcome sign. However, what the strategy report lacked, and the Clinton administration still lacks, is an attempt to fashion a coherent strategy combining security, economic, and political goals, and the resolve to pursue those goals in partnership with America's allies.

Asia is a diverse region that, in general, lacks liberal institutions for managing security and interdependence. In the Asia of the 1990s, working toward nationalism, sovereignty, and a balance of power is a political imperative. It is remarkable that these old and basically European ideas are being revived as the most important guides for foreign policy in Asia generally and in China particularly. China and most other Asian states are realists in international relations, but powerful economic trends are driving them toward interdependence, borderless economies, and open regionalism. Asian and Western nations still have fundamental differences on approaches to common economic problems. Nevertheless, they all advocate in principle at least, economic liberalism, open trade and investment, and technology transfer. Therefore, it is desirable that the economic imperatives that bind the United States to Asia prevail over the political imperatives.

Whether this will happen depends on the turn of domestic politics in each Asian state because most countries tend to define their foreign policy from a domestic political perspective. Most of the countries in Asia now face uncertain political futures; leadership transitions are underway in China, Russia, Japan, South Korea, North Korea, Taiwan, and elsewhere. How China evolves in the long run and North Korea evolves in the short run will vitally affect the future of Asian security and interdependence.

Given these realities, there is no alternative to American leadership in Asia. Only the United States, with the help of other countries that share its interests and values, can marshall the power needed to shape the future of Asia. However, the United States will have to design a strategy to cope with Asia's overlapping security, economic, and political challenges, one that is flexible enough to handle different issues in different places. Secretary of State Warren Christopher was certainly right when he said: "Our strategic alliance with Japan—as well as with South Korea and our other allies—is essential to American security and prosperity. And our engagement is essential to a secure, prosperous, and more democratic Asia. This administration has placed Asia at the core of its long-term foreign policy strategy."[6]

While such words are reassuring to many in Asia, Washington must back its words with credible deeds by implementing its strategy of conditional engagement and leadership in collaboration with its partners. A balance of power must be the overall goal in managing Asian security affairs. To prevent a regional hegemon from emerging and North Korea from developing nuclear and other weapons of mass destruction, the United States must strengthen its bilateral security relationships with Japan, South Korea, and Australia, among others. It must maintain forward military deployment while promoting the confidence-building measures of the ASEAN Regional Forum and other regional frameworks. Such measures will be neces-

---

THE TEN PRINCIPLES OF CONDITIONAL ENGAGEMENT

1. No unilateral use of offensive military force
2. Peaceful resolution of territorial disputes
3. Respect for national sovereignty
4. Freedom of navigation
5. Moderation in military force buildup
6. Transparency of military forces
7. Nonproliferation of weapons of mass destruction
8. Market access for trade and investment
9. Cooperative solutions for transnational problems
10. Respect for basic human rights

sary as long as Asia lacks a strong security coalition capable of thwarting hegemonic ambitions and the proliferation of weapons of mass destruction.

Washington must link economic issues with security issues, investing substantial material and human resources in the pursuit of its leadership strategy and strengthening multilateral norms, and it should resist the temptation to take unilateral action to satisfy domestic constituencies. Here it should follow South Korea's example. Seoul succeeded in brokering China's participation in APEC by mediating between Beijing and Taipei in 1991, and it succeeded in normalizing diplomatic relations with China in 1992 by taking advantage of Beijing's desire to attract trade and investment to Shandong and other northeastern provinces.

The United States will no doubt continue to pursue a policy of enlarging democracy, but this will lead to conflict with the Asian states that insist on their own versions of democracy and "Asian values." In promoting democracy, therefore, the United States must carefully consider local conditions in Asia. Moreover, the United States will have to allow for a division of roles so that Japan can assume more responsibility for promoting economic and political cooperation, and ASEAN and South Korea can take on bridge-building roles.

If the United States is serious about being engaged in Asia and exercising leadership there, the strategic ends and means of its policies must be coherent and consistent. In dealing with China, for example, it should not let Beijing "pick and choose" among options to avoid confrontation.[7] Of course, it is not necessary to provoke China. Washington has acknowledged that by trying to avoid the use of words such as "threat" or "containment" in discussions of Beijing's behavior in the Spratly Islands and the Taiwan Strait; those words may well become self-fulfilling prophecies. However, Washington must be willing to take the lead in building Asia's agenda for security and economic cooperation. Its strategy of peaceful engagement and constructive leadership must become a self-fulfilling prophecy.

AMERICA'S ROLE: FROM A HEGEMON TO A BALANCER

IN ASIA, the United States is moving from the regional security role of Cold War hegemon to that of a balancer. Although
American foreign policy is still suffering from the post–Cold
War blues, there are signs that Washington is feeling its way
toward a balance-of-power strategy designed to counter a
potential hegemon. By deciding to keep 100,000 forward-
deployed American troops in Northeast Asia, the Clinton
administration appears to be positioning its conditional
engagement strategy to guard against the dangers inherent in
China's uncertain future, the nuclearization or violent
unification of the Korean peninsula, and the proliferation of
nuclear and biological weapons in general, while supporting the
multilateral dialogue in the ASEAN Regional Forum and other
attempts to create a Northeast Asian security dialogue.

Only the U.S. presence can prevent the creation of a power
vacuum in Asia that would intensify the Sino-Japanese rivalry.[8]
It is not necessary to assume there will be "an endless shifting
balance of power" in Asia, as Jonathan D. Pollack points out in
chapter 6. History teaches a shift in the balance of power takes
a long time. The China-centered order in Asia, for example,
lasted almost two millennia, until 1885, when the Japan-cen-
tered order replaced it; that lasted until 1945, when the United
States became the regional hegemon. Although the United
States can no longer maintain this role, it should be the natural leader of a coalition to enforce a balance of power, control
nuclear proliferation, and manage instability—however
difficult it is to define those terms.

The Clinton administration's position that "maintaining
productive relationships with the world's most powerful states
is vital—not for the sake of good relations alone, but because it
allows us to pursue our objectives in a safer and more favorable
environment."[9] Because there is no NATO-type collective security structure in Asia, the U.S.-Japanese alliance is the key to

maintaining a balance of power and defending U.S. security and economic interests in the region. It not only keeps the United States engaged in Asia through its forward military deployment but prevents Japan from becoming militarily independent, from "leaving the West and returning to Asia." Therefore, an American leadership strategy should not be directed at China alone, but also designed to anchor Japan firmly in its bilateral security relationship with the United States so that it can remain free of nuclear weapons and defensively postured. The American military presence is the essential glue that holds Japan's and South Korea's bilateral security relationships with the United States together and that allows the ASEAN countries to have some measure of confidence in America's balancing role. In light of Japan's inability to make an unambiguous apology for its World War II aggression and the failure of the no-war resolution in the Diet on the fiftieth anniversary of World War II's end. South Korea and the members of ASEAN worry about a rising tide of Japanese nationalism and conservatism. Consequently, the renewal of the U.S.-Japanese alliance takes on a new urgency and must be understandable even to China. According to a poll conducted by the Chicago Council on Foreign Relations in 1994, 85 percent of the American public and 96 percent of governmental and private sector leaders believe that the United States has a vital interest in Japan. Moreover, more than three-quarters of the leaders are in favor of permanent membership for Japan in the U.N. Security Council. More than half (55 percent) of the leaders believe that Japan should be encouraged to assume some military role in the world, while slightly less than half (43 percent) are opposed.[10]

The United States must be a balancer in the region not only to engage China economically but to constrain, if not contain, China's aggressiveness and ambition to project power and to act as a counterweight against China's uncertain intentions, lack of military transparency, and tradition of using barbarians against barbarians to achieve its ends. So long as China practices balance-of-power politics and adheres to a strict interpretation of sovereignty, territorial integrity, and noninterference in the context of its "Five Principles of Peaceful Coexistence," the United States has no choice but to insist on the importance of military transparency and confidence-building measures in its relations with China. China's weapons acquisition program and its rapidly increasing military capabilities may not pose a threat now. But as former Commander in Chief of the U.S. Pacific Command Admiral Richard C. Macke warns, the United States must regard Beijing with suspicion when its strategic intentions are not made clear, when it is reluctant to use its influence to help resolve the Korean question, when it refuses to clarify its territorial claims over the Spratly Islands, and when it goes so far as to build a military installation on the Mischief Reef within the 200-mile exclusion zone of the Philippines.[11]

Washington says that it does not wish to regard China as a threat because doing so may become a self-fulfilling prophecy. But more than half (57 percent) of the American public and slightly less than half of the public and private sector leaders (46 percent) believe that the development of China as a world power could become a critical threat to vital U.S. interests in the next decade.[12] Moreover, in recent years, the Chinese have reversed a longstanding policy of welcoming the U.S. military presence in Asia as a stabilizing factor. They distrust American and Japanese motives, even as they invite American and Japanese economic cooperation in accomplishing "socialism with Chinese characteristics." China has refused to admit that it sold missile parts to Pakistan and has ignored a U.S. offer to lift some bans on the sale of high-technology to China in return for such an admission.[13] Considering these facts, a prudent U.S. strategy must be ready to meet the Chinese military challenge in the future with a credible countervailing force; meanwhile, it must reengage the Chinese military to probe its intentions and reach understandings on transparency and confidence building measures. Beijing's postponement of a trip last year by

Minister of Defense Chi Haotian to the United States to retaliate for Washington's decision to allow Taiwan's president to make a "private" visit to the United States, indicates how difficult it will be to establish a pattern of mutually beneficial military cooperation with Beijing.

Apparently Beijing believes that Washington has been conspiring to contain China by helping Taiwan assert its independence, denying China entry into the World Trade Organization (WTO), and interfering in its domestic politics over the human rights issues. U.S. House Speaker Newt Gingrich's proposal for recognizing Taiwan only fueled Beijing's suspicions. While Chinese President Jiang Zemin is preoccupied with a power struggle to succeed Deng Xiaoping as China's leader, the military is increasing its influence over the conduct of Chinese foreign policy. It was against this background that Beijing, in July 1995, arrested Harry Wu, the human rights activist with American citizenship, ordered the test-firing of six missiles in the sea about 140 kilometers north of Taiwan, and expelled two American officers on espionage charges.

To call a halt to this chain of action and reaction, Secretary of State Christopher met with Chinese Foreign Minister Qian Qichen in Brunei, and the two agreed to continue high-level dialogues in August 1995 without settling U.S.-Chinese differences. This was an important step because, as former Secretary of State Henry Kissinger points out, "Stability in Asia is most likely if China and the United States cooperate."[14] It is certainly desirable that Washington and Beijing reach broad understandings on the strategic, economic, and political issues that divide them.

Recently, Japan has begun to collaborate with the United States in its policy of engagement and leadership toward China. In a defense white paper released in July 1995, Tokyo expressed worries about the expansion of Chinese naval and air force capabilities. When Beijing went ahead with a nuclear weapons test in May 1995, a few days after the nuclear Nonproliferation Treaty (NPT) to which China is a signatory was extended and only two weeks after Prime Minister Tomiichi Murayama went to Beijing and asked the Chinese not to carry out the test, Tokyo decided to suspend $70 million in future aid payments to China and refused to readjust an estimated $5 billion increase in Chinese interest repayments caused by appreciation of the yen. By taking this tougher approach, Tokyo is working to tie Beijing into the emerging institutions for economic and security cooperation, such as APEC and the NPT.[15]

A policy of engagement is consistent with South Korea's national interest and strategic culture because it may directly or indirectly encourage China to play a constructive role in achieving peace and stability on the Korean Peninsula. South Korea has expanded its economic and political cooperation with China in the hope that Beijing will persuade, if not pressure, Pyongyang to enter into direct negotiations with Seoul on denuclearization, peace, and cooperation. China has become South Korea's third largest trading partner, and South Korea is China's sixth largest partner. Beijing has voiced its support for such dialogues, but it has so far failed to use its substantial leverage to influence North Korea's policies and behavior. Politically, Beijing has tried to play off Seoul against Pyongyang by treating the Korean issue as ancillary to China's relations with the United States and Japan.

It is time for the United States to begin to see the Korean Peninsula and the Agreed Framework, signed between the United States and North Korea in October 1994, in the larger context of Asian regional security, because meeting the North Korean challenge may well remain the number one threat to East Asian security indefinitely. Primarily concerned with the task of global nonproliferation and desirous of keeping North Korea within the nonproliferation regime, Washington hastily wrapped up the agreement at the expense of South Korea's concerns about North Korea retaining its capacity for nuclear weapons development, even in crude forms. If North Korea is allowed to enjoy permanent ambiguity about whether it has already developed one or two nuclear devices and to eventually get away with actual nuclear capabilities, it will speed up nuclear proliferation in South Korea, Japan, and Northeast Asia as a whole.

Yet U.S. officials tend to see the Korean issue as a fire across the water. While they understand the importance of a nuclear-free peninsula, they are reluctant to shed blood or risk war to force North Korea to abandon the nuclear option once and for all. However, there is no question a nuclear-armed North Korea would be highly destabilizing for Asia as a whole.

Here again, China's intentions are unclear. Although Beijing has been busy expanding China's economic interdependence with South Korea and advocating peaceful solutions to the problems that divide the peninsula, it has endorsed North Korea's foreign policy by withdrawing its representative from the Military Armistice Commission at Panmunjom in November 1994, backing Pyongyang's quest for negotiating a peace agreement directly with the United States rather than with South Korea, and refusing to join the Korean Peninsula Energy Development Organization, which will provide substitute energy sources like heavy oil to North Korea.

Ultimately, the quest for a nuclear-free Korean Peninsula, a peace agreement, and unification must be met through a dialogue between the two Koreas. Seoul insists on the use of South Korean designed light-water reactors for North Korea under the Agreed Framework and on a central role in building them not for money and prestige. Rather, the reason is that if an American firm serves as the principal contractor and a South Korean firm takes on a subsidiary role South Korea's effectiveness in any dialogue with North Korea would be reduced. Seoul also sees Pyongyang's acceptance of South Korean reactors as a litmus test of whether Pyongyang is prepared to enter into serious discussions on denuclearization, peace, and reconciliation, or whether it is still only interested in driving a wedge between Seoul and Washington.

While the Agreed Framework defused the tensions caused by North Korea's nuclear weapons development program, it may have encouraged Pyongyang in its refusal to deal directly with Seoul. Also left unaddressed by the accord is the ominous threat posed by North Korea's formidable conventional forces deployed along the Demilitarized Zone and its large stockpile of chemical weapons, offensive artillery, and missiles capable of reaching South Korea and Japan. Pyongyang's attempts to circumvent the Military Armistice Commission and negotiate a peace agreement with Washington at the expense of South Korea, ostensibly in place of the armistice, pose a difficult challenge to the armistice and deterrence system that has kept the peace on the Korean Peninsula since 1953. In the interest of maintaining regional security, therefore, the United States, South Korea, Japan, and other Asian nations must join in an effort to stop North Korea from playing a game of nuclear brinkmanship. It is heartening in this regard that Congress has passed a joint resolution urging North Korea to resume dialogue with South Korea and implement the Agreed Framework, and requiring the president to report to Congress on these implementations.

Denuclearization and unification must proceed cautiously. The uncertainty presented by Korea derives not only from the possibility of a nuclearized North Korea but from the prospect of a messy process of unification that may destabilize the major-power relationship among the United States, Japan, China, and Russia. Beijing's priority seems to be the prevention of the violent collapse of the North Korean regime, which could send millions of refugees across the Yalu and Tumen Rivers into Manchuria. It also wishes to discourage North Korean leader Kim Jong Il from making militarily provocative moves against South Korea and deny North Korea the acquisition of a serious nuclear capability. Beijing may tolerate the (ambiguous) possession of a few nuclear devices by North Korea because it fears that unification on South Korea's terms would eliminate a strategic buffer against American and Japanese power.[16]

The United States, Japan, and South Korea must convince

China that a nuclear-free, peaceful, and unified Korea can contribute to regional stability and interdependence. Unification will not come by design; if anything, it will come by default. A reunited Korea should be on friendly terms with all other neighboring powers. A unified Korea will also be a more powerful state, which means that the Asian balance-of-power system would encompass five rather than four powers. Given the Korean Peninsula's strategic location—at the intersection of the geopolitical interests of China, Russia, and Japan—it will be in the interests of a reunited Korea to maintain a security relationship with the United States.

There is little prospect for the development of a multilateral security framework in Asia in the foreseeable future other than the ASEAN Regional Forum and its track-two organization, the Council for Security Cooperation in the Asia-Pacific (CSCAP). These forums for consultation on security issues allow participants to convey their intentions and engage in preventive diplomacy. For some time to come, however, they will remain talk shops. In Northeast Asia, where most of the important strategic issues are concentrated, there is no subregional security dialogue, mainly because China and North Korea are reluctant to engage in such talks. China does not want to be left out of multilateral dialogues, but it much prefers bilateral negotiations. And Beijing adamantly objects to Taipei's participation in CSCAP, even in its nongovernmental capacity. Certainly, these cooperative security efforts should be exploited to the fullest, but they are limited by the divergent leaderships, agendas, and perspectives of Northeast and Southeast Asia.

An Asian collective security regime, in which an attack on one is regarded as attack on all, or an Asian "concert of powers," in which nations coalesce around common values or threats, is a long way off. In all probability, a loose balance-of-power system comprising four or five major actors, depending on when Korea is reunified, is likely to continue. Washington's decision to recognize Vietnam and ASEAN's decision to admit it to membership in July 1995 must also be seen from the perspective of balance-of-power politics. So although it is noteworthy that after a majority of the 19 participants at the second meeting of the ASEAN Regional Forum in July 1995 called for increased military transparency China agreed for the first time to give its Asian and Pacific neighbors more information about its defense program, there is no viable alternative to the United States acting as a balancer of Asian interstate relations.

AMERICA'S ECONOMIC ROLE:
FROM IMPORTER TO EXPORTER

DURING THE Cold War, the United States served as the largest importer of goods and services from Asia and as Asia's lender of last resort. Now, the United States is the world's largest debtor nation and seeking to become a greater exporting nation by aggressively expanding its market access in Asian countries. Indeed, the United States now looks on Asia as the largest potential market for its goods and services, especially in the areas of high technology, intellectual property, and telecommunications.

The United States remains the largest export market for most Asian countries although the share of Asian exports to the United States has been declining since 1992. Faced with fiscal and trade deficits, the United States has been pressuring Asian countries, in bilateral discussions and in multilateral fora such as APEC and the WTO, to open their markets. Having developed a measure of comparative advantage in manufacturing and commodities, Asian countries have tried to resist these pressures, which has made trade friction an undercurrent of the U.S. relationships with Japan and China and, increasingly with ASEAN. On balance, however, both the United States and Asia share responsibility for creating liberal, rule-based, trading systems that would benefit all sides.

U.S. trade with Asia-Pacific countries in 1993 totaled more than $374 billion and accounted for 2.8 million American jobs.[17] The East Asian economic miracle is not a myth, as some have argued, but a reality,[18] fueled by savings, investments, technology, and pragmatic macroeconomic policies. The World Bank has predicted that Asia will lead global economic growth in the next century; the countries in East Asia, with their strict adherence to macroeconomic fundamentals and export-oriented strategies, will account for about 50 percent of the growth of the global GDP.[19]

As comparative advantage has shifted toward Asia, the United States has begun to view Japan, China, Taiwan, South Korea, and many other Asian countries as unfair traders whose practices threaten American domestic prosperity and jobs. Japan, with a 1994 current-account surplus of $129 billion, $66 billion of which was from the United States, is seen as the prime offender. One school of thought contends that the U.S.-Japanese imbalance is caused by the structural differences between the consumer-oriented capitalism of the United States and the production-oriented capitalism of Japan. Japanese industry, it notes, invests at nearly twice the rate of American industry,[20] and imports of manufactured goods represent only 2.9 percent of Japan's GDP.[21] According to this view, the trade surpluses that Japan enjoys with virtually every country are the root cause of the yen appreciation.

Frustrated by its inability to lower mounting trade deficits with Tokyo—despite the yen's appreciation since the Plaza Agreement in 1985—Washington has repeatedly sought a commitment from Tokyo to buy more U.S. products. Tokyo, however, has resisted Washington's demands on the grounds that they would result in managed trade. For example, the negotiations over Japanese imports of U.S. auto parts in Vancouver in May 1995 went nowhere, mainly because the negotiators' domestic political situations did not allow them to make concessions. This was especially true of the Japanese negotiators, given the economic trouble facing the Japanese auto industry since the yen soared against the dollar. When Washington announced its decision to impose a 100 percent punitive tariff on Japanese luxury cars beginning on June 28, 1995, the Japanese lodged a complaint with the WTO, contending that such a tariff would violate global trade rules barring unilateral sanctions. Most Asian countries sympathized with Japan on this issue. Although they have been eager to have Japan open its markets to their exports, they were afraid they would also become the target of U.S. sanctions.

Washington and Tokyo went to the brink and then pulled back, reaching a compromise just as the tariff was to go into effect. Tokyo announced a "voluntary" plan to increase production and investments in the United States, and Washington lifted the planned tariff against Japanese luxury cars. The dispute over air cargo rights followed a similar pattern. To placate domestic constituencies, each side claimed that the other side blinked in the end. This succession of confrontations created an awareness that such brinkmanship must be avoided between the world's two largest trading nations if cooperation is to be maintained in a larger regional context.

Having come close to a trade war with Japan, the United States is determined not to allow the same thing to happen with China. America's trade deficit with China, $29 billion in 1994, was second only to its trade deficit with Japan. In February 1995, the United States barely averted a trade war with China by reaching an agreement on the protection of intellectual property rights. Faced with sanctions on $1.1 billion of its exports to the United States, China had no choice but to accede to American demands. Significantly, Beijing promised for the first time to inspect compact disc and laser disc factories in China and destroy pirated goods, thus compromising its rigid doctrine of sovereignty. In return, Washington agreed to consider acceding to China's entry into the WTO under the less restrictive rules governing developing countries. In this way, Washington followed a policy of trying to engage China in the global regime by making it play by the rules of reciprocity and open trade.

The United States has been trying to advance free trade, open regionalism, and the creation of a Pacific community by working to anchor China, Japan, and ASEAN in APEC. To thwart the creation of an East Asian economic bloc, the United States has also been trying to accelerate the pace of establishing the free trade and investment zone that the developing countries promised to complete by 2020. Most important, the United States is worried that Japan may promote the formation of such an economic community by saying no to Washington's pressures, taking advantage of the growing intra-Asian trade that is outpacing trans-Pacific trade, and using the clout that it has gained from the 20 percent rise in the value of the yen since the beginning of 1995. Professor Chalmers Johnson predicts that Japan will form a yen bloc by restoring the Greater East Asian Co-Prosperity Sphere, which would in effect divide the world into three trading blocs rather than the two—the European Union and APEC—that the United States anticipates.[22] Some Japanese are advancing these ideas in the name of "returning to Asia" under Japanese leadership.

Such a move toward the "re-Asianization of Asia" would be dangerous because it would strain not only the economic but also the security ties between the United States and Asia. APEC does have security implications for the United States because it connects China to an interdependent America and Asia; it is also a means of anchoring the U.S. military presence in Asia. As a result, Pacific globalism within the context of WTO rules is preferable to the idea of restoring "Asia for Asians."[23]

Economics and security are inevitably linked, if not indivisibly. In Asia, that is the implicit trade-off: the United States expects Asian countries to make economic concessions in return for security commitments. Commenting on the U.S.-Japanese confrontation on trade issues, Singapore's senior minister, Lee Kuan Yew, warned in a speech given in Tokyo: "Japan risks serious deterioration in bilateral relations with the United States if it persists with current practices. Such deterioration

must eventually affect the U.S.-Japan security alliance. Therefore, Japan must weigh its trading interests against its needs for
an indispensable U.S. counterweight to a China growing in
weight and influence, and a Russia which is still well-armed but
unstable."[24] Asian countries know that they can no longer
count on automatic American military cooperation to accom-
plish "goals as nebulous as 'stability'." American foreign policy
commentator, Alan Tonelson, contends that the United States
must use its economic power to extend its influence instead of
its military clout: "Asians may doubt America's military capability, but they still urgently need American capital, technology and, above all, markets. Thus, tightly regulating Asian access
to these assets is America's best bet for expanding its access to
Asian markets and helping to shape Asia's future."[25] In a speech
given in Singapore in May 1995, Assistant Secretary of State
Winston Lord echoed this line of reasoning: "Over time, if the
U.S. domestic perception is that the United States was being
shut out of Asian markets, [Americans] might well·begin to
question the maintenance of forces in the region," and Congress would likely not renew funding for the Seventh Fleet.[26]
Thus, warnings about the possibility of eroding public support
for the U.S. forces in Asia are being used to secure concessions
on trade issues, even as Washington insists that there is no formal linkage between security and economic issues.

The world's leading industrialized states, the Group of
Seven, failed at their meeting in Washington in April 1995 to
tackle the problem of the overvalued yen except to make vague
pledges to continue to cooperate closely in the international
exchange market. Ignoring the requests from Tokyo and Bonn
for coordinated macroeconomic policies, Washington vowed
instead to protect its domestic economic interests. This prompted then Minister of Transportation Shizuka Kamei to state, "The
recent behavior of the United States makes me suspect that it
may be using Japan and saying, 'There are very diligent Japanese
whom you can use as slaves and produce good results'. "[27] It is in

the interest of both sides to avoid such a war of words.

With respect to its allies in Asia, particularly Japan and South Korea, it is better for the United States to keep economic and security issues on separate tracks. Washington should call upon its allies to increase their burden-sharing payments in support of the American military presence in Asia with the express warning that American public support for maintaining the presence is likely to decline if the allies say no. Threats of economic sanctions or reduced military deployment may not only weaken U.S. influence but also undermine the credibility of the U.S. security commitment.

The United States will inevitably link economic benefits to cooperation on security issues involving its adversaries. Such a strategy has already yielded dividends in China, even though Beijing did not yield to Washington's demands for suspending the shipment of fissile materials and missiles to Iran and Pakistan. However, China is now so preoccupied with its economic development that it has indicated a willingness to enter into dialogues with Taiwan, the United States, Japan, and other Asian countries. As Admiral Liu Huaqing points out: "We hope to modernize our navy, but the problem is that we have no resources. And if we compete with economic needs, we will be in competition with the economy, and that is not in China's interests."[28]

Washington is therefore in a stronger position to induce Beijing to be more cautious in its military behavior and responsive to the issue of military transparency by linking trade issues not to human rights but to security issues such as the export of missiles and weapons of mass destruction, the North Korean nuclear challenge, and the Spratlys. Since China exports four times as much to the United States as it imports from the United States, and gains enormously in foreign exchange and high technology by doing so, the United States can and should lead the efforts to make China play by the rules of reciprocity and transparency in both the economic and security spheres in the Asia-Pacific.

AMERICA'S POLITICAL ROLE:
FROM OBSERVER TO PROMOTER OF DEMOCRACY

DURING THE Cold War, the United States subordinated the promotion of democratization in foreign countries to its policy of containing the Soviet Union. With the end of the Cold War, it has begun to see itself as a promoter of democracy throughout the world. When Washington tries to apply the strategy of the "enlargement" of democracy to Asia, however, it invariably runs into conflict with Asian countries that defend their versions of democracy, human rights, and "Asian values."

In a world in which there is no longer a direct threat to their physical security, both the United States and the Asian countries have to look at their security and economic issues through the lens of domestic politics. Without support in their legislatures, the press, and among the general public, their foreign policies cannot succeed. This is especially true in countries where political transitions are underway or the tide of nationalism is rising, as seems to be the case in most Asian countries.

With the Republican Party as the majority in Congress for the first time in 40 years and a Democratic president, the politicization of U.S. foreign policy was inevitable. Moreover, Congress is likely to strongly influence the making of American foreign policy for some time to come. For example, the recent Sino-American confrontation over the visit of Taiwan's president to the United States was actually a clash between the military in Beijing and the Republican Congress. Therefore, any innovation in Washington's Asia policy must have congressional support.

The Clinton administration has moderated its value-based foreign policy since it delinked human rights and trade in dealing with China and granted most-favored-nation status in June 1994. But this does not mean that the administration has abandoned its human rights policy altogether. Secretary of State Christopher reaffirmed the administration's commitment in the spring of 1995: "Securing and expanding the community of democratic nations and respect for human rights are consistent with American ideals and advance our interests. Democratic nations are far less likely to go to war with each other and far more likely to respect international law. They are more likely to promote open markets and free trade, and to pursue policies that lead to sustained economic development."[29] Here again is an example of the American tendency to link security, economics, and politics.

By trying to engage China, Vietnam, and North Korea in the international community of democratic nations and market-based economies, the United States is promoting what these countries call "peaceful evolution," but they maintain the idea that there is an Asian brand of socialism. Unlike European communism, Asian socialism did not collapse, because Asian communist regimes originated at least at part in nationalist movements, their first-generation leaders are still in power, historically the state preceded civil society, and economic reforms have preceded political reform. Whether these Asian "socialist" regimes will follow the Eastern European example and collapse, or the East Asian example and become developmental dictatorships ("capitalist developmental states," in Chalmers Johnson's phrase) on their way to becoming functioning democracies is not yet clear. If China turns into another East Asian developmental state, it is bound to experience democratization as the middle class in urban areas grows rapidly. Vietnam may well follow this path. North Korea's future is highly uncertain. Whatever kind of political change takes place in these countries, one thing is clear: the United States will continue to promote democracy and other universal values like human rights and environmental protection.

The outcomes of the leadership transitions in post-Deng Xiaoping China and in post-Kim Il Sung North Korea will critically influence security in Northeast Asia. Whether or not the regimes in these countries collapse will depend on domestic developments, but to cope with the external effects of their internal political transformations, Washington, Tokyo, and

Seoul must prepare contingency plans with all possible scenarios in mind. The aim should be not to intervene but to limit the impact that volatile change may have on regional stability.

No less important will be the outcome of leadership and party realignments in Japan. Since the Liberal Democratic Party's 38 years of one-party rule ended in July 1993, four prime ministers have taken office. In 1995, three incidents shook the Japanese establishment and the Japanese people's confidence in it. The devastating earthquake in the Kobe region in February 1995 destroyed confidence in the quality of Japanese engineering, and the slow response of the government angered the local residents and stunned the outside world. The death and casualties caused by the sarin gas attack in March in the heart of Tokyo—allegedly the work of the Aum religious cult—undermined confidence in public safety. And the steep appreciation in the yen, which reached as high as 80 to the dollar in April 1995, seriously weakened the competitiveness of Japanese exports. Nevertheless, Washington persisted in a policy of benign neglect, despite Tokyo's repeated pleas for help. Surprisingly, the Japanese bureaucracy showed little appetite for dealing with the yen problem by attacking the regulations that protect vested interests in Japan or by reducing the trade surplus to encourage more imports.

Against this background, independent candidates were elected as mayors of Tokyo and Osaka, perhaps indicating that at last a civil society strong enough to take on the entrenched government bureaucracy, is forming. The bureaucracy had seemed to become stronger since Japan's political parties began to fragment two years ago. Until a stable ruling coalition emerges in Japan, it will be difficult for Japan to assert a coherent and active foreign policy, let alone take on a constructive leadership role in Asia, as the United States expects.

Several prominent Asian leaders have taken issue with Washington's assertion of universal democratic values by arguing that "Asian values" are either superior or equally important to Western values. Singapore's Lee Kuan Yew contends that "the exuberance of democracy leads to undisciplined and disorderly conditions which are inimical to development" and that "what a country needs to develop is discipline more than democracy."[30] Some important Japanese officials have sounded a similar theme. What is noteworthy about such statements is that they are addressed toward Americans. In effect, these protests are U.S.-bashing. These views attest to a rising tide of nationalism and self-confidence; in particular, they show Asians' refusal to be preached to by Americans. If the United States tries to push its policy of "enlargement of the world's free community of market democracies" too hard, its relations in Asia, particularly Southeast Asia, will be strained. Any attempts by Washington to link human rights, labor standards, and environmental protection to trade negotiations will meet strong opposition in Asia.

What Asians expect from the United States is a better understanding of their unique situations in terms of improving human rights and labor and environmental standards. They are not so much advocating distinctive Asian values as they are desirous of realizing universal values such as democracy and human rights within Asian cultural, political, and economic contexts. In effect, they are calling for a better understanding and some accommodation from Americans for their different ways of living and looking at life. These voices deserve fair consideration by the United States. Assistant Secretary of State for East Asia Winston Lord made such a gesture, meeting the Asians halfway, when he stated: "Each country must find its own way, given its history and economic situation, and its culture; but we believe there are some universal principles, and we believe open societies are in countries' self-interest for development as well as for security."[31]

It is unlikely that all Asians take a united stand on the issue of Asian values. There are no doubt many Asians who, like many in the West, recognize the universal characteristics of human rights and democracy, and there are no doubt many in Asia who do not—just as there are those in the West who do not. Therefore, what the United States should do is respect Asian values where they exist, while exploring common interests and values with Asians through close consultation and exchanges among people from all walks of life. The United States can do this without necessarily compromising its moral standards. In reality, these debates about values reflect conflicts in national interests and political processes.

AMERICAN LEADERSHIP AND A DIVISION OF ROLES

COHERENT AND STEADY U.S. leadership coupled with a fair division of roles among Japan, South Korea, ASEAN, Australia, and others is crucial if Washington is to sustain a strategy of conditional engagement in Asia. The United States can and should build a coalition of nations with shared interests and common values, and the coalition should try to integrate China, North Korea, and Vietnam into the global system through a combination of incentives and disincentives in the economic, military, and political arenas.

The United States is first among equals in Asia and therefore has little choice but to lead. If it is unwilling to take on the role of leader, it will be unable to shape a secure, interdependent, and democratic future in Asia. The current debate between proponents of unilateralism and multilateralism in the United States is based on a false distinction. Senate Majority Leader Bob Dole went too far when he said that the choice is whether to allow international organizations to call the shots, as in Bosnia, or to make multilateral efforts work for American interests, as in Operation Desert Storm. But he is right when he said that "leadership consists of proposing and achieving a solution" and "by saying what you mean, meaning what you say, and sticking to it."[32]

What Asia expects of the United States is steady leadership from the White House, which will make the American policy of engagement credible to both adversaries and friends. America can no longer exercise hegemony in Asia, but with the help of such partners as Japan, South Korea, and Australia it can maintain peace, prosperity, and democracy in the region. The United States must maintain the Seventh Fleet and the forward deployment of American troops at their current levels in the Pacific, develop economic relationships that avoid unilateral confrontation, deepen political ties with countries that share its values, and avoid confusing allies and adversaries. It is more than ironic that America's relations with Japan and China, Asia's two most important powers, have deteriorated while its relations with North Korea and Vietnam have improved. This situation must be rectified as early as possible.

The United States must pursue a strategy of conditional engagement by enlisting the support of Japan, an economic superpower that can share the burden of political and economic leadership commensurate with its status as the largest provider of credit and aid in Asia. Although Japan's record and the lack of consensus and leadership in its domestic politics prevent Tokyo from taking on such a role, on issues of Asian security and interdependence it makes a clear-cut break with the past and embraces the idea of building a new Pacific community with the United States instead of trying to sit on the fence between America and a future East Asian economic community. Japan should immediately open its domestic market further to the United States and other Asian countries and become more generous in providing technology, human resource training, peacekeeping operations support, and development aid to other Asian countries.

Tokyo also should link economic cooperation and aid to progress in arms control and confidence-building measures in its policies toward China, North Korea, Russia, and other countries that possess weapons of mass destruction. Tokyo's move in this direction in May 1995, when it cut off aid to China over the issue of nuclear testing, was a welcome first step. By getting China to play by global rules compatible with U.N. and wTO principles while engaging it economically through disincentives and incentives, the United States and Japan can bring China into the global community.

The Japanese government, however, must resist domestic political pressures to have Washington remove most of its troops from Japanese soil or to abrogate the U.S.-Japan security treaty in favor of an autonomous military posture, for such moves would help destabilize Japan and countries throughout Asia. Moreover, in its economic diplomacy Japan must avoid moves that could undermine U.S. domestic support for the security treaty.

The U.S. leadership role is compatible with the diplomatic bridge-building activities of South Korea, Australia, and ASEAN, which took the lead in launching the ASEAN Regional Forum in July 1994. South Korea has been trying to build bridges between China and Taiwan, and among the advanced and developing countries by brokering their participation in APEC. Seoul's foreign policy complements the American strategy of engagement and leadership because it is firmly committed to accomplishing a peaceful reunification of the two Koreas, sustaining a security alliance with the United States and economic and political partnerships with Japan and ASEAN, and fostering friendly relations with China and Russia. Its goal is a Korean unification that does not threaten regional peace and stability.

ASEAN's efforts to promote cooperative security and economic cooperation have been instrumental in facilitating regional dialogues, and Washington has supported ASEAN's attempts to build institutions through a gradual process of consensus formation, which is beginning to yield results. At the ASEAN Regional Forum meeting in July 1995, for example, Chinese foreign minister Qian Qichen pledged that China would step up military exchanges with the ASEAN countries.

Now that the United States is no longer willing to allow Asia to be a free rider in terms of security, some degree of linkage between economic incentives and military expansion is inevitable if an American leadership and engagement strategy is to be effective, especially toward potential adversaries. Offering carrots to North Korea, for example, will not be enough to induce Pyongyang to implement the Agreed Framework in letter and spirit. Nor will the promise of economic engagement alone deter an ambitious and proud China from exporting missiles and acquiring power-projection capabilities beyond its legitimate security interests. Given the preoccupation of these countries with economic reforms, however, tough economic sanctions will be as effective as military threats in influencing their behavior as military threats. Building a fallback security coalition is therefore a good investment for the long-term national interests of the United States and its partners.

The United States and its partners must demand that China and North Korea play by WTO, U.N., and International Atomic Energy Agency rules and make it clear that adherence to those rules is a precondition to being accepted as responsible members of the international community. If Washington is serious about exercising decisive leadership in Asia, it must draw lines whenever a country violates the rules, not interfere in the country's domestic politics but impose a measure of stability and order in Asia and the Pacific.

Military transparency and economic reciprocity are essential to promoting security and economic cooperation. Therefore, the United States should not relent in its demands for the enforcement of these two principles. Transparency is the first step in building confidence among nations and achieving arms control. Reciprocity has been Washington's theme song in its trade negotiations and in dealing with its security partners, particularly Japan and South Korea, Washington has also escalated its demands for burden sharing. Currently, Japan and South Korea are contributing $5 billion and $300 million a year respectively toward the cost of maintaining U.S. forces on their soil. In addition to these cost-sharing arrangements, these allies can share military technologies and facilities to help cope with conflicts that may occur on the Korean Peninsula or in East Asia.

Asian countries must be prepared to accommodate reasonable U.S. demands. Leadership and coalition building are expensive, and the costs should not fall disproportionately on the American taxpayer. South Korea, for example, is ready to share the costs with Japan, the United States, and others by carrying out joint military exercises and entering into security dialogues to ensure regional stability and promote interdependence.

Former Assistant Secretary of Defense Joseph S. Nye was right when he pointed out that "North Korea is a clear and present danger. Not only is it on the brink of a nuclear weapons capability, but it has also 1.1 million under arms, with two-thirds of them deployed along the Korean Demilitarized Zone. Moreover, it is developing a new generation of ballistic missiles."[33] Hence, coping with the North Korean problem is the most pressing issue for Asian security in the short run. However, engaging China and drawing it into the Asia-Pacific community is the most serious long-term challenge. Meeting these challenges successfully will require decisive and steady leadership from a United States with a firm sense of direction.

NOTES

1. *A National Security Strategy of Engagement and Enlargement* (Washington, D.C.: The White House, February 1995), p. 28.
2. Richard N. Haass, "Paradigm Lost," *Foreign Affairs* 74 (January/February 1995), p. 52.
3. Department of Defense of Office of International Security Affairs, *United States Security Strategy for the East Asia-Pacific Region* (Washington, D.C., February 1995), p.2.
4. Ibid, p. 5.
5. Kishore Mahbubani, "The Pacific Impulse," *Survival* 36, no. 1 (spring 1995), pp. 105-20.
6. Warren Christopher, "America's Leadership, America's Opportunity," *Foreign Policy*, no. 98 (spring 1995), p. 12.
7. Jim Hoagland, "They Leave China Free To Pick and Choose," *International Herald Tribune*, June 3-4, 1995.
8. Robert A. Manning and Paula Stern, "The Myth of the Pacific

Community," *Foreign Affairs* 73 (November/December 1994), p. 90.

9. Christopher, "America's Leadership," p. 10.

10. John E. Rielly, "The Public Mood at Mid-Decade," *Foreign Policy*, no. 98 (spring 1995), pp. 80, 86.

11. *International Herald Tribune*, March 8, 1995.

12. Rielly,"Public Mood at Mid-Decade," p. 86.

13. *International Herald Tribune*, February 14, 1995.

14. Henry Kissinger, "Four Proposals to Get the U.S. and China Off Their Collision Course," *International Herald Tribune*, July 24, 1995.

15. Brian Bridges, "Here Comes a New Phase of China-Japan Rivalry," *International Herald Tribune*, August 1, 1995.

16. See Henry A. Kissinger, "No Compromise, But a Rollback," *Washington Post*, July 6, 1994.

17. *United States Strategy for the East Asia-Pacific Region*, p.2.

18. See Paul Krugman, "The Myth of Asia's Miracle," *Foreign Affairs* 73 (November/December 1994), pp. 62-78.

19. Sumit Sharma, "World Bank Official: Asia Will Lead Global Growth," *Journal of Commerce*, April 13, 1995.

20. Clyde V. Prestowitz Jr., "Japan Does Things Differently and Keeps Getting By All the Same," *International Herald Tribune*, April 18, 1995.

21. *Far Eastern Economic Review*, April 20, 1995, p. 80.

22. Chalmers Johnson, Japan, *Who Governs? The Rise of the Developmental State* (New York: W.W. Norton, 1995), pp. 315-24.

23. Yoichi Funabashi, "Introduction: Japan's International Agenda for the 1990's," *Japan's International Agenda*, ed. Yoichi Funabashi (New York: New York University Press, 1994), p. 18.

24. *The Sunday Times*, (Singapore), May 21, 1995.

25. Alan Tonelson, "For a Successful Asia Policy, America Needs More Economic Clout," *International Herald Tribune*, April 28, 1995.

26. *The Straits Times*, (Singapore), May 21, 1995.

27. *International Herald Tribune*, April 29-30, 1995.

28. *International Herald Tribune*, January 3, 1995.

29. Christopher, "America's Leadership," pp. 14-15.

30. Cited in David I. Hitchcock, *Asian Values and the United States: How Much Conflict?* (Washington, D.C.: Center for Strategic and International Studies, 1994), p. 1.

31. Cited in Ibid., p. 27

32. Bob Dole, "Shaping America's Global Future," *Foreign Policy*, no. 98 (Spring 1995), p. 37.

33. Joseph S. Nye Jr., "The Case for Deep Engagement," *Foreign Affairs* 74 (July/August 1995), p. 95.

10

ASEAN and Conditional Engagement

Amitav Acharya

THE RESPONSE of the Association of Southeast Asian Nations (ASEAN)—comprised of Brunei, Malaysia, Indonesia, the Philippines, Singapore, Thailand, and Vietnam—to any new American strategic framework for the Asia-Pacific region will depend on the extent to which such a framework addresses ASEAN's major security concerns, especially those arising from the growth of Chinese power; helps to keep the United States actively involved in the region's security affairs, especially in maintaining a stable regional balance of power; and complements and strengthens ASEAN's own initiatives on regional security.

There is little doubt that the ASEAN states prefer an American strategy of engagement to one of isolationism. ASEAN also welcomes a U.S. policy that engages, rather than isolates or contains regional powers, such as China. A policy framework that ensures a leadership role for the United States in integrating China into the regional order is in ASEAN's interest.

The leaders of ASEAN states take a realist's view of cooperation in international relations. While engagement may seem preferable and more workable under present circumstances than containment, ASEAN members will benefit if Washington maintains the capability to act as a check on potential Chinese or Japanese militarism. A policy framework that sets standards and promotes rule-governed behavior among the key regional actors is the litmus test of an engagement strategy. The United States should adopt a policy of opposing an Asian nation only if a clearly defined and thoroughly tested engagement strategy fails.

The appeal of a strategy of conditional engagement to ASEAN will very much depend on the nature of the terms that Washington negotiates with China and other regional actors— what Jonathan Pollack in his chapter calls the "rules of acceptable behavior." Any attempt on the part of the United States to impose a set of conditions on the region will be resisted and ultimately rejected. However, rules that are compatible with ASEAN's security objectives and that operate through ASEAN-sponsored multilateral channels will receive ASEAN's support.

ASEAN SECURITY INTERESTS: THE CHINA FACTOR

DESPITE ASEAN's reputation for political unity and cohesion, each ASEAN member faces a different predicament and has a different perspective on regional security issues. The divergence in their perceived threats and strategic priorities has inhibited security cooperation. The strategic uncertainties of the multipolar post–Cold War world, and the recent expansion of ASEAN to include Vietnam, are likely to put ASEAN's "consensual and consultative" decisionmaking style under further stress.

There are some broad areas of commonality in the ASEAN states' security interests. All members recognize that the end of the Cold War is a mixed blessing. Among the positive consequences that ASEAN can count from this are the political settlement of the Cambodian conflict, the end of the long and bitter ideological polarization of Southeast Asia, the collapse of the communist insurgencies that were threatening ASEAN regimes, and the removal of the regional threat posed by the Soviet navy. However, those sources of insecurity have been replaced by new concerns. In general, ASEAN policymakers seem to miss the components that provided the relative stability of the Cold War: the fairly simple framework of strategic bipolarity, the predictability of alignments, the balance of power maintained by superpower military deployments, and the ability of the superpowers to quell regional conflicts by restraining their clients. They see the post–Cold War era as a more dangerous period because the balance of power tends to be more fluid, threats are more complex, alignments less predictable, and the prospects for conflict resolution less certain.

The major security concerns of the ASEAN states arise from the changing balance among the major Asia-Pacific powers, territorial disputes, both within ASEAN and the wider regional disputes in the South China Sea, domestic instability caused by ethnic separatist movements, and the demands for regime change that are being generated by rapid economic growth. While domestic political instability and threats to national cohesion remain significant factors in the ASEAN states' security planning, there has been a discernable shift in attention to external security threats.

The external sources of insecurity include a host of intra-ASEAN territorial disputes: between Malaysia and Singapore over Pedra Branca Island off the coast of the Malaysian state of Johor; between Malaysia and Indonesia over Sipadan and Ligitan Islands in the Sulawesi Sea near the Sabah-Kalimantan border; between Malaysia and Thailand over a 1922 treaty that allows Thai military personnel to conduct cross-border operations; between Malaysia and Brunei over the Limbang area in Sarawak; and between the Philippines and Malaysia over Sabah. In addition, there are over a dozen maritime boundary disputes in the South China Sea, the Gulf of Thailand, and the eastern Sabah-Sulu Archipelago region. Most intra-ASEAN conflicts are low-intensity in nature, however, and should not be viewed as serious threats to regional stability. ASEAN's worst-case scenarios involve the larger powers surrounding Southeast Asia, especially China.

China's size, proximity, and power ensures it a dominant place in the ASEAN states' strategic perceptions. Indeed, for Malaysia's prime minister, Mahathir Mohammed, the growing economic and military power of China is the "most worrisome" development in East Asia in the post–Cold War era.[1] Three factors have played a major role in shaping ASEAN's concerns about Chinese power. The first is China's involvement in the South China Sea, particularly the dispute over the Spratly Islands. The ASEAN states view the South China Sea as the most likely flashpoint of future conflict. Vietnam's entry into ASEAN makes it the first ASEAN member to have a history of direct military confrontation with China. With four ASEAN members—Brunei, the Philippines, Malaysia, and Vietnam—directly involved in the Spratlys dispute and one, Indonesia, uneasy about Chinese intentions towards Natuna Island, the South China Sea has become a China-ASEAN dispute. Moreover, the dependence of ASEAN members on maritime trade means the organization is deeply concerned about possible Chinese control over the strategic sea lanes in the South China Sea. Even Singapore, which strongly supports engagement with China and is not a party to the dispute, has declared the freedom of air and sea passage through the South China Sea a big issue in which the island republic, the world's most trade-dependent nation, has a vital interest. Singapore's leaders have raised the issue of navigation safety in the South China Sea in discussions with their Chinese counterparts.[2]

China's occupation of Mischief Reef, which is within waters claimed by the Philippines, came to public notice in 1995 and shattered the assumption long-held within ASEAN that Beijing would be more moderate in dealing with noncommunist ASEAN parties to the dispute than it had been with Vietnam, with whom China had fought naval battles in 1988. The fact that China chose the least-capable ASEAN member (in military terms) against which to assert its claim could only fuel suspicion that this was a calculated and opportunistic move to expand China's military presence in the South China Sea at the expense of ASEAN members. ASEAN is increasingly skeptical that China is seeking a peaceful solution to the dispute; Chinese declarations on this issue are often ambiguous and contradictory. For example, ASEAN welcomed Chinese foreign minister Qian Qichen's announcement last year that Beijing would accept the Law of the Sea as a basis for resolving the South China Sea dispute and begin working toward that goal in multilateral talks with ASEAN, but a Chinese foreign ministry spokesman soon reasserted China's "indisputable sovereignty over the islands and their adjacent waters" and referred to bilateral channels as the best way of managing the conflict.[3]

Citing the Chinese military buildup in the South China Sea, B. A. Hamzah, director-general of the Malaysian Institute of Maritime Affairs, warns that China's ultimate strategic objective is to "convert the entire South China Sea into a Chinese lake."[4] In the Philippines, Orlando Mercado, chairman of the Philippines Senate Committee on National Defense and Security, points to China's "double-edged strategy of maintaining friendly ties with its neighbors while slowly and clandestinely expanding its military presence in strategic waters" and carrying out "officially-approved freelance piracy, illegal fishing and poaching" in the South and East China Seas.[5]

Another source of ASEAN's concerns about China is the changing balance of power in the Asia-Pacific. More than any other regional power, including Japan or India, China is seen as a major beneficiary of the end of the Cold War. In the words of two senior Malaysian defense officials, China is the one power "potentially capable of posing a major strategic threat to the region."[6] These officials view China's defense modernization program as a means of creating an offensive power-projection capability. Among other things, China's military modernization program involves the expansion of rapid-reaction forces, the extension of the range and capability of the Chinese navy, the provision of air cover for the fleet, the training of highly mobile airborne troops, and the acquisition of "amphibious offensive capability" through the creation of a marine corps. The new Chinese military strategy "treats the ocean as strategic space and the navy as an instrument for control of the ocean. This strategy envisages the encounter and defeat of enemies in the ocean rather than at its doorstep."[7]

ASEAN's perceptions of China also continue to be influenced by the ethnic Chinese population in the region. Malaysia and Indonesia have historically been suspicious of their ethnic Chinese citizens, and anti-Chinese riots took place in Indonesia as recently as 1994. China's protest against Indonesia's handling of these riots drew a sharp response from Jakarta, which accused Beijing of interfering in Indonesia's domestic affairs. Although China's decision in the 1980s to stop supporting communist insurgencies in ASEAN states—whose cadres, especially in Malaysia and Indonesia, included a large number of ethnic Chinese—has removed a major obstacle to improved Sino-ASEAN relations, the relative wealth ethnic Chinese in these societies remains a source of resentment. Moreover, in Malaysia and Indonesia the surge of investment by ethnic Chinese businessmen in mainland China has become a politically sensitive issue, with opposition politicians in Malaysia questioning the loyalty of their ethnic Chinese businessmen. Thus, the emergence of China as a major power will have significant implications for inter-ethnic relations within some ASEAN states, which in turn will color their regimes' perceptions of China as a security threat.

To date, ASEAN governments have been reluctant to publicly voice their security concerns about China, which they occasionally see as unduly provocative and contrary to the "ASEAN way" of dealing with conflict. Malaysian prime minister Mahathir has been quoted as saying that the "U.S. naval fleets in East Asia were a waste of money as there was nothing to fear from either Japan or China."[8] Military leaders in the region have been less reticent in raising the alarm about China.

Benny Murdani, a former defense minister of Indonesia, speaks of the "lack of trust" with respect to China's strategic intentions and capabilities. The defense minister of Singapore has stated that "everybody in the region is fearful that an economically stronger China may choose to exercise that strength in a manner that is not in the interests of the region."[9]

ASEAN countries worry about the prospect of being on the receiving end of direct military pressure from Beijing, and they are troubled by the likely implications of China's growing military power for regional stability as a whole. They fear that Chinese military assertiveness will set the stage for an intense Sino-Japanese rivalry, as well as a Sino-Indian competition. Try Sutrisno, former commander of the Indonesian armed forces and currently the country's vice president, warns that a decrease in U.S. military power in Asia would encourage the stronger Asian states, such as China and Japan, to "emerge and vie for influence in the region."[10] A related concern of ASEAN members is that a strong and belligerent American response to Chinese power would stoke nationalist and hard-line sentiments in China and will be highly destabilizing for the region. Thus, Singapore's senior minister, Lee Kuan Yew warns that a Sino-U.S. confrontation will mean that "the medium and small countries of the region will have to live with the results of an aroused and xenophobic China."[11]

As Paul Evans and I have noted elsewhere, within the Asia-Pacific region there are different perspectives on the causes and implications of China's military buildup.[12] Two broad views can be discerned. The relatively benign view is that China's leadership is principally concerned with economic reform and domestic stability rather than regional expansion through military power. China's economic development strategy cannot be sustained in a tense regional climate, which would be inevitable if Beijing were to attempt sustained military expansion. China's dependence on foreign trade, markets, and investment will thus constrain its ability to threaten its neighbors or seek regional hegemony. An outward-looking Chinese military would surely subvert the inward-looking political strategy of the Chinese leadership, which is seeking legitimacy through economic performance. Moreover, according to this benign view, China's military control over the South China Sea is still insignificant, and Beijing faces serious logistical and technological constraints in developing its power-projection capability. China may succeed in denying other claimants any access to South China Sea resources, but it cannot secure exclusive control over them, especially since they cannot be exploited without Western technology and capital. While China's defense budget has increased, so have others in the region. Those who hold this view also point out that China's military procurement from abroad is geared to modernizing hopelessly obsolete equipment and that, in any case, it is not clear how long China can sustain double-digit increases to its defense budget. Last, but not the least, it is argued that a stronger and more modern Chinese military might be beneficial for regional security because it would deter Japanese regional ambitions.

Many military analysts and policymakers have assumptions about the scope and purposes of Chinese military power that are virtually opposite. They note that China's military buildup is proceeding rapidly despite a substantial easing of its security concerns as a result of the demise of the Soviet Union, the weakening of Vietnam's armed forces due to the loss of Soviet aid and Hanoi's attention to domestic reform, and a slowdown in India's military buildup because of economic and political constraints. They see a clear albeit long-term effort by China to increase its power-projection capabilities, which is shifting the regional balance of power in favor of Beijing. The most affected regions will be the South China Sea and Southeast Asia, which are natural spheres for the exercise of Chinese hegemony. Furthermore, the Chinese threat to Southeast Asia appears to have shifted from political subversion to direct military coercion. The end of the Cold War has contributed to this shift by removing some of the constraints on China's ability to use force in support of its territorial claims, especially since China no longer has any incentive to seek ASEAN's diplomatic support against Vietnam on the issue of Cambodia. Beijing's current commitment to the peaceful settlement of disputes is dismissed as a tactic to buy time until it completes its military modernization program. Proof of this can be found in the contradictions between China's declared policy and its actions on the Spratly Islands issue. While recognizing the disputed status of the islands and supporting a negotiated settlement, China has steadily increased the number of islands under its occupation and claimed sovereignty over them through national legislation.[14]

ASEAN's security fears about China surely are tempered by a recognition of the opportunities that exist for economic and political cooperation. China's economic reforms have created major trade and investment opportunities for the ASEAN states, but they might also divert foreign investment away from ASEAN. China is the focus of Singapore's attempts to develop an "external economy." Even Malaysia, despite its deep-rooted suspicion of China, has moved aggressively to exploit business opportunities there. The ASEAN states and China hold similar views on human rights and democracy and agree on the need for political cooperation in countering Western perspectives and pressure on these issues. Moreover, the ASEAN countries recognize that China has an interest in maintaining a close political relationship with them. China is likely to find ASEAN's support useful in dealing with the West, not only on human rights issues, but also on trade matters. This may have a moderating impact on China's hard-line policy on territorial disputes. As one Singaporean journalist puts it, "By appeasing ASEAN on the South China Sea question, they [the Chinese] will be able to better handle the Americans."[15]

The close Sino-ASEAN political relationship that emerged during the 1980s was predicated on China's need for ASEAN's diplomatic backing against its main Cold War adversaries, Vietnam and Russia. But the end of the Cold War and the settlement of the Cambodian conflict removed one of the foundation's for Sino-ASEAN political understanding. Agreements in principle on economic interdependence and "soft authoritarian" government are not enough to overcome the deeply ingrained suspicions about China's strategic aims in some ASEAN circles.

All of this suggests that security planners in the ASEAN states will agree with the overall emphasis of a conditional engagement strategy: that China is the most critical security issue for the Asia-Pacific region in the post–Cold War era. China is not the only security concern for ASEAN, but it is clearly among the most important. And although the ASEAN states refuse to publicly raise or discuss the China threat, they are concerned about the buildup of Chinese military power, Chinese policy toward the South China Sea, and Beijing's potential for regional domination.

ASEAN'S SECURITY IN THE POST-COLD WAR ERA

ASEAN's security goals in the post–Cold War era are to: deny any nation the power to dominate the Asia-Pacific; maintain the region's rapid economic growth to sustain the legitimacy of existing regimes and contain demands for political change; peacefully manage the region's territorial disputes; prevent an arms race in the region; keep the United States strategically engaged in the region; ensure greater political, economic, and cultural integration among the 10 countries of Southeast Asia; and acquire greater bargaining power for Southeast Asia in international institutions, including a major voice for ASEAN in emerging regional economic, political, and security institutions.

The pursuit of these objectives in the post–Cold War strategic environment has led ASEAN to change its approach to regional order. In general terms, ASEAN has moved from an indirect, inward-looking, subregional, exclusionary approach to security issues toward a more direct, outward-looking, extra-regional, and inclusive approach. During the Cold War, ASEAN remained more or less preoccupied with security issues within the Southeast Asia subregion, such as the threats posed by communist insurgency and the Vietnamese invasion of Cambodia, and with its stated goal of keeping Southeast Asia insulated from the great-power rivalry. It is now assuming the more ambitious role of managing regional order throughout the wider Asia-Pacific region, which entails creating a stable balance among the region's principal powers.

Two aspects of ASEAN's changing approach to regional order are especially noteworthy. The first is the expansion of ASEAN itself. Vietnam became the organization's seventh member in July 1995, Cambodia and Laos have acquired observer status, and Myanmar has signed the Treaty of Amity as the first step in gaining observer status and eventual full membership. With a population of 72 million (the second largest among ASEAN members after Indonesia's) and an armed force of 800,000 (the largest in Southeast Asia), Vietnam adds significantly to ASEAN's political clout and bargaining power, especially in dealing with China. Some analysts have speculated that the entry of Vietnam into ASEAN has already contributed to China's flexibility on regional security matters, for example, Beijing's recent acceptance of international maritime conventions as a basis for a negotiated settlement of the South China Sea dispute.[16] By the same token, Vietnam's inclusion has raised concerns that it might dilute ASEAN's unity and consensual decisionmaking style, which has been founded on a highly informal and interpersonal basis since the organization's creation.

The second notable aspect is ASEAN's central role in instituting the primary vehicle for multilateral security dialogues among the Asia-Pacific countries. Its effort culminated in the birth of the ASEAN Regional Forum (ARF) in 1994. ARF's members include the seven ASEAN members and the United States, Canada, Japan, South Korea, China, Cambodia, Australia, New Zealand, Papua New Guinea, Russia, and the European Union. ASEAN's interest and role in creating ARF came in response to a number of developments. As a result of growing economic linkages and the transregional interests and roles of powers such as the United States, Japan, and China, the security concerns of Northeast Asia and Southeast Asia have increasingly overlapped. Therefore, security management in Southeast Asia could no longer be insulated from the changing balance of power in the wider Asia-Pacific region. Moreover, earlier proposals for a new multilateral security framework for the Asia-Pacific—made by the Soviet Union, Australia, and Canada—presented a serious challenge to ASEAN. Rather than let outside powers seize the initiative, it devised an indigenous framework that would give itself a central role in any multilateral approach to regional security affairs.

After a quarter century of evolution, ASEAN now has a self-confident and mature identity. The relative prosperity of its members and its proven ability to survive difficult internal and external challenges have earned ASEAN respect from outside powers, and it commands their support for its approach to regional order. The growing prosperity of ASEAN members gives them the ability to sponsor international initiatives and institutions, such as ARF. ASEAN's changing approach to security issues has important implications for a strategy of conditional engagement. Although its members place great value on the U.S. military presence in the region, they are not likely to blindly accept any American-sponsored strategic framework, especially if it undermines ASEAN's interests and initiatives.

ASEAN AND U.S. REGIONAL SECURITY POLICY

THE END OF THE Cold War has brought about more of a consensus among ASEAN members on the stabilizing role of the U.S. military. During the Cold War, Indonesia and Malaysia, which were officially nonaligned nations, desired neither superpower to maintain major military deployments in the region. Singapore and Thailand, on the other hand, strongly supported the U.S. military presence. Indonesia now openly recognizes the need for the United States to play the role of regional balancer, and even Vietnam sees the American presence as a critical counterweight to China. Almost all the ASEAN members have moved to strengthen their defense relationships with the United States. Singapore, Brunei, Indonesia, and Malaysia have each offered to allow the United States to build logistical and repair facilities for American naval and air craft, and the Philippines is seeking renewed military cooperation with the United States, especially in light of the conflict with China over Mischief Reef.

ASEAN might react very differently to each of the four U.S. regional security alternatives outlined by Jonathan Pollack: strategic autonomy, liberal internationalism, preemptive containment, and conditional engagement. Strategic autonomy, implying an isolationist America, represents one of the worst security fears of ASEAN policymakers because if adopted, it would lead to a serious reduction in the U.S. military presence in the region. In addition to removing a counterweight to Chinese military power, it would require ASEAN to become more self-reliant, spark a military buildup—possibly an arms race—and revive Japanese militarism. Given the memory of Japan's wartime deeds, ASEAN will not accept a Japanese role in regional security outside the framework of the U.S.-Japan security relationship. Many ASEAN security planners fear that a creeping Japanese remilitarization could develop out of Japan's effort to protect sea lanes, which entails policing areas as far as 1,000 miles from its shores. If Japan's naval power continues to grow more self-reliant, any rupture in the U.S.-Japan security relationship would be especially destabilizing. As Lee Kuan Yew warns, "The impact of such developments will be to divert the focus of Southeast Asia from economic development towards defense. Increased defense forces will lead to increased suspicions and tensions."[17]

Neither China nor Japan is acceptable to ASEAN states as a security guarantor. Thus, ASEAN regards an American policy of strategic autonomy as the least desirable scenario. Yet many ASEAN policymakers, in their search for a new security order, are beginning to foresee it as a long-term possibility. Despite repeated assurances by American officials that the United States intends to remain a strong Pacific military power and a recognition that technological advances have made it possible for the United States to project its power rapidly from remote Pacific or continental U.S. bases, there is a growing feeling within ASEAN that the American military presence—indeed, the ability of the United States to provide a security umbrella in the region—can no longer be taken for granted. Domestic factors, such as the declining American economic performance and the U.S. public's reaction to trade disputes with Asian countries, may ultimately drive Washington to drastically reduce its military presence in East Asia. Similarly, improved security prospects in the region, such as a peaceful reunification of Korea, would remove much of the rationale for a sustained American presence.

If ASEAN policymakers view strategic autonomy as destabilizing, they are likely to see an American strategy of liberal internationalism, premised largely on the pacific effects of economic interdependence, as naive. The argument that interdependence contributes to peace and stability has many critics. Skeptics argue that European economic interdependence did not prevent the outbreak of World War I. And the current prospects for war between China and Taiwan, despite their significant economic interdependence, cannot be ruled out. The fact that North Korea remains outside the framework of Asia-Pacific economic interdependence also creates a problem. Although ASEAN countries see the growing economic ties within Asia as a positive development, they also know that interdependence can be a double-edged sword that leads to trade frictions, disputes over migrant labor, competition over investments, and a host of other economic conflicts that can negatively affect political and security relations. Moreover, in ASEAN capitals, American liberal internationalism is often associated with the less savory aspects of U.S. global hegemony, including a tendency to impose American values and methods of governance on Asian societies. An American

assumption of a liberalizing mission toward authoritarian
domestic political systems in Asia is seen in some ASEAN capitals,
including Singapore, Kuala Lumpur, Hanoi, and Jakarta as being
selective, self-serving, and counterproductive.

A security approach based on preemptive containment is
also not acceptable to ASEAN. Notwithstanding their fear of
China, the ASEAN states agree that the best way to deal with Beijing is engagement, not containment. ASEAN cannot pursue a
containment strategy by itself because the collective military
capability of its members, Vietnam included, is no match for the
Chinese military. Moreover, a containment strategy would
require ASEAN to become a military alliance, something its members continue to reject in no uncertain terms. Such a strategy
would mean more security dependence on outside powers, particularly the United States, at a time when ASEAN is pursuing
greater self-reliance and regional autonomy. Accepting a containment strategy under American leadership would be tanta-
mount to acknowledging the failure of its own political approach
to regional order, which is based on the principles of inclusiveness and "cooperative security" (i.e., security with as opposed to
security against a likely adversary). To the extent that ASEAN sees
itself as the centerpiece of a new Asia-Pacific regional security
framework, the adoption of a containment strategy would be an
admission of failure because it would also mean accepting
renewed great-power intervention and rivalry in Southeast Asia.

To reject containment does not, however, imply a total
aversion to a strategic posture based on deterrence and disincentives. ASEAN states are likely to hedge against the failure of
their cooperative security approach by retaining more conventional balancing options. Given the problems of developing a
credible multilateral forum—especially China's opposition to
such a forum—the aspirations of ASEAN multilateralists to "contain China by other means" could prove unrealistic. Countering
Chinese military power through unilateral means (arms acquisitions) or external security alliances remains an essential secu-

rity option. ASEAN states lack the military ability to deter or balance China singlehandedly. Nonetheless, they may be able to develop a "denial" capability, one that substantially raises the costs of Chinese aggression or attempts to control vital sea lanes in the region. The dramatic growth of defense spending among ASEAN members and their emphasis on naval and air force capabilities underscores the emphasis they place on this strategy.

To the extent that the strategy of conditional engagement would keep America "engaged" in the region and prevent an outright confrontation with China, it would serve ASEAN's security interests. An acceptable strategy of conditional engagement would also address ASEAN's desire to prevent Japanese remilitarization and inhibit China's potential for regional hegemony.

The virtual alliance concept—a loose network of access arrangements between the United States and regional states—is integral to the conditional engagement strategy and consistent with ASEAN's approach to security issues. As Indonesian foreign minister Ali Alatas puts it, although the U.S. military presence in the region has become a "part of life," it "need not take the form of military bases."[18] To some extent, the shape of U.S.-ASEAN defense cooperation under a virtual alliance parallels ASEAN's own approach to intra-regional defense cooperation. Although the ASEAN countries continue to reject the need for developing a formal military alliance among themselves, that does not rule out significant, if informal, multilateral military cooperation against a future external threat. To date, defense ties among the ASEAN states, such as intelligence exchanges, joint exercises, and sharing of training facilities, have been developed on a bilateral basis only. In the view of ASEAN leaders, a military pact may be too provocative to potential adversaries (Vietnam in the past, China now), and an alliance requires the perception of common threat. The ASEAN countries not only worry about different external threats but harbor distrust and antagonism regarding each other, and as a result they engage in contingency planning against their ostensible partners, as in the case of Singapore and Malaysia. Nonetheless, the rapid proliferation of overlapping bilateral defense ties among the ASEAN members in the 1980s has resulted in what might be called a virtual defense regime within ASEAN, known in ASEAN military circles as a "defense spider's web." At the very least, defense linkages among ASEAN states have contributed to greater mutual trust and, more significant, to an increased potential for inter-operability among ASEAN military units in a crisis. Thus, even if ASEAN now resists signing a formal defense pact, member states could conceivably cooperate on an informal basis should the need arise. Malaysian defense minister Najib Razak said as much in 1993: "There is nothing to prevent ASEAN from acting collectively if there is the political will to do so. If there is a need to have an ASEAN military force, it could be done almost overnight."[19]

The virtual nature of intra-ASEAN defense cooperation holds implications for the U.S.-ASEAN security relationship and the conditional engagement strategy. Joint military exercises with individual ASEAN states could facilitate greater defense cooperation among the ASEAN states themselves. The Cobra Gold exercises between the United States and Thailand, for example, are now open to military observers from other ASEAN states. In 1994, Singaporean officers became the first outsiders to observe the entire process. If the Team Spirit exercises between the United States and South Korea are permanently halted, joint U.S. exercises with the ASEAN states will assume greater significance.

Despite a history of deep mutual distrust, Singapore and Malaysia have been able to cooperate militarily within the framework of the Five Power Defense Arrangement which includes Australia, New Zealand and the United States. An invitation from Washington to Malaysia to join in military exercises with the Philippines could promote defense cooperation between the two ASEAN members and enhance their ability to counter the Chinese threat in the Spratlys. They have found it difficult to develop military ties because of their longstanding dispute over Sabah. Gradually opening up such exercises to even more nations could be an important component of a conditional engagement strategy, complementing other areas of U.S.-ASEAN defense cooperation, such as military education and training (which has been slowed by human rights concerns in Congress), arms transfers, and U.S. participation in the development of indigenous defense industries in the ASEAN states.

A conditional engagement strategy could be creatively tailored to meet ASEAN's post–Cold War defense needs, but that alone will not ensure a positive response by the ASEAN states. ASEAN's acceptance of a conditional engagement strategy will depend upon the rules of behavior that would form the basis of such a strategy, the manner in which the rules were developed and implemented, and on how such a strategy fits into ASEAN's own multilateral approach to regional security.

ASEAN AND THE RULES OF BEHAVIOR

A CENTRAL ELEMENT of the conditional engagement strategy, as described by Jonathan Pollack, is a set of "rules of acceptable behavior," or "norms of behavior, combined with a few specific do's and don'ts." The ASEAN states are generally supportive of rule-governed conduct in interstate relations. In fact, ASEAN takes credit for being the first regional grouping in the Asia-Pacific to develop a code of conduct for its members and encourage peaceful interstate relations. As Musa Hitam, a senior Malaysian statesman, notes:

> Because of ASEAN, we have been able to establish the fundamental ground rules for the game of peace and amity between us all. What are these fundamental ground rules? First, the principle of strict non-interference in each other's internal affairs. Second, the principle of pacific settlement of disputes. Third, respect for each other's inde-

pendence. Fourth, strict respect for the territorial integrity of each of the ASEAN states. The ASEAN states have
declared these ground rules . . . [and] we have enacted
them, we have imbibed them, and most important, we
have acted and lived by them.[20]

ASEAN's ground rules[21] were formally enumerated in two major
documents: the 1967 Bangkok Declaration announcing ASEAN's
creation, and the Treaty of Amity and Cooperation signed at the
first summit meeting of ASEAN leaders in 1976. Among these
rules, five derived from the 1976 treaty are especially relevant to
the discussion. The signatories agreed to show respect for the
independence, sovereignty, and territorial integrity of all
nations; acknowledged the right of every state to govern itself
free from external interference, subversion, and coercion;
pledged non-interference in the internal affairs of one another;
agreed to seek the "settlement of differences and disputes by
peaceful means"; and promised not to threaten the use of force.[22]

The first meeting of the ASEAN Regional Forum (ARF) held
in Bangkok in July 1994 agreed to "endorse the purposes and
principles" of ASEAN's Treaty of Amity and Cooperation "as a
code of conduct governing relations between states and a unique
diplomatic instrument for regional confidence building, preventive diplomacy and political and security cooperation."[23] As a
signal of its commitment to inclusiveness, ASEAN, which has
been reluctant to let nonmembers sign the treaty, is now prepar-

---

THE TEN PRINCIPLES OF CONDITIONAL ENGAGEMENT

1. No unilateral use of offensive
   military force
2. Peaceful resolution of territorial
   disputes
3. Respect for national sovereignty
4. Freedom of navigation
5. Moderation in military force
   buildup
6. Transparency of military forces
7. Nonproliferation of weapons of
   mass destruction
8. Market access for trade and
   investment
9. Cooperative solutions for
   transnational problems
10. Respect for basic human rights

ing a protocol that would enable them to declare their support for adherence to the treaty's principles of cooperation.[24]

In 1995, on the occasion of the second ARF meeting, held in Brunei, the Philippine foreign secretary, Domingo Siazon, called for the "rule of law and reason, a mutually accepted code of behavior, in place of the arbitrary assertion of sovereignty" over the islands in the South China Sea.[25] Russia also suggested the need for what its former foreign minister, Andrei Kozyrev, called a "code of conduct for interstate contacts" in the Asia-Pacific region, to be based on a declaration drafted by Russian diplomats and circulated at the Brunei meeting, "On Principles of Security and Stability in the Asia-Pacific Region."[26]

Of the ten principles of the conditional engagement strategy, the principles on no use of force, peaceful territorial resolution, and the respect for sovereignty are almost identical to the ones enshrined in ASEAN's Treaty of Amity and Cooperation. The principles on freedom of navigation, nonproliferation, market access, and transnational problems are broadly consistent with ASEAN's commitment to regional cooperation. The remaining principles—moderation in military buildup, transparency of military forces, and respect for human rights—would also be generally acceptable to ASEAN. However, there are likely to be differences in interpretation over what constitutes moderate growth and adequate transparency of a state's military forces. ASEAN countries are reluctant to make their defense postures completely transparent, a reluctance they share with China. And although the strategy's proposed distinction between human rights and democratization would be important in terms of gaining ASEAN's acceptance, it might not be enough. ASEAN countries accept the universal nature of human rights, but they argue, like China, that the defense of human rights may vary depending on a nation's cultural, historical, and political circumstances. Some ASEAN leaders argue that human rights standards should conform to "Asian values," which include a recognition of the priority of societal rights over individual rights, of "society over self." Moreover, some ASEAN members, notably Indonesia, Singapore, Vietnam, and Malaysia, believe that economic rights, including the right to development, ought to have precedence over political and civil rights. Thus, negotiating an acceptable standard of human rights under the rules of acceptable behavior could prove difficult.

A policy of basing relations with China upon its acceptance of a set of rules of behavior mirrors Lee Kuan Yew's advice to Washington on how to deal with the rise of China. In 1993, at a meeting in Japan, Lee deplored the fact that China was increasingly being treated by various American groups as "a Third World, aid-dependent country." The way to deal with China, Lee said, was for the United States to take the lead in co-opting China into the management of international and regional order. This could be done by laying out the terms and conditions for China's participation. "If China refuses cooperation, if China wants trade, technical cooperation, and technology but keeps acting as a spoiler, then the position is totally different. I think the U.S., Japan and Europe will then be quite justified to say that this is a rogue outfit like the Soviet Union and should be treated as such."[27]

Even though ASEAN may find the proposed rules of behavior consistent with its own goals, it will not want the United States to impose them unilaterally. Such rules should be applied with multilateral backing and not only to China but to all Asia-Pacific countries equally. Thus, the substance of these rules will be less of an issue than the manner in which the United States goes about negotiating and implementing them. Ideally, the ASEAN states would have such rules negotiated and implemented in a low-key, consensual manner.

MULTILATERALISM, CONDITIONAL ENGAGEMENT, AND ARF

To ENSURE ASEAN's support for a strategy of conditional engagement, Washington will have to accord ARF a prominent place in the policy. One implication of such an acknowledgement is that Washington will have to recognize the importance of a multilateral approach to regional security. The Bush administration greeted multilateralism with open hostility (calling it "a solution in search of a problem") out of fear that it would undermine existing U.S. bilateral security arrangements in the region. The Clinton administration realizes that the Asian proponents of multilateralism, especially ASEAN, strongly support the U.S. military presence and regional alliance system. Accordingly, it has revised U.S. policy. Multilateralism is now one of the ten major goals of a new U.S. policy in Asia,[28] but its endorsement is qualified. Current U.S. policy on multilateralism envisages a concentric circle of security institutions, that includes its existing bilateral alliances, the newly developed security consultations within the ASEAN Post-Ministerial Conferences, and the ARF. The policy endorses multilateral action, where appropriate, by the actors most interested in resolving specific security problems, such as the one presented by the Korean Peninsula. But some within the Clinton administration remain ambivalent about the usefulness of a multilateral approach. As Joseph Nye, then an assistant secretary of defense, stated:

> East Asia is an area that ended the Cold War without major multilateral institutions, in contrast again with Europe, and this administration has made major efforts to add multilateralism. But let me make an important point here. The U.S. strategy is not based on multilateralism, the strategy is based on reaffirmation of the bilateral alliances we have: Japan, Australia, South Korea, so forth. And what we are doing is adding a set of multilateral institutions . . . around this core of the bilateral relationships. So while we are indeed stressing the increased importance of multilateral institutions, it's not at the cost of our primary attention to reinforcing the traditional security alliances we have in the region.[29]

This reaffirmed Secretary of State Warren Christopher's earlier statement that regional security dialogues "in no way supplant America's alliances or forward military presence in Asia."[30] The ASEAN nations, recognizing the salience of existing American security arrangements, will not quarrel with the strategic aspects of the Clinton agenda. But to the extent that conditional engagement goes beyond retaining the U.S. military commitments in the region and adds political rules of behavior, ASEAN will be uneasy unless such rules are applied through the ARF.

The ASEAN Regional Forum meeting in Brunei last year approved a set of concrete measures to promote security cooperation in the Asia-Pacific, such as voluntarily exchanging information on defense postures, increasing dialogue on security issues at the bilateral, subregional and regional levels, maintaining senior-level contacts and exchanges among military institutions, and encouraging the participation of ARF members in the U.N. Conventional Arms Register. Admittedly, these are modest initiatives, but ASEAN believes that they will lead to a range of measures for enhancing regional security, including confidence-building measures, preventive diplomacy, and, in ASEAN diplomatic jargon, an "elaboration of approaches to conflicts"—a less ambitious concept than "conflict resolution," which was unacceptable to China.

The ASEAN Regional Forum is in some respects limited as an instrument of regional security because of ASEAN's and China's extremely cautious approach toward institution-building. The ASEAN countries generally prefer informal ad hoc consultations to formal structured cooperation. This will make it difficult for ARF to take the initiative in conflict-resolution, confidence-building, and arms control. ARF does not include Taiwan or North Korea, parties to two of the region's ongoing conflicts. Also excluded initially, are South Asian actors, especially India, whose power-projection capabilities have already caused major concern in some ASEAN states. ARF also has a problem of adaptability. The ASEAN approach to regionalism and the so-called ASEAN way of conflict avoidance were conceived at a time when the threat of communist expansion served as the cement for an otherwise divided and disparate membership. ASEAN's internal norms and decisionmaking procedures, which remain largely interpersonal and informal, may not be appropriate to a wider and much more complex regional setting. Finally, many countries in the region continue to see bilateral alliances and bilateral resolution of conflicts as more practical and effective than multilateral approaches. They view multilateralism as an unknown quantity, in contrast to the proven efficacy of America's bilateral alliances for preserving regional stability.

The ASEAN states, however, are firmly committed to security multilateralism and intent on being in the "driver's seat" in developing ARF's agenda. A U.S. policy framework that is acceptable to ASEAN, must be consistent with ASEAN's goals and approach in developing ARF, which are as follows:

- ARF should evolve gradually and cooperation should be voluntary and consensual. It should not have a predetermined road map, and its main goal should be to promote dialogue and consultations rather than to build a formal and rigid security organization.

- ASEAN members should be in the "driver's seat" in ARF. While ASEAN should try to accommodate the concerns of all of ARF's members, it should have control over the ARF agenda. The larger powers within ARF should not seek to dominate it. They should recognize the equality of all members and the leadership role of ASEAN.

- ASEAN's code of conduct, based on the 1976 Treaty of Amity and Cooperation, should become the basis of interstate relations within ARF.

- ARF must not become a military pact, nor should it designate any country as an adversary. Security and defense cooperation among ARF members may be undertaken bilaterally or perhaps multilaterally, but the formation of military alliances should be discouraged.

- ARF should seek to engage China and bring it into a multilateral security structure. Any policy of containing China will be counterproductive and should be discouraged. (It should be noted, however, that following the Mischief Reef incident involving China and the Philippines, some ASEAN countries have become doubtful about whether engaging China will work.)

- ARF should not become a forum for the discussion of the human rights records of Asian governments, nor should it be used by the Western powers to promote their liberal democratic agenda.

- ARF should be the only region-wide security forum. The Asia Pacific Economic Cooperation (APEC) forum should focus exclusively on economic and trade issues. Any politicization of APEC should be avoided. Although some ASEAN policymakers and analysts recognize the need for a separate subregional security forum in Northeast Asia, they insist, however, that such a forum should be consistent with the principles and norms laid down by ARF and not be dominated by the major powers.

As we have seen, there are three main factors that will affect ASEAN's response to a strategy of conditional engagement—the extent to which such a strategy addresses ASEAN's major security concerns, the extent to which it keeps the United States involved in maintaining regional security, and the extent to which it complements and strengthens ASEAN's own security initiatives. The latter factor is likely to be the most problematic. ASEAN will not support the U.S. strategy unless care is taken to reconcile conditional engagement with ASEAN's homegrown multilateral approach and to avoid a unilateralist American approach to developing and implementing the strategy.

The conditional engagement strategy does address ASEAN's most serious security concern in the post–Cold War era—how to deal with Chinese military power. While the ASEAN states face a variety of other security challenges, most of them are low-intensity and ASEAN, based on past performance, should be able to handle them within its own institutional framework. The conditional engagement strategy is also in ASEAN's interest because it straddles an acceptable middle ground between the extremes of containment and appeasement.

ASEAN is likely to view the rules of behavior as a key element in a conditional engagement strategy. While substantively, the proposed rules should be acceptable to ASEAN, much depends on how the United States goes about negotiating them and setting them in motion. ASEAN will seek a central role in developing any set of norms for governing interstate relations. ASEAN will also want to ensure that such rules are developed in the context of ARF. Toward this end, ASEAN will demand a firmer U.S. commitment to multilateralism, notwithstanding its currently perceived limitations.

To be sure, the United States cannot, and should not, expect a unified ASEAN response to its security strategy for the Asia-Pacific. Moreover, if the U.S. military presence is reduced and American credibility declines, some ASEAN states can be expected to gravitate towards China. Others may seek to balance Chinese power by seeking security guarantees from other major powers. ASEAN will be watchful to see whether the U.S. policy establishment is able to abide by the principles and goals laid down in a strategy of conditional engagement. ASEAN policymakers are well aware of the bureaucratic inertia, interagency rivalry, and public opinion pressures that can derail even the most carefully thought-out U.S. strategy. American policy toward China is likely to remain a source of serious disagreement between those who favor conditional engagement and those who believe in a more hard-line, containment-oriented approach. An inability on the part of the United States to maintain consistency in implementing a conditional engagement approach will undermine American credibility and prompt ASEAN to search for alternative approaches.

NOTES

1. Michael Richardson, "China's Military Secrecy Raises Suspicions," *Asia-Pacific Defense Reporter* (June-July 1993), p. 24.
2. "China, U.S. Hope Maritime Safety Not Compromised in Spratly Dispute," *Agence France Presse Dispatch*, August 1, 1995.
3. See Amitav Acharya, "The ARF's Challenges," *Trends* 60 (August 26-27, 1995), Singapore: Institute of Southeast Asian Studies, p. 1.
4. Michael Richardson, "Beijing Casts Long Shadow Over the Nations of Southeast Asia," *International Herald Tribune*, May 30, 1994.
5. "Highlights, Luncheon Speech of Senator Orlando Mercado, Chairman, Senate Committee on National Defense and Security," ADTEX '95 panel discussion "Defense and Information Technology for Regional Cooperation," April 20-21, 1995, New World Hotel, Manila, p. 1."
6. Siti Azizah Abod and Jamil Rais Abdullah, "Defense Reorientation in Southeast Asia: Political and Military Implications," Paper presented to ADTEX '95 panel discussion "Defense Reorientation in Southeast Asia," April 20-21, 1995, New World Hotel, Manila, p. 6.
7. Ibid., pp. 6-7
8. Cited in J. N. Mak, "The ASEAN Naval Build-up: Implications for Regional Order," paper presented to the conference, "CBMS at Sea in the Asia Pacific Region: Meeting the Challenges of the 21st Century," Kuala Lumpur: Malaysian Institute of Maritime Affairs, August 2-3, 1994, p. 14.
9. Michael Richardson, "Modern Weaponry Makes Neighbors Uneasy," *International Herald Tribune*, December 2, 1992.
10. Michael Richardson, "Asia Sees a Risk in Tokyo-Beijing rivalry," *International Herald Tribune*, October 20, 1992.
11. "SM Lee, Kissinger Rap U.S. Policy towards China," *The Straits Times Weekly Edition*, November 20, 1993, p. 5.

12. Amitav Acharya and Paul Evans, "China's Defence Expenditures: Implications for Regional Security," *Eastern Asia Policy Papers* 1, (Toronto: University of Toronto—York University Joint Centre for Asia-Pacific Studies, 1994.)

13. Michael Leifer, "The Maritime Regime and Regional Security in East Asia," *Pacific Review* 4 (1991), pp. 130-33.

14. Mark Valencia, "The Regional Imperative," *Far Eastern Economic Review*, August 13, 1993, p. 20.

15. Yang Razali Kassim, "ASEAN Chalks Up Valuable Diplomatic Gains," *Business Times*, August 1, 1995.

16. One Southeast Asian diplomat has been quoted as saying: "I think ASEAN implicity sees the admission of Vietnam as containment of China. Vietnam has perhaps the strongest standing army in Southeast Asia. And I think Vietnam sees [ASEAN membership] as bolstering it as a front line state against China" (cited in Bill Tarrant, "Asia-Pacific Security Security Talks Focus on Spratlys," *Reuters World Service*, July 31, 1995). See also, Bill Tarrant, "China Seen Defusing Tensions in South China Sea," *Reuters World Service*, August 2, 1995.

17. Lee Kuan Yew, "Japan's Key Role in the Industrialisation of E. Asia," *The Straits Times*, February 14, 1992.

18. K. T. Arasu, "ASEAN Seeks Continued U.S. Military Presence," *Reuters World Service*, August 3, 1995.

19. Interview in *Jane's Defence Weekly*, December 18, 1993, p. 32.

20. Text of keynote address by Datuk Musa Hitam, delivered at the East-West Conference on ASEAN and the Pacific Basin, Honolulu, October 29, 1985, pp. 5-6.

21. Noordin Sopiee also refers to the "ground rules of inter-state relations within the ASEAN community with regard to conflict and its termination." He mentions four such rules: (1) "system-wide acceptance of the principle of the pacific settlement of disputes"; (2) "non-interference and non-intervention in the domestic affairs of member states"; (3) "respect for each other's territorial integrity and independence," and "the principle of not inviting external intervention on one's behalf in the pursuit of disputes." See "ASEAN and Regional Security" in *Regional Security in the Third World*, ed. Mohammed Ayoob, (London: Croom Helm, 1986, p. 229)

22. Tamthong Thongswasdi, *ASEAN after the Vietnam War: Stability and Development through Regional Cooperation*, Ph.D. diss., Claremont Graduate School, 1979, p. 123.

23. "Chairman's Statement," first meeting of the ASEAN Regional Forum (ARF), July 25, 1994, Bangkok, p. 2.

24. Lee Kim Chew, "ASEAN Has Entered New Phase in Development,"

The Straits Times (Singapore), July 28, 1994, p. 1.

25. "Siazon Calls for Code of Behavior in Spratlys," *Kyodo News Service* (Japan Economic Newswire), July 29, 1995.

26. "Kozyrev Attends ASEAN Conference," *BBC Summary of World Broadcasts*, part 1, former U.S.S.R.; Russia; SU/2371/B, August 2, 1995.

27. "Give China Role to Keep World Peace," *The Straits Times Weekly Edition*, November 6, 1993, p. 6.

28. Susumu Awanohara, "Group Therapy," *Far Eastern Economic Review*, April 15, 1993, pp. 10-11.

29. Transcript of Defense Department special briefing on East Asia strategy report by Joseph S. Nye, Jr., Assistant Secretary of Defense for International Security Affairs, February 27, 1995 (Washington D.C.: Federal News Service), p. 4.

30. "Asian and Pacific Links: A Sort of Safety," *The Economist*, July 31, 1993, p. 26.

11

The New Multilateralism and the Conditional Engagement of China

Paul M. Evans

FOR THE THIRD TIME in the twentieth century, the United States faces the fundamental challenge—and the opportunity—of adjusting its security policy toward the Asia-Pacific and of helping to establish a new regional security framework. The Washington Conference system, created in 1921-22 in the aftermath of the First World War, was much more than a naval arms control arrangement. It replaced what the historian Akira Iriye has called the "diplomacy of imperialism" with an international banking consortium set up to make loans to China. The Anglo-Japanese alliance was abrogated in favor of the Nine Power Treaty and other multinational agreements. Under these new rules of the game particularist agreements were swept away and principles were formulated to guide the conduct of other states with respect to China, among them the condemnation of spheres of influence, support for equal foreign opportunities in China, and confirmation of Chinese sovereignty, independence, and administrative integrity.[1]

After the war in the Pacific, America, faced with the victory of Chinese communism and the outbreak of the Korean conflict, was the prime mover behind a system of bilateral alliances and diplomatic arrangements centering on resistance to communism and the containment and isolation of communist China. In the 1970s, the definition of the threat shifted from China to the Soviet Union, but the United States maintained its bilateral security ties with key Asian partners.

By 1990 it was clear that the Cold War order in the Asia-Pacific was losing relevance, yet five years later, the new order is still amorphous. What is apparent is that the post-Cold War security framework in the region will almost certainly not be built as a response to a specific threat nor created by a single diplomatic conference. Rather, it will emerge from a more gradual process of accretion, adjustment, and evolution.

Nor will it be imposed from the outside. For the first time in a century and a half, the future of Asia is primarily in Asian hands. In this era of national states as opposed to empires, Asia is no longer racked by revolution but is in the midst of unprecedented economic growth and dynamism. The emergence of new patterns of trade and production within Asia and across the Pacific in the context of a global economy have intensified economic, political, social, and cultural connections throughout the region. Governments are increasingly self-confident and assertive. In geopolitical terms, while the United States remains the most powerful and comprehensive actor in the region, multipolarity is on the rise. Ronald Montaperto, a senior fellow at

---

THE TEN PRINCIPLES OF CONDITIONAL ENGAGEMENT

1. No unilateral use of offensive military force
2. Peaceful resolution of territorial disputes
3. Respect for national sovereignty
4. Freedom of navigation
5. Moderation in military force buildup
6. Transparency of military forces
7. Nonproliferation of weapons of mass destruction
8. Market access for trade and investment
9. Cooperative solutions for transnational problems
10. Respect for basic human rights

the National Defense University, accurately observes that the "nations of Asia are actively engaged in nothing less than a basic redefinition of the ways in which they order their relations with each other and with the trans-Pacific world."[2]

The increasingly complex international relations of the Asia-Pacific are much more than the sum of isolated national policies. Economic growth and integration are reshaping Asia. The consequences for political and security relations are immense but rarely examined in systemic fashion. One dimension is a new and visible self-confidence among Asian states, seen in their reaction to supposed Western intrusion in areas like human rights and trade policy. Another dimension is a growing uncertainty about the intentions and capabilities of the great powers. Can the United States sustain its forward deployment? Will Japan remilitarize? Will Russia collapse or veer toward aggressive nationalism? Whither China?

Another deeper uncertainty concerns what form a new security order will take. Asian intellectuals and policymakers have rarely articulated the mechanisms for maintaining peaceful relations between states that for 300 years have been a constant topic of discussion on the European scene. Moreover, the possibilities for Asia as a whole and the Asia-Pacific in particular are numerous, ranging from hegemonic and balance of power systems at one end of the spectrum, to various kinds of cooperative or common security systems at the other.

It is in this context that we must assess the search for an appropriate regional order and the outline of American policy. Neither the United States, China, nor any other single power is in a position to dictate the emerging order. Similarly, a new order will not be determined by any bilateral relationship, even one as important as the Sino-American relationship. Yet Sino-American relations will be a principal determinant of how fast and in what direction a new regional order will be built. The state of U.S.-Chinese relations will determine what can be accomplished in the region, and every country in Asia will calibrate its policies and expectations according to American and Chinese actions.

Viewed in wider perspective, the turbulent relations between the United States and China reflect not just the clash of national interests but two distinct approaches to international relations. With this in mind, the central issue becomes how the United States and the region should react to the rise of Chinese power. This is not just because of China's growing economic and military weight or because of worries about increasingly assertive Chinese nationalism. It is because of widespread uncertainty and apprehension about China's immediate intentions and its long-term ideas about the regional and world order. Repeated statements of benign intent by Chinese officials, invocations of the "Five Principles of Peaceful Coexistence,"[3] and even concrete steps by Beijing to improve bilateral relations with most of its Asian neighbors are increasingly ineffective in meeting international concerns.

It is in America's, and the region's, long-term interest to develop regularized processes for confidence building, preventive diplomacy, and conflict resolution. The major challenge for the United States and East Asia will be the construction of an institutional framework commensurate with the economic dynamism, geopolitical multipolarity, and national self-confidence that characterize the region. There is little enthusiasm in Asia for importing or imitating the institutions and approaches that have been developed in postwar Europe. This is partly a matter of recognizing divergent historical and cultural influences. It is also based on skepticism about the durability of peace in Europe and a reluctance to embrace the ideas of political integration and supranational institutions along the lines of the European Union. Nor can the leaders of the Asia-Pacific resurrect some golden past, for the simple reason that the state system is comparatively new to at least the Asian part of the region. Instead, the leaders need to create something new: a rule-governed regional system constructed on a base of Asian-inspired rules.

What progress has been achieved in creating such a rule-governed regional system or even habits of dialogue and consultation, Asian-style, that must be its precursors? Where does China fit into the regional process? And how can an American-led strategy for the conditional engagement of China contribute to the multilateral efforts currently in motion?

THE LOGIC OF CONDITIONAL ENGAGEMENT OF CHINA

CONDITIONAL ENGAGEMENT of China, as outlined by Jonathan Pollack, properly avoids stigmatizing or singularizing China. Rather, its objective is to devise a program to integrate China into a web of bilateral and multilateral arrangements that will encourage China's continued economic growth and promote stability in Asia. In the event this integration fails, mechanisms for constraining the growth and exercise of Chinese power will have to be established.

Several aspects of the strategy are appealing. First, the adjective "conditional" refers not to American engagement in the region (with the possibility that America will disengage if China does not meet particular conditions) but to the kind of policy that will be pursued as part of a continued American presence. Second, it is appropriate to a period of instability and uncertainty in which there is no consensus about the future configuration of power and the future direction of Chinese policy is indeterminate and, more important, still malleable and amenable to outside pressures. Third, it involves sending clear signals to China's leadership without resorting at the first sign of trouble to a policy of containment or isolation. Despite China's provocative actions in constructing new structures in early 1995 on Mischief Reef, a disputed area close to the Philippines, and testing missiles near Taiwan in the aftermath of Taiwan's President Lee Teng-hui's visit to the United States in June, it is premature and self-defeating to engage in what *the Economist* calls a strategy of "economic and strategic containment."[4] Fourth, it emphasizes the value of constructing rules and norms, and the importance of

China's participation in creating them; experience, at the United Nations and elsewhere has shown that China is much more likely to respect rules and processes it helps to formulate. Fifth, it acknowledges that although a policy of conditional engagement can be led by the United States it will only be successful if it has substantial regional support and is implemented through bilateral and multilateral mechanisms.

Moreover, conditional engagement suggests guidelines for assessing Chinese behavior that are interesting–if not definitive–starting points for discussion. China would be judged on whether it was willing to: forgo the unilateral use of force; desist from making irredentist claims; engage in the cooperative management of any "endgame" in North Korea; agree to a measured program of military acquisition; lend no support for the development of weapons of mass destruction; maintain transparency in defense doctrine and capabilities; and contribute to the building of a collaborative security structure.

The concept of conditional engagement also gives rise to a variety of questions:

- Is it appropriate for America? Does the United States have the political will and capacity to be vigilant and consistent in pursuing broad-based principles rather than its immediate interests in its relations with China? Can its "integration-based" as opposed to "threat-based" logic find support in Congress and among the public? Is it possible to generate political support for a strategy of engagement that does not identify human rights, democratization, and internal political change in China as central aims of U.S. policy?

- Is it acceptable to China? As Jianwei Wang suggests in his chapter, it can be made so, but a great deal of difficult discussion lies ahead, not only on principles and perceptions, but on issues like the South China Sea, defense modernization, and the future of Taiwan, Hong Kong, and Tibet.

- Recognizing that it is a strategy that cannot be implemented unilaterally, is it likely to be understood and accepted in the region? Are these "minimal" guidelines acceptable to China and other states in the region? How can such ideas as irredentism, transparency, and cooperative management be defined to the satisfaction of the United States, China, and the other states in the region? How and by whom will compliance or noncompliance be measured?

These are difficult questions. The answer to each depends on the way the overall strategy is linked to regional processes already in motion. Especially important in this respect is the gathering momentum of Asia-Pacific multilateralism. As Jonathan Pollack and others correctly argue, these multilateral processes and institutions are largely new to East Asia, do not form the principal feature of the region's current security architecture, and have an uncertain future.[5] Rather than focus on these multilateral efforts in their current forms, it is more useful to think of where they seem to be going and what they can offer if properly nurtured. They promise to be useful for managing existing regional conflicts, building confidence, and reducing tensions. But they also have the potential to transform regional arrangements so as to manage the rise of Chinese power far more effectively than the United States acting alone —or with its current allies—could do.

THE NEW MULTILATERALISM

MULTILATERALISM in the Asia-Pacific has taken on a new form different in character and leadership from the multilateralism of the Cold War years, when the idea was to create collective defense alliances through such organizations as the Southeast Asia Treaty Organization. This can be seen in at least five overlapping areas:

1. *Ad hoc cooperation* on specific disputes and areas of potential conflict. The Cambodian peace process was one example of such cooperation; the Indonesian-sponsored (and Canadian-funded) workshops on the South China Sea is another. And it is at least arguable that the ongoing efforts to resolve the North Korean nuclear issue are becoming increasingly multilateral in character, in part because of the involvement of such international institutions as the International Atomic Energy Agency and the newly established Korean Peninsula Energy Development Organization and in part because of the extensive consultations involving Washington, Tokyo, Seoul, Beijing, and Moscow.

2. *"Subregional" cooperation* in the creation of formal institutions, especially in Southeast Asia. The maturation of the Association of Southeast Asian Nations (ASEAN) and its gradual expansion to include all of the nations of Southeast Asia is the most important example of a formal routinized multilateral arrangement for political, economic, and security cooperation. ASEAN is important not only in the Southeast Asian context but as a leading force in Asia-Pacific-wide efforts to increase dialogue and mutual reassurance. This outward orientation has not come without considerable internal debate, but it presents the United States and Japan with an opportunity to foster a region-wide consensus on objectives and instruments.

3. *Formal governmental efforts at the regional, Asia–Pacific level.* The most significant of these has been the creation, in mid-1993, of the ASEAN Regional Forum (ARF).[6] In addition, there are at least four smaller, more exclusive annual or regular gatherings of diplomats, including the annual "quintilaterals" that bring together policy planners from Australia, Canada, Japan, South Korea, and the United

States. There are at least five regular multilateral military conferences and a growing number of multilateral military exercises. The U.S. Pacific Command has played a leading role, organizing several regionwide programs for military personnel and recently creating the Asia-Pacific Center for Security Studies in Honolulu.[7]

4. *Global institutions and processes.* The United Nations is playing an increasingly visible and significant role in regional matters. One dimension is the global norms, commitments, and principles established through such mechanisms as the nuclear Nonproliferation Treaty (NPT) and the U.N. Conventional Arms Registry, which are supported by almost all of the countries of the region. The United Nation's largest and most expensive entry in recent years under the heading of regional security was through its involvement in the U.N. Transitional Authority in Cambodia (UNTAC). U.N. regional organizations including the Economic and Social Commission for Asia in the Pacific (ESCAP) and the Regional Center for Peace and Disarmament in Asia and the Pacific have sponsored research projects, seminars, governmental dialogues, and public conferences on an array of security-related issues.

5. *Nongovernmental, track-two programs.* There are more than 30 nongovernmental, or "track-two," programs for the discussion of Asia-Pacific security matters, the most ambitious among them the Council for Security Cooperation in Asia Pacific.[8] These programs are diverse in their composition and objectives. They vary considerably in their definitions of the region and of security, in their interest in policy-related as compared to more theoretical issues, in the level of government participation and funding, in the extent to which they are based on original research and conceptualization, and in their size, longevity, and leader-

ship. But most extend beyond the like-minded to involve participants spanning the ideological and national spectrum. No fewer than eighteen countries have either sponsored or hosted such programs. One of these distinctive characteristics has been the "track-two" nature of many of the meetings. While these meetings deal with policy-related matters and include government officials (often of senior rank), the officials are there both as representatives of their government and in a private and personal capacity. The track-two concept has proven especially valuable in a region where there is little tradition of multilateral diplomacy and where significant sensitivities to formal government institutions still exist. In 1994, there were more than 90 such track-two multilateral meetings on regional security issues, significantly, almost all of these had a trans-Pacific axis and only two were exclusively Asian.[9]

The leadership of the multilateral process can best be described as diffuse. In the late 1980s and early 1990s at least eight governments proposed new mechanisms for multilateral security cooperation. Unsurprisingly, much of the early diplomatic and intellectual energy came from medium-size powers such as Australia, Canada, and the members of ASEAN, all of which have an abiding interest in institution building. One of the most significant features of the ensuing process has been that the great powers have continued to encourage these smaller powers to play leading roles. Japan has quietly but effectively supported several multilateral initiatives, especially the series of meetings that began in 1991 and led to the creation of the ASEAN Regional Forum. The Soviet Union was instrumental in launching the multilateral push in Asia in the mid-1980s, and Russia has continued to support the process, although it has not played a leadership role either conceptually or organizationally.

America's role has shifted significantly in the past five years. From skepticism and resistance in 1990, the U.S. government has moved toward active support for the regional dialogue process.[10] The U.S. government has supported ARF, encouraged an American-led track-two dialogue focusing on security cooperation in Northeast Asia, and recently created through the Pacific Command, the Asia-Pacific Center for Security Studies, the largest center in the region focusing on the non-war fighting aspects of regional security. Such multilateral activities are no longer seen either in Washington or Asia as diminishing or replacing bilateral alliances and friendships but as complementing them.

American nongovernmental organizations have encouraged the growth of multilateralism in the Asia-Pacific and other regions. Foundations and research institutes were well ahead of the government in organizing multilateral programs for dialogue, training, and research in the 1980s.[11] The capacity of these private institutions to initiate and sustain regional activities, usually in partnership with Asian counterparts, is a significant asset for the United States in shaping thought among governments and intellectuals in the region.

The achievements of these multilateral processes should not be blown out of proportion. Despite the recent publicity they have generated and their apparent momentum, their development has been characterized by caution, modest aims and expectations, and a comparatively slow-paced, incremental agenda. Discussions so far have focused on confidence-building measures, especially instruments for increasing transparency in defense doctrine and military capacities and intentions, and for conflict prevention. The Cambodian peace process is the only example of coordinated conflict resolution in the region. Nor has there been much progress in multilateral approaches to arms control. The level of institutionalization is also low; ARF, for example, does not have a permanent secretariat and is moving cautiously in establishing inter-sessional support groups.

Moreover, multilateralism's penetration into East Asia has been neither consistent nor universal. The historical pattern and current prospects of Northeast Asia are very different from those of Southeast Asia. Despite vigorous efforts by Canada, Mongolia, Russia, South Korea, Japan, and the United States to establish inclusive nongovernmental and government forums, discussions of security issues in Northeast Asia and the North Pacific have made very limited progress. Multilateral institutions are few and their focus is limited to economic and environmental issues. Some capitals, especially Pyongyang, even seem to be allergic to track-two multilateral dialogue on political security matters. North Korea has participated in very few multinational gatherings on Northeast Asia since the nuclear issue came to the fore in March 1993.[12]

Yet, it is also unwise to underestimate the significance of multilateral instruments in defining and building a new regional order. In combination, the activities of the late 1980s and early 1990s have done a great deal to legitimate multilateral discussion, increase the comfort level for new forms of intellectual and diplomatic communication, create a shared vocabulary, raise possibilities, lessen divisions, and, ironically, encourage new forms of bilateral cooperation (as, for example, between Japan and Korea).

CHINA AND REGIONAL MULTILATERALISM

IT IS NOT EASY to sum up China's reaction to the new multilateralism. In part this is because there is a major disjunction between Beijing's interest in multilateral and plurilateral economic institutions ranging from the Pacific Economic Cooperation Council and the Asia-Pacific Economic Cooperation (APEC) forum to the World Trade Organization (WTO) and the General Agreement on Tariffs and Trade (GATT) and its more guarded response to multilateral efforts addressing political and security issues. On security matters, the Chinese approach has been neither static nor obstructionist, but it has been of a different character than that of the other major states in the region. China's attitude toward regional security forums is at once skeptical, reluctant, and defensive. Its officials want a seat at the table but are reluctant to see the agenda of multilateral discussions widened or the pace of concrete multilateral efforts (in the ARF, for example) quickened.

With respect to the track-two process, research institutes attached to government ministries and agencies in China have initiated multilateral meetings only infrequently. In some instances they have made their attendance contingent on specific demands, including the omission of the South China Sea dispute from the official program. In almost every instance they have insisted that they will not participate in discussion of political-security issues if representatives from Taiwan are present, and their anxiety over the matter has increased markedly since Taiwan's President Lee Teng-hui's visit to the United States in the summer of 1995.

The case of China's participation in the Council for Security Cooperation in Asia Pacific (CSCAP) demonstrates some of the complications of engaging China in the new multilateralism. Some in CSCAP believe that China's involvement is essential to the vitality of the organization and to the broader strategy of engagement; others believe that it would be valuable but cannot come at the cost of conditions that violate the integrity of a nongovernmental organization committed to regional inclusiveness. The issue, as most CSCAP members see it, is less the inclusion of Taiwan (although this is seen as important) than giving Beijing the right to dictate terms.

Beijing in turn does not regard CSCAP as a nongovernmental organization but as a semigovernmental one. In taking a position on Taiwan's participation, it draws a firm distinction between the economic and cultural spheres on the one hand and political-security matters on the other, arguing that the latter are the exclusive preserve of sovereign states. China was a charter member of ARF but was not involved in the formation of CSCAP in November 1992. Thus some Chinese analysts see joining CSCAP as boarding a moving train; some of them have privately suggested that China's best course is to create its own track-two process.

China, of course, is not alone in its skepticism about the value of multilateral approaches to security, its attempts to keep specific issues off the multilateral agenda, or its maximization of bargaining power through its favoring of bilateral talks over multilateral ones. But the level of anxiety about regional multilateralism is greater in China than any other state except North Korea. China is not just a state but a civilization with a long tradition of interaction with its Asian neighbors and the West. The clash between Chinese conceptions of world order and those of foreign powers and international institutions has been a defining motif of China's relations with the world for more than a century and a half. In an era of rising Chinese power fueled by unprecedented economic growth, China's leaders are manifesting a traditional penchant for nationalism and balance of power thinking. The growing apprehension about China in Asia and across the Pacific is not merely a reaction to expanded Chinese capacities; it also reflects deeply rooted perceptions of Chinese cultural superiority coupled with territorial and psychological grievances.

Chinese experience and interests also militate against Beijing looking favorably on regional multilateralism. For most of the last two thousand years, China conducted its foreign relations under a tribute system based on hierarchy and what would now be called bilateral diplomacy. China's experience with multilateral institutions—including the League of Nations, the United Nations before 1971, and COMECON in the 1950s and 1960s—was scarcely a positive one, leaving it feeling betrayed, manipulated, and excluded. China also worries that key questions of sovereignty and territory, especially those concerning Taiwan and the South China Sea, will be "internationalized." Finally, rising powers rarely seek to gain entrance into international institutions that threaten to limit their spheres of action. That many governments, especially in Southeast Asia, take the view that the purpose of regional security institutions is to "enmesh" China—perhaps to bring collective pressure to bear on such issues as the South China Sea, perhaps more generally to engage China in the regional give-and-take in the grueling calendar of ASEAN events—is not lost on Chinese officials or defense analysts.

These factors are part of China's broader approach to world order. China prefers to place the emphasis on creating an ethos of trust rather than on formal institutions; on the sort of confidence building that focuses on unilateral declarations of benign intent, such as its "Five Principles of Peaceful Coexistence"; and on bilateral relations rather than formal multilateral treaties or intrusive verification regimes.

Chinese officials and intellectuals have expressed dissatisfaction with multilateral dialogues, complaining that China has frequently been unfairly singled out for criticism on its claims to the Spratly Islands, nuclear testing, transparency on matters of military capacity and doctrine, defense expenditures, and human rights. Their response has usually been defensive and occasionally angry, reflecting their deeply felt belief that the status quo powers, including the United States and Japan, are denying China the right to take the same path toward becoming a major power that they themselves took. This is clear in such areas as defense expenditure and transparency. The creation of a regional consensus on such issues, fostered by the regional multilateral process in conjunction with U.N. efforts, is making objections to "Western" norms less tenable. This is so because although regional opinion is influenced by the United States and Japan, it is not dominated by them.

These factors suggest that Chinese engagement in regional multilateralism will be cautious and limited for the near future. There are signs, however, that Beijing's attitude could become more positive over the longer run. In global forums like the United Nations, China's participation has been sophisticated and proactive. Beijing agreed to participate in ARF, although within the forum it has been the strongest voice for a slow-paced approach and reduced mandate for the inter-sessional working groups and meetings. China has not favored the formation of a sub-regional governmental process focusing on Northeast Asia or the Korean Peninsula, but it has participated in most of the track-two dialogue channels, albeit with a commitment to a slower agenda than most of the other participants.

In the track-two setting, Chinese officials and representatives of research institutes usually attend meetings to which they are invited, except in instances complicated by Taiwan's participation. Most important, China has continued to pursue a policy of openness in other areas. Significantly, it has shown a deep interest in economic organizations. And even in the political-security arena, Chinese research institutes and academic organizations have kept open the channels of communication with their counterparts outside China, participating in bilateral conferences and research and training programs. The flow of Chinese students and researchers abroad to study international relations is unabated.

China is thus at a crossroads with respect to its participation in regional multilateralism. Until recently, experts in Beijing tended to view multilateralism as inevitable and to believe that not participating in the process could be more dangerous than selective involvement.[13] In the wake of President Lee's visit to the United States, the collision over membership in CSCAP, and Beijing's worries about the direction of ARF and the speed with which it is moving, this view is being questioned. But the current emphasis in regional processes is on inclusiveness. No serious voice in the region is arguing for the isolation of China as in the 1950s and 1960s. If China is excluded from regional processes, its isolation will be self-imposed.

NEXT STEPS

THE CURIOUS truth about the new multilateralism is that it is in itself a form of conditional engagement for China as well as other participants. In the context of a soft multilateralism of dialogue and consultation, lines of communication and diplomatic interaction are created. While this has not led to the establishment of a firm set of rules or norms, the habit of dialogue is a first step in that direction.

For the moment, the objective of the architects of the multilateral process is to develop a soft process for inclusive dialogue and consultation rather than a hard organization for conflict management or resolution. Beijing's full participation would not only lead toward China's full integration into the region but would serve in the interim as a confidence-building measure. Few doubt that it is better to speak with China than about China. Should Beijing, however, decline to participate, the process will continue to move ahead. And were China to use force against one or more of its neighbors, what is currently an inclusive process could quickly turn into a loose coalition or even a collective defense arrangement.

It is conceivable, though far from desirable, that the main multilateral forums in the Asia-Pacific region that now champion inclusive dialogue could be reconfigured as organizations of the like-minded in an alliance-like stance. They would be more broadly based, and thus more effective, than the Cold War coalition formed by America's bilateral alliances. The convergence of regional opinion in support of economic openness and political reform is a major basis of the current process. ASEAN's style and pace cause concern in some quarters, and it is clearly difficult for that organization, given its makeup, to take a lead in managing the problems of Northeast Asia. But it is ASEAN that is setting the tone and direction of many of the most significant dialogues now under way.

Successful multilateral arrangements in the Asia-Pacific, as in Europe, may present a problem for American policymakers. The nations of the region do not want economic and human rights issues linked, for example, as U.S. administrations have done and threatened to do. And they may not always see eye to eye with Washington on the best ways to liberalize trade and open markets, or on how to manage specific disputes, as with Cambodia. But they will promote the rule-governed system that is in America's, and the region's, long-term interest.

A strategy of conditional engagement of China will have to be pursued at many levels and through multiple channels. The United Nations and other global institutions will have crucial roles to play with respect to arms control and nonproliferation, nuclear as well as conventional. At the regional level, China can be engaged most effectively on an Asia-Pacific basis rather than a narrower Northeast Asian/North Pacific basis, at least for the moment. Continuing bilateral dialogue, negotiations, and exchanges with China will also remain a vital part of the mix, not least because this is China's preferred level of interaction.

Regional institutions, organizations such as the Group of Seven, the International Monetary Fund, the World Bank, and other international financial institutions must work out common approaches to problems like measuring China's defense expenditures and assessing Chinese intentions. The United States can play a key role in setting the benchmarks in the areas that Jonathan Pollack has singled out and by entering into bilateral negotiations with China on their application. But any benchmarks set will be far more effective if they are the products of a multilateral process in which China participates. The track-two process faces special challenges, particularly on the issue of Taiwan's participation. It is possible that both China and Taiwan may participate in some activities but not in others.

If conditional engagement of China is to succeed in the regional multilateral context, two things must occur. Some innovative and systematic thinking must go into the question of how the strategy can be achieved and maintained. Very few of the region's leaders have outlined their views on what a framework for a peaceful and stable Asia would look like. It is as if a highway is being built with impressive speed and great determination toward an unknown destination. Where European thinkers and policymakers have debated for 300 years the causes of war and the appropriate instruments for ensuring peace, this subject has rarely been part of the security discourse in Asia.

Peace may well be, as many argue, a by-product of economic growth, good intentions, and effective diplomacy. But, just as those committed to market-led economic growth in the Asia-Pacific have found it useful to do some long-term thinking about new economic institutions through such mechanisms as APEC's Eminent Person's Group, those charged with thinking security would do well to engage in a similarly creative process. What are alternative ways in which peace can be created, how can regional processes fit in? What are the virtues and defects of the concert of powers, cooperative security, security communities, and collective defense systems? Must something entirely new be created to fit the historical realities and social and political complexities of the Asia-Pacific? Peace through democracy and peace through federation (or political integration) have few Asian adherents in this era of intensive state building, but what of the medium and long terms?

A more focused examination of regional security principles must also be undertaken. The CSCAP working groups and the South China Sea workshops are already looking into this.[14] The Russian Foreign Ministry has circulated its preliminary sketch of regional principles and suggested that an ARF-related process be established for purposes of discussion. One approach is to begin with the principles and norms that are emerging in Asian practice. Here the obvious starting point is ASEAN's founding principles, including the Treaty of Amity and Cooperation. How these intersect with other formulations such as Beijing's "Five Principles of Peaceful Coexistence" would be an interesting starting point for the examination of how far any national or subregional perspective could be transformed into a regionwide approach. Similar efforts could focus on specific geographical areas of conflict (including the Korean Peninsula and the South China Sea) and on functional issues such as arms transfers and production, nonproliferation, and defense spending. Immediate consensus on any of the foregoing is unlikely due to deep-seated disagreements over, among other things, the nature and

implications of democratic institutions and the concept of non-
interference in the domestic affairs of nations. But conditions
are ripe for a first systematic foray at the nongovernmental level
into the question of regional security principles.

The enunciation of principles is a Chinese specialty, and
movement in the direction of a regional approach to formulating principles should prove an iterative process, one in which
Chinese intellectuals and officials could play a major role. This
could well work to engage China in a regional dialogue, especially if the Chinese military is involved.

Boldness here should entwine with modesty. History provides some sobering lessons. The security framework of the
1920s led to an active trans-Pacific network, in the form of the
Institute of Pacific Relations, that has strong similarities to the
current track-two process. In the Pacific as in Europe, regional
networks and international institutions failed to preserve peace
in the face of militarism, fascism, and calculated aggression.
There is no guarantee that the networks and the institutions of
the late twentieth century will be more successful. On the other
hand, it is very difficult to conceive of a durable peace being
established without them.

Conditional engagement of an emergent China is far more
likely to succeed than such a strategy would have with the rising
powers of Germany and Japan in the prewar years. Chinese
nationalism, even at its most virulent is of a stay-at-home variety, even though the geographical boundaries of the home provide enormous scope for conflict with neighbors. Moreover, in
the absence of a threat of immediate military conflict between
the great powers in the Asia-Pacific, there is a momentary window of opportunity for setting in place some kind of inclusive
rule-governed order. The development of the ASEAN Regional
Forum and the prolific track-two process hold out the hope that
this can be accomplished. But the key will be recognition of a
convergence of interests between the United States and its traditional allies working in concert with ASEAN. It would be in the

interests of all for China to be a central participant in the creation of such a rule-based regional order. But the process of creation will move forward, if necessary, without a Chinese voice.

NOTES

1. Akira Iriye, *After Imperialism: The Search for A New Order in the Far East, 1921-1931* (Cambridge: Harvard University Press, 1965).
2. See Ronald Montaperto, "Thinking About China," *PacNet* (Pacific Forum/CSIS), no. 27, August 4, 1995.
3. The "Five Principles of Peaceful Coexistence" are: mutual respect for sovereignty and territorial integrity; mutual non-aggression; mutual non-interference in internal affairs; equality and mutual benefit; and peaceful coexistence.
4. "Containing China," *The Economist*, July 29, 1995, pp. 11-12.
5. This argument is made even more forcefully in Barry Buzan and Gerald Segal, "Rethinking East Asian Security," *Survival* 36 (Summer 1994), pp. 3-21.
6. ARF is composed of Australia, Brunei, Canada, China, the European Union, Indonesia, Japan, Malaysia, New Zealand, Papua New Guinea, the Philippines, Russia, Singapore, South Korea, Thailand, Vietnam, and the United States. In addition to an annual meeting at the ministerial level, it organizes intersessional meetings of senior officials and has sponsored a series of track-two meetings on topics including confidence-building measures, preventive diplomacy, and peacekeeping.
7. With an anticipated multinational staff of more than 125, it will be by far the largest center in the region on the non-war fighting aspects of regional security.
8. See Paul M. Evans, "The Dialogue Process on Asia-Pacific Security Issues: Inventory and Analysis," in *Studying Asia-Pacific Security: The Future of Research, Training and Dialogue Activities*, Paul M. Evans, ed. (Toronto: Joint Centre for Asia-Pacific Studies, 1994). See also "Compendium of Multinational Activities in East Asia Prepared by Rear Admiral Larry G. Vogt," in Ralph Cossa, *The Japan-U.S. Alliance and Security Regimes in East Asia: A Workshop Report*, (Tokyo: Institute for International Policy Studies and Alexandria, Va.: Center for Naval Analysis, 1995). The Strategic and Defence Studies Centre at the Australian National University also publishes a semiannual calendar of upcoming security-related meetings. The Dialogue Monitor Project at the Joint Centre for Asia-Pacific Studies

systematically reports on various government, nongovernmental, and track-two meetings of a multilateral nature that focus on Asia-Pacific security issues.

9. See *Dialogue Monitor: Inventory of Multilateral Meetings on Asia Pacific Security Issues*, No. 1 (Toronto: Joint Centre for Asia-Pacific Studies, July 1995).

10. See *United States Security Strategy for the East Asia–Pacific Region* (Washington, D.C.: U.S. Department of Defense, February 1995), especially pp. 12-14). In a subsequent speech, former Assistant Secretary of Defense for International Security Affairs Joseph Nye, said, "Our alliances are the core around which multilateral institutions and dialogue may be built, forming concentric rings of security" (*PacNet*, no. 26, July 21, 1995).

11. My impression is that the principal funders of the multilateral track-two process and of the gatherings of military personnel have been, first, the United States; second, Japan; third, Canada and Australia; and fourth, South Korea.

12. See "Japan's 'Forum of Security Dialogue' Opposed," statement issued by the Foreign Ministry of North Korea, *Foreign Broadcast Information Service* EAS-95-014, January 23, 1995. The key passage reads: "In Northeast Asia, unlike in other regions, there remain complicated bilateral problems that must be solved between states. It is self-evident that, even if Northeast Asian countries sit around a table under these circumstances, nothing can be expected from it and, if regional character is attached to bilateral problems, complication and confrontation will be fostered. Last year, the ASEAN Regional Forum came into being in the Asia-Pacific region. This is the only forum of security dialogue in this part of the world."

13. For a helpful summary, now slightly dated, see Banning Garrett and Bonnie Glaser, "Multilateral Security in the Asia-Pacific Region and Its Impact on Chinese Interests: Views from Beijing," *Contemporary Southeast Asia* 16 (June 1994), pp. 3-21.

14. The workshop series was started by Indonesia with Canadian support and focuses on managing conflict in the South China Sea. Participants include all countries with claims in the area—Brunei, China, Taiwan, Malaysia, the Philippines, and Vietnam—plus Laos and Cambodia.

Background
and Acknowledgements

臨淵羨魚不
如退而結網

Background and Acknowledgements

THE FRAMEWORK of conditional engagement emerged from the deliberations of three study groups that met from the fall of 1994 through the spring of 1995, conducted under the Council on Foreign Relations Asia Project. The ambitious goal of the Asia Project was to propose a comprehensive long-range strategy for the United States in Northeast and Southeast

Asia that would reflect the radical economic and political transformation of the region since the end of the Cold War. The study groups, on security, economics, and transnational problems, such as drug trafficking, organized crime, illegal migration, human rights, refugees, and environmental degradation, constituted the first phase of the Asia Project. During the second phase, a smaller "blue-ribbon" policy panel was charged with reviewing the findings of the study groups, integrating them into a comprehensive U.S. foreign policy strategy, testing that strategy against informed public and private opinion during two extensive trips in Asia, and presenting the final proposed strategy to the U.S. government. In the course of their debates, participants in both the study groups and the policy panel concluded that China is the pivotal variable and the biggest long-term challenge for U.S. policy in Asia.

The security study group began by looking at various big-picture models of an American strategy toward Asia: strategic autonomy (sometimes called neo-isolationism), liberal internationalism, preemptive containment (or neo-containment), and conditional engagement. Early in its discussions, the security group split along a theoretical fault line between the liberal institutionalist approach and the realist approach. These two fundamentally different ways of looking at the world led to widely divergent proposals for dealing with China: liberal institutionalists suggested that the economic integration of China into the world community would transform and moderate Beijing's behavior, and realists countered that economic integration would just make China one more player in the jostling competition between states. The conditional engagement strategy that ultimately was generated from the Asia Project is an empirical approach; that is, it is agnostic with respect to both the liberal institutional and realist views. It proposes some principles for acceptable behavior by all parties and recommends that the course of economic and security engagement be dependent on the degree of Chinese compliance with those principles.

This volume began as an attempt to extract a useful structure from the study group discussions and working papers and evolved into a strategic proposal for dealing with the challenge presented by China. As a result, this volume may be viewed as an extended study group report, the outline of a proposed strategy for dealing with China, and an assessment of the intractable problems that confront any China strategy.

This volume is not, however, a consensus report. Some of the Asia Project study group and policy panel participants emphatically disagree with the concept of conditional engagement, and many take strong exception to some of the proposals made in this volume. The details of conditional engagement were worked out piecemeal during the study group sessions over a nine-month period and are being assembled for the first time in this volume. Not all of the paper writers participated in all of the meetings; some of them had only limited exposure to the details of conditional engagement, because the strategy emerged gradually. In order to "test" conditional engagement in more detail from various perspectives, several of the papers were written after the study group's last session. Therefore, the discussion of conditional engagement in chapters 1 through 5 represents the views of this author alone; likewise, the views expressed in chapters 6 through 11 are only those of the respective authors.

Ralph A. Cossa, Doak Barnett, Alastair Iain Johnston, Lonnie Keene, Kevin P. Lane, Ronald N. Montaperto, Hisahiko Okazaki, Stephen A. Orlins, Phillip C. Saunders, William H. Overholt, John D. Langlois, Douglas Paal, Jianwei Wang, and Gerald Segal were kind enough to read and comment on the first draft of my chapters, and share with me the wisdom of their years of experience grappling with China policy. I am indebted to my colleagues at the Council on Foreign Relations, especially Elizabeth C. Economy, Richard Haass, Miles Kahler, Kenneth H. Keller, Nicholas X. Rizopoulos, Gideon Rose, Bruce Stokes, and Ruth Wedgwood, who were remarkably gracious in validating the concept of conditional engagement, elaborating on the argument, and critiquing several drafts of my chapters. I also particularly benefitted from discussions with Morton I. Abramowitz, Burwell B. Bell III, Jan C. Berris, Richard K. Betts, Ronnie C. Chan, Chang Lunkai, Richard Evans, Leslie Fong, Stephen Friedman, Yoichi Funabashi, Daniel R. Fung, Richard Garbaccio, William H. Gleysteen, Jr., Donald P. Gregg, Harry Harding, Paul S.P. Hsu, Anwar Ibrahim, Takashi Inoguchi, Marius B. Jansen, Mohammed Jawhar bin Hassan, David E. Jeremiah, Richard L. Johnston, Jr., Virginia A. Kamsky, Koichi Kato, Lonnie Keene, Kim Kyung Won, David M. Lampton, Lee Hong Koo, Kenneth Lieberthal, Winston Lord, Charles E.

Morrison, Masashi Nishihara, Marvin C. Ott, Christopher Patten, Robert A. Peirce, Russell A. Phillips, Jr., Alan D. Romberg, J. Stapleton Roy, Hung-mao Tien, C.H. Tung, Richard H. Ullman, Michael R.J. Vatikiotis, Ezra F. Vogel, Fareed Zakaria, and David Zweig.

I would also like to thank Leslie H. Gelb for his unflagging support in this undertaking. Research, editing and logistics were performed by the ever-efficient Asia Studies program associates, Anna Kang and Nancy Yao, and by the Asia Studies intern, Job E. Campbell. Research assistance was also provided by Phillip C. Saunders, Q. Ken Wang, and May Ng of Princeton University; Phillip deserves credit for intellectual authorship of many ideas scattered throughout the text, but particularly those in chapter 4. Thanks also to David Kellogg and his team, and Alice H.G. Phillips for her copyediting. Special thanks to Linda Wrigley for her editing, and especially Joseph Saxon O'Keefe whose editing and production expertise were integral to the final product.

I am extremely grateful to the chairmen of the study groups—Harold Brown, W. Michael Blumenthal, and Robert B. Oxnam—and to the Asia policy panel members, including Stephen W. Bosworth, David B.H. Denoon, Donald Oberdorfer, Richard H. Solomon, and Robert A. Scalapino; to the authors of all the Asia Project working papers, not just those reproduced in this volume; and to the participants in the Asia Project study groups for generous investments of time and energy.

Discussions with scholars and officials on the policy panel's road trips to Northeast and Southeast Asia, especially those in the People's Republic of China, were instrumental in the analysis of conditional engagement.

The Council on Foreign Relations would like to express its appreciation to the institutions whose financial support made the Asia Project possible, including the Center for Global Partnership of the Japan Foundation, Epoch Foundation, Korea Foundation, Rockefeller Brothers Fund, and the following corporate sponsors: American International Group and the C.V. Starr Foundation, China Commercial Times, Morningside/Springfield Group, and NYNEX Corporation.

This volume has been a thoroughly collaborative exercise. the concept and insights of conditional engagement reflect the contributions of many people; any errors of fact or judgment are mine alone.

James Shinn
New York City

ASIA POLICY PANEL

W. Michael Blumenthal
Lazard Frères & Co. LLC

Robert B. Oxnam
Bessemer Trust Co., N.A.

Stephen W. Bosworth
Korean Peninsula Energy
Development Organization

Robert A. Scalapino
University of California-
Berkeley

Harold Brown
Center for Strategic and
International Studies

James Shinn
Council on Foreign Relations

David B.H. Denoon
New York University

Richard H. Solomon
United States Institute
of Peace

Donald Oberdorfer
Nitze School of Advanced
International Studies

ASIA PROJECT PARTICIPANTS

Amitav Acharya
Byung-joon Ahn
Alice H. Amsden
Susumu Awanohara
John R. Baker
Burwell B. Bell III
Jan C. Berris
Richard K. Betts
Daniel E. Bob
Carter Booth
Peter Borré
Marshall M. Bouton
L. Paul Bremer
John Bresnan
Richard Bush
Laura Campbell
Jack C. Chow
Thomas J. Christensen
Edward T. Cloonan
Bernard D. Cole
Kathleen B. Cooper
Ralph A. Cossa
Robert P. DeVecchi
William Drennan
Elizabeth C. Economy
Daniel C. Esty
Paul M. Evans
Peter D. Feaver

Fereidun Fesharaki
Stephen Flynn
Wendy Frieman
Yoichi Funabashi
R. Michael Gadbaw
Peter F. Geithner
Paul H. B. Godwin
Benjamin Gomes-Casseres
Gerrit W. Gong
Joseph A. Greenwald
Donald P. Gregg
Gerald Hane
Harry Harding
Marianne Haug
David A. Henson
J. Tomilson Hill
Robert M. Immerman
Takashi Inoguchi
Naoko Ishii
Merit E. Janow
David E. Jeremiah
Alastair Iain Johnston
Richard L. Johnston, Jr.
Sidney R. Jones
Miles Kahler
Yutaro Kamae
Virginia A. Kamsky
James A. Kelly

The names of the Asia Project participants are noted for information purposes only. *Weaving the Net* is not a consensus report and does not necessarily reflect the opinions of any Project participant, sponsor, or member of the Asia Policy Panel. The opinions expressed in *Weaving the Net* are solely those of the authors of each respective chapter.

Joe Klein
Andrew B. Kim
B.C. Koh
Hirotsugu Koike
Yoshihisa Komori
Roger M. Kubarych
David M. Lampton
Terrill E. Lautz
Edward C. Luck
Mark Mason
Jessica T. Mathews
Isao Matsuura
Kiichi Mochizuki
Ronald N. Montaperto
Edward L. Morse
Emily M. Murase
Douglas P. Murray
Robert A. Myers
K.A. Namkung
Thomas J. Navratil
Masashi Nishihara
Marcus Noland
Sadako Ogata
Hideichi Okada
Michel Oksenberg
Stephen A. Orlins
Marvin C. Ott
Larry D. Outlaw
William T. Pendley
Linda J. Perkin
Russell A. Phillips, Jr.

Jonathan D. Pollack
Louise Ran
Gowher Rizvi
Lester Ross
Nafis Sadik
Richard J. Samuels
David E. Sanger
Susan C. Schwab
Frances J. Seymour
Daniel A. Sharp
Dingli Shen
Christopher J. Sigur
Sichan Siv
Paul J. Smith
John B. Starr
James Sterngold
Bruce Stokes
S. Thanarajasingam
Hung-Mao Tien
Naranhkiri Tith
Alan Tonelson
Yasuhiro Ueki
Michael R. J. Vatikiotis
Mary Wadsworth-Darby
Jianwei Wang
Q. Ken Wang
Clifton R. Wharton, Jr.
Jennifer S. Whitaker
Maya Wiley
L. Patrick Wright
Atsumasa Yamamoto

ASIA PROJECT PAPER AUTHORS

Alice H. Amsden, Massachusetts Institute for Technology, "'Post Industrial' Policy in East Asia"

Elizabeth C. Economy, Council on Foreign Relations, "The Environment for Development in the Asia-Pacific Region"

Stephen Flynn, U.S. Coast Guard Academy, "Ailing Sovereignty: Drugs and Organized Crime in East Asia"

Takashi Inoguchi, United Nations University, "Five Scenarios for Asian Security: Affluence, Amity and Assertiveness in Its Changing Configuration"

David E. Jeremiah, Technology, Strateigies Alliances, "East Asia-Pacific Regional Security"

Sidney R. Jones, Human Rights Watch/Asia, "The Impact of Asian Economic Growth on Human Rights"

Mark Mason, Yale University, "Foreign Direct Investment in East Asia: Trends and Critical U.S. Policy Issues"

Marcus Noland, Institute for International Economics, "Implications of Asian Economic Growth"

Jonathan D. Pollack, RAND Corporation, "Designing a New American Security Strategy for Asia"

Phillip C. Saunders, Princeton University, "Implementing Conditional Engagement" (forthcoming)

Paul J. Smith, Pacific Forum/csis, "Asia's Economic Transformation and it Impact on Intraregional Labor Migration"

James Sterngold, *The New York Times*, "Asian Commercial Practices: Japan, Korea, China"

The names of the Asia Project participants are noted for information purposes only. *Weaving the Net* is not a consensus report and does not necessarily reflect the opinions of any Project participant, sponsor, or member of the Asia Policy Panel. The opinions expressed in *Weaving the Net* are solely those of the authors of each respective chapter.

Michael R.J. Vatikiotis, *Far Eastern Economic Review*, "Fission or Fusion: What Kind of Commercial Culture Will Emerge in Southeast Asia?"

Jianwei Wang, University of Wisconsin, "Coping With China as a Rising Power"

ABOUT THE AUTHORS OF *WEAVING THE NET*

AMITAV ACHARYA is associate professor, Department of Political Science, York University, Toronto. He is also a research fellow of the Centre for International and Strategic Studies at York and the University of Toronto—York University Joint Centre for Asia Pacific Studies. His areas of teaching and research interest are international relations (security studies) and Southeast Asian Studies. Prior to his appointment to York University, he was a lecturer in the Department of Political Science, National University of Singapore and a fellow of the Institute of Southeast Asian Studies, Singapore. His recent publications include: *A New Regional Order in Southeast Asia: ASEAN in the Post–Cold War Era* (1993) and *An Arms Race in Post–Cold War Southeast Asia: Prospects for Control* (1994). In addition, he has contributed to a number of scholarly journals including: *Australian Journal of International Affairs, Pacific Affairs, Journal of Peace Research, Contemporary Southeast Asia,* and *Pacific Review.*

BYUNG-JOON AHN is a professor of political science at Yonsei University in Seoul, Korea. Professor Ahn serves as an advisor to the Foreign Ministry, Defense Ministry, and Unification Board. He was president of the Korean Association of International Relations in 1988 and is also director of the Korea-Japan Forum and many other academic associations. His previous positions include distinguished visiting professor at George Washington University, visiting scholar at the University of California at Berkeley, and Dean of Academic Affairs at Yonsei University. He received his B.A. at Yonsei University, his M.A. from the University of Hawaii, and his Ph.D. from Columbia University. He has written many articles in the *Journal of Asian Studies, China Quarterly, Foreign Affairs,* and other journals, and has over 10 publications in both English and Korean including: *Post–Cold War International Politics and Korean Unification* (1993); *Political Economy of Chinese Modernization* (1992); and *SDI: Its Implications for Asia and the Pacific* (1987).

PAUL M. EVANS is the director of the University of Toronto-York University, Joint Centre for Asia-Pacific Studies and professor of international politics at the University of Toronto-York University. He is also directing a research project for the Canadian International Development Agency on "Regional Economic Integration in Eastern Asia," and is also the co-chair of the Canadian member committee of CSCAP and co-director of CSCAP's "North Pacific Working Group," focusing on frameworks for stability on the Korean Peninsula. Dr. Evans received his B.A. and M.A. degrees at the University of Alberta and his Ph.D. at Dalhousie University. He did his post-doctoral work at the University of Toronto and Harvard University. Dr. Evans is the author of numerous books and essays on Asia-Pacific security issues and multilateral organizations including *John Fairbank and the American Understanding of Modern China, Reluctant Adversaries: Canada and the People's Republic of China, 1949-1970,* and *Studying Asia-Pacific Security: The Future of Research, Training, and Dialogue Activities.*

MASASHI NISHIHARA is director of the First Research Department of the National Institute for Defense Studies in Tokyo. He is also professor of international relations at the National Defense Academy and research associate at the Research Institute for Peace and Security in Tokyo. Previously Dr. Nishihara held research and teaching positions at Kyoto Sangyo University, Australian National University, and the Rockefeller Foundation. From 1986 to 1995 he served on the Council of the Inter-

national Institute for Strategic Studies in London. Dr. Nishi-
hara received his B.A. from the Law Department of Kyoto
University, and his M.A. and Ph.D. in political science from the
University of Michigan. He is the author of many works on
Japanese security issues and international relations, including
The Japanese and Sukarno s Indonesia (1982), *East Asian Security and
the Trilateral Countries* (1985), *Senryaku Kenkyu no Shikaku* (*An
Angle on Strategic Studies*) (1988), *New Roles for the Japan-U.S. Secu-
rity Strategy in Japan Review of International Affairs* (1991), *North-
east Asia and Japanese Security in Japan's Emerging Global Role* (1993),
Trilateral Country Roles in Keeping the Peace in the Post–Cold War Era
(1993), and *UNPKO and Japan-U.S. Security Treaty* (co-editor, 1995).

JONATHAN D. POLLACK is senior advisor for International Policy at RAND, Santa Monica, California. Between 1990 and
1994, he served as RAND's corporate research manager for
international policy and headed the International Policy
Department. A specialist on East Asian political and security
affairs, his recent publications include: *Should the United States
Worry About the Chinese-Iranian Security Relationship?* (1994); *A
New Alliance for the Next Century: The Future of U.S.-Korean Security Cooperation* (co-author 1995); *China's Air Force Enters the 21st
Century* (co-author, 1995); and *East Asia's Potential for Instability
and Crisis* (co-editor 1995).

JAMES SHINN is the C.V. Starr Senior Fellow for Asia at the
Council on Foreign Relations in New York City. He is the
director of the Council's multi-year Asia Project, a comprehensive review of American foreign policy in Northeast and
Southeast Asia. Mr. Shinn served in the East Asian Bureau of
the U.S. Department of State during the Carter administration, working on political and economic issues, including the
Tokyo Round of the Multilateral Tariff Negotiations. He
joined State after several years with the Chase Manhattan Bank
in Asia. He was the co-founder of Dialogic Corporation, a

manufacturer of voice and facsimile systems, which had revenues of $165 million in 1995. Prior to Dialogic, he held a variety of management positions at Advanced Micro Devices, a semiconductor firm based in California's Silicon Valley, including three years as general manager of AMD's subsidiary in Japan. He holds a B.A. in economics from the Woodrow Wilson School of Public and International Affairs at Princeton University and an M.B.A. from the Harvard Business School.

JIANWEI WANG received his B.A. and M.A. from Fudan University in Shanghai, China and his Ph.D. from the University of Michigan. Previously, Dr. Wang was a Research Fellow in the Program on International Politics and Economics at the East-West Center and at the United Nations Institute for Disarmament Research in Geneva. He has also held research and teaching positions at the University of Michigan, George Washington University, Stanford University, and Fudan University. He is currently teaching at the University of Wisconsin at Stevens Point. He is also an Associate Senior Fellow at the Atlantic Council of the United States. A specialist in Chinese foreign policy, Sino-American relations, and security affairs in East Asia, Dr. Wang is currently working on two book manuscripts, *Sino-American Mutual Images in the Post-Tiananmen Era: A Regression or Sophistication?* and *Modernizing China's Diplomacy*. His monograph on the U.N. peacekeeping mission in Cambodia (UNTAC) will be published soon.